Beckenham's
Thirty Glorious Years
1935-65

Pat Manning with

Cliff Watkins & Ian Muir

Using new research and the memories
of people from the neighbourhoods of
Beckenham, Penge, Anerley and West Wickham

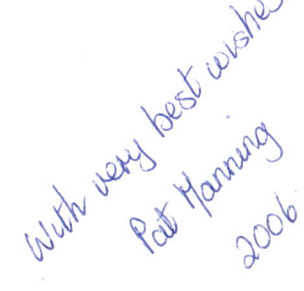

First published in Great Britain 2005

Copyright © 2005 Pat Manning

ISBN 0-9540202-3-5

Published by

Jenna Publishing

29 Birchwood Ave. Beckenham. BR3 3PY

ben-ja@ntlworld.com

In memory of Jenna who walked the woods with me

Front cover: Beckenham Town Hall (p3), Dr J H Bennett, the first Mayor (p5), AFS marching along Rose Walk in 1939 (p47), Rupert Holloway leading out the Cypher's first XI (p74), Three Little Maids (p94).

Back cover: Alison Prince's 'Boy on the Beach' (p128), Spitfire crashlands at Ravensbourne (p93), 1937 Coronation floats (p9), Boxer Frank Morris (p130), Beckenham's mace used today by London Borough of Bromley (p3 and 4).

Designed by Chris Edwards, Lancasters www.lancasters.co.uk
Printed and bound by Antony Rowe Limited

Every care has been taken to ensure the accuracy of the information herein and to find owners of photographs and text for permission for their use.

Contents

Foreword

Introduction

Acknowledgements

Chapter 1	The Beginning	1
Chapter 2	Beckenham's first Mayor is Dr J H Bennett 1935/36	5
Chapter 3	Alderman Parker is the Coronation Mayor 1936/37	8
Chapter 4	Dr Edden from Eden Park is Mayor 1937/38	11
Chapter 5	Alderman Frank William Healey is Mayor as war breaks out 1938/39	13
Chapter 6	Beckenham sees out the phoney war with Mayor Alderman Robert William Jeff 1939/40	16
Chapter 7	Mayor Cllr W J Sampson comes with the blitz and stays for three years 1940/43	21
Chapter 8	Alderman C A Campbell is Mayor during doodlebug year 1943/44	29
Chapter 9	A most eventful year with Cllr Richard Steven Jackson, 1944/45	32
Chapter 10	Alderman Guy Brook is the post-war Mayor 1945/46	35
Chapter 11	The Auxiliary Fire Service 1938-1945	39
Chapter 12	A year of construction for Mayor Cllr James Hilton Atkins, 1946/47	48
Chapter 13	Mayor Thomas Boyd Boyd serves from November 1947 to May 1949	53
Chapter 14	Getting back to normal with Cllr Thomas Mallett 1949/50	57
Chapter 15	Things were looking up for Cllr Edward Charles Dixon 1950/51	61
Chapter 16	Cllr Charles Percy Christie, Festival of Britain Mayor, 1951/52	65
Chapter 17	Cllr White prepares for the coronation, 1952/53	68
Chapter 18	Alderman Sampson returns to honour the Queen 1953/54	72
Chapter 19	'Ben Curtis' Mayor 1954/55 is a name to be remembered	77
Chapter 20	Mayor Cllr William Duncan 1955/56 from a Beckenham family	80
Chapter 21	Cllr David Robert Knox-Johnston Mayor 1956/57 has a famous son	83
Chapter 22	Cllr Henry Herbert Brook Brown was Mayor 1957/58	86
Chapter 23	Cllr Kathleen A Moore is a double first in 1958/59	89
Chapter 24	Lancastrian Cllr William Sidney Robbins becomes Mayor 1959/60	92
Chapter 25	Alderman Henry Thomas Parkin wears the double chain first 1960/61	96
Chapter 26	Cllr Alfred Waller's daughter becomes the youngest Mayoress 1961/62	100
Chapter 27	Deputy Mayor Cllr Smithers succeeds as Mayor 1962/63	103
Chapter 28	Mayor Cllr Mrs Daisy West of West Wickham 1963/64	107
Chapter 29	Cllr Alfred Johnson is Beckenham's last Mayor 1964/65	110
Chapter 30	The Borough 19 Story	114
Chapter 31	Rob Bonnet tells of his childhood in Beckenham	117
Chapter 32	Some Personalities of the time	125
Epilogue	London Monuments	133

Foreword

Beckenham and its past have long held a passionate fascination for me. I was born and brought up there a little after the 30 Glorious Years began, but my childhood, schooldays and early married life took place during this time.

My family has always had the concern and welfare of Beckenham in its affection, beginning when my grandfather, T.W. Thornton, arrived in the "village" in the late nineteenth century, buying the Stationers shop on the High Street, a part which later became known as Thornton's Corner. T.W. also acquired the proprietorship of the Beckenham Journal, and some years later, using its pages to promote a successful campaign, he was instrumental in ensuring Kelsey Park was retained permanently for the enjoyment of future generations. My father, Victor Thornton, who became owner and editor of the Beckenham Journal, was a well-known local figure, and no less enthusiastic about his town. He worked tirelessly for the community, and accomplished many impressive events of note during his lifetime, including performing in and producing a number of theatrical performances on special occasions.

Since retirement I have revived my interest in the history of Beckenham, and, like Pat Manning, have been delving into its past, with particular reference to my family's involvement. Pat and I share the same love and attachment to our background in Beckenham, and many of the names mentioned in her book drift across my mind, bringing either vivid memories of personal acquaintance, or occasions also remembered through individual involvement or in the course of family conversation.

I have read that love and knowledge go hand in hand, so those who care for Beckenham should relish this book with the information it divulges of the times and the personalities who, during these thirty years, helped to ensure Beckenham remains forever glorious.

Valerie Sheldon, October 2005

Mayor Cllr Mrs Anne Manning and Valerie at the unveiling of the plaque at Thornton's Corner in 2004

Introduction

By 1935, Beckenham was no longer a place of manors and farms but a suburban neighbourhood of solid enduring houses that survived bombs, doodlebugs, rockets and gunfire and even developers. We like to think that the community feeling and interest in local affairs that existed then remains today.

Certainly the resurgence of various 'Friends' organisations, Conservation areas, Historical Societies and Residents Associations shows that the people of Beckenham and West Wickham are just as interested as ever in their part of the London Borough of Bromley into which they were made to fit in 1965.

In this book I hope to bring the names of past Beckenham residents alive as we look at Beckenham's thirty glorious years of being a borough in its own right. I must confess it is 'my' Beckenham and not the Beckenham of a history book!

Date	Mayors	Deputies
Nov 1935-Nov 36 (1935-36)	Ald Dr J H Bennett	Ald J Crease
1936-37	Ald R T Parker	Ald F Healey
1937-38	Cllr R P S Edden O B E	Ald J A Collister
1938-39	Ald F Healey	Ald R W Jeff
1939-40	Ald R W Jeff	Ald F Healey
1940-41	Cllr W J Sampson	Cllr R S Jackson
1941-42	Ald W J Sampson	Cllr R S Jackson
1942-43	Ald W J Sampson	Cllr R S Jackson
1943-44	Ald C A Campbell	Cllr J S Yates
1944-45	Cllr R S Jackson	Cllr T Boyd Boyd
1945-46	Ald C G Brook	Cllr K R Maynard
1946-47	Cllr J H Atkins	Cllr T W Mallett
Nov 1947-May 49	Cllr T Boyd Boyd	Ald R S Jackson
May 1949-May 50 (1949-50)	Cllr T W Mallett	Cllr G C W White
1950-51	Cllr E C Dixon	Ald J H Atkins
1951-52	Cllr C P Christie	Ald W J Sampson
1952-53	Cllr G C W White	Cllr G M R Lord
1953-54	Ald W J Sampson	Cllr E C Dixon
1954-55	Cllr C B Curtis	Cllr G C W White
1955-56	Cllr W Duncan	Ald C P Christie
1956-57	Cllr D R Knox-Johnston	Ald W J Sampson
1957-58	Cllr H H Brook Brown	Ald T Boyd Boyd
1958-59	Cllr Kathleen A Moore	Cllr W Duncan
1959-60	Cllr W S Robbins	Ald G C W White
1960-61	Ald H T Parkin	Cllr A W Waller
1961-62	Cllr A W Waller	Cllr E R Smithers
1962-63	Cllr E R Smithers	Cllr A T Johnson
1963-64	Cllr Mrs D E L West	Ald J H Atkins
1964-65	Cllr A T Johnson	Cllr M Williams

Notice that originally the Mayoral Year ran from November to November until it was changed in 1947 to run from May to May giving Cllr Boyd Boyd and Ald Jackson eighteen months in office.

Acknowledgments

Cliff Watkins has edited many of the images included here. Previously he devised the book Beckenham the Home Front published for June 18, the date of the concert celebrating the music of WWII. I appreciate his time and expertise in the production of this book.

Ian Muir also edited many of the images used in this book. Previously we had worked together to produce Monks Orchard and Eden Park, published by Halsgrove in October 2004.

The rich source of times gone by in the pages of the Beckenham Journal and Kentish Times available in Bromley Central and Beckenham libraries.

Chris and Mark Edwards, graphic designers of Beckenham, for their work assembling this book.
My thanks are due to the following for whose help I have been very thankful:

Rob Bonnet, BBC sports commentator,
Felicity Boyden (née Edden), daughter of Dr Edden former Mayor, Adremian
Margaret Buckingham (neé Parsons) Adremian
Ray Burden, whose father was a fireman
Mavis Crawford (née Leeks), daughter of AFF Commander Reginald Leeks, Adremian
Marjorie Davy (formerly Snell, née Sear), Adremian
Alan Dowsett, Beccehamian
Peggy Duffin, Beckenham Soroptimist
Monica Duncan (née Weeks) daughter-in-law of Mayor William Duncan, Adremian
Mary Feltham, long time member of the Eden Park TG
Olive Hamer (formerly Mountjoy, née Beasley), Adremian
Arthur Holder, local librarian
Tony Johns, nephew of historian, Rob Copeland
Peter Johnson and sister Sylvia O'Brien, children of the last Mayor of Beckenham
Jerwood Library of Performing Arts for the picture of Joe Mitchenson & Raymond Mander
Jill Jones, secretary of the Adremians
Shirley Morris of the BBLHS, Adremian
Patricia Newman née Carroll, former concert pianist, Adremian
Alison Prince, writer and painter, Adremian
Chris Purnell (née Smith) widow of Ted Purnell of Cypher's cricket. Adremian
Joan Rees (née Burns), whose father was in Beckenham's AFS, Adremian
Mollie Russell Smith formerly Frost, aka Lunggren, writer and artist
Eileen Sampson, daughter-in-law of the late Mayor Sampson
Audrey Sarjeant (née Handy) Adremian
Valerie Sheldon (née Thornton) daughter of Victor Thornton, Adremian
Phyllis Teare (formerly Munro, née Crease), granddaughter of James Crease who named Crease Park
Bill Tonkin, husband of the late Nancy Tonkin (née Banks) and collator of her collection
Carol Walklin (née Jeffries) granddaughter of Beckenham's first Mayor, Dr Bennett
Margaret Watson (née Lovegrove), Adremian
Cliff Watkins, photographer, writer and historian who provided the article on Carey Blyton
Peter Wiseman, local writer of army biographies, whose grandmother survived the Clockhouse V1

One
The Beginning

'I dedicate this tree to the future Councils of the Borough of Beckenham. As this tree grows in grace and beauty may the Council grow in power and usefulness.'

Sir Josiah Stamp Thursday 26 September 1935

There had been various forms of local government in Beckenham. Parish business was the responsibility of the Common Law Vestry until the Public Health Act of 1872 when it passed into the hands of the Rural Sanitary Authority. Then changes came thick and fast with the Parochial Committee followed by the Local Board from 1880 when the High Street was decked with flags and bunting wishing 'Success to the Local Board' and 'Prosperity to Beckenham.' Great celebrations heralded the advent in 1894 of the Beckenham Urban District Council that resulted from a new Local Government Act but the UDC worked towards becoming a Borough in its own right.

Beckenham prepared for its charter by building the Town Hall in Church Avenue on the site of the Rectory, the Robert Adam design of 1788. One Adam fireplace saved from the Rectory and incorporated in the Town Hall can still be seen in the Civil Centre at Stockwell Close today. The Duke of Kent opened the Town Hall in 1932 and Beckenham amalgamated with West Wickham in 1934.

Baron the Rt Hon Josiah Charles Stamp became the Charter Mayor whose responsibility was to set up the new organisation and in 1935 Beckenham was granted a Borough Charter.

On Charter Day, 26 September 1935, the Rt Hon Lord Mayor of London, Sir Stephen Killick, entered West Wickham where he was met by the Charter Mayor's Procession. They drove through West Wickham High St to Beckenham Town Hall along Beckenham Rd, Wickham Rd and Bromley Rd. To the sound of pealing bells, they were met at the Town Hall by the guard of honour of the Queen's Own Royal West Kent Regiment. The Lord Mayor of London planted a memorial tree at the SW corner of the Town Hall. Although the Town Hall is long gone, there is a large conifer still there, possibly that planted by the Mayor of London.

After formalities on the balcony and in the Council Chamber, the party travelled to the Croydon Rd Recreation ground through the decorated streets.

THE BEGINNING

The Lord Mayor and Charter Mayor stopped at the War Memorial where the British Legion under Commander Reginald Palmer OBE had arranged a Guard of Honour for the laying of wreaths by the two Mayors while the rest of the party went on to the Recreation ground.

At the Recreation ground, the Mayors were greeted by the March from Scipio played by the Royal Artillery Band as they drove round the assembled children, scouts, guides and invited guests, arriving at the platform for the final ceremony of handing over the Charter.

After the presentation of the Charter in Croydon Rd Recreation ground, the main event of the day for the people was the afternoon parade of decorated vehicles in two sections, Beckenham and West Wickham. The first assembled at Ravenscroft Rd and the second at Monks Orchard Rd.

They met at the War Memorial, turned up Rectory Rd and then went through the High Street on the way to the recreation ground, taking about three hours. There were ten classes including Historical Tableaux such as the stagecoach carrying Dr Samuel Johnson on a visit to John Cator at Beckenham Place. Children of 10 to 16 could enter their decorated cycles and decorated motor or horsedrawn vehicles, private and trade provided other classes.

After the judging, a Fancy Dress Gymkhana followed and then Open Air Dancing to Mr Petchey's Orchestra. Music in Kelsey Park accompanied floodlighting and illuminations at dusk. Charter Day was rounded off with a Gala dance at the Regal Ballroom until 1a.m. with tickets at 3/- each. Friday was 'Children's' Day as the schools met on the Elgood Playing Field (where Kelsey Park School is today). The Mayor presented a silver souvenir to each school and there was a March Past, a PE display and Folk Dancing by them all. At the other end of the scale, the retired of 70 and over were entertained to tea either at the lecture hall West Wickham or the Regal Ballroom where the Oldest Inhabitant received a silver medallion.

Very few photographs of the day are held in the public records but they can be seen on the microfilm of the Beckenham Journal in 1935. Leading the tableaux in class 10, were floats 80 and 81 of the Kent & Clock House Traders and St Mary's Home of Compassion shown on the next page.

THE BEGINNING

The last meeting of the UDC was held after 41 years on Monday 20 October 1935 followed by a commemorative service at the Beckenham Methodist church on Sunday 3 November. Afterwards two more trees were planted outside the Town Hall, one by Cllr Healey to represent the UDC and the other by the Charter Mayor. Sir Josiah Stamp's words were 'I dedicate this tree to the future Councils of the Borough of Beckenham. As this tree grows in grace and beauty may the Council grow in power and usefulness.' The mace, the symbol of authority, was given to the new Borough by the Charter Mayor. Hall-marked Silver 'Fire' Gilt, it had 'Borough of Beckenham' 1935 carved in Gothic letters round the bowl.

The Borough Arms in ceramic enamels took the centre of the bowl, flanked by hops, cherries and cob-nuts. Four brackets joined the bowl to the embossed staff and an arched crown surmounted the whole.

An irreverent story about the new Town Hall was that the next day when the postman came to deliver the mail, there was no letter box!

Among the buildings planned for the next few years were a fire station in Glebe Way, a branch library in West Wickham, a central post office by the Beckenham war memorial, a central Beckenham library by the swimming baths, an extension to the Cottage Hospital, a joint maternity hospital for Beckenham & Penge in Stonepark Ave and an Odeon cinema at Elmers End Green.

THE BEGINNING

Gifts to the new borough

The Mace	Sir Josiah Stamp GCB,GBE
The Mayor's Chain and Badge	Dr J H Bennett
The Mayoress' Chain and Badge	Beckenham Women
The Deputy Mayor's Chain and Badge	Beckenham teachers and pupils
Robes of office for Mayor, Deputy and Town Clerk	Henry John Cator JP
Chain and Pendant for the Mayoress evening wear	Cllr F W Chamberlain
Holders for the Mace	Local Government Officers
Mayoral Chair	Sir Louis Newton Bt
Town Clerk's Chair	Cllr F W Chamberlain
Deputy Mayor's Chair	H J Wallington KC
Silver Loving Cup	Arthur Lees CBE
Silver Inkstand	Sir Edward and Lady Campbell
Silver Spade and Replica	County Cllr John Bennett
Gold Swan Pen	Messrs Mabie Todd & Co
Union Jack for Municipal buildings	Mrs John Place
Borough Flag	A M Woodman

Mayor Cllr Duncan and Deputy Mayor Ald. Christie are wearing the red, fur trimmed robes presented to the borough of Beckenham by Henry John Cator. The Mayor's chain and badge show clearly against his jabot and the Deputy Mayor's chain and badge are reproduced below. The Mace Bearer proudly carries the Mace while the Town Clerk completes the Civic Party in May 1955.

The medallions are inscribed with the names of the Deputy Mayors

Two
Beckenham's first Mayor, Dr J H Bennett 1935/36

'Anyone would be proud of being Mayor of Beckenham but it is startling to realise that you have elected me the first mayor!'

Dr James Bennett was the first reserve Charter Mayor to Sir Josiah Stamp and was elected the first Mayor of Beckenham on 9 November 1935. He was proposed by Cllr James Crease in appreciation of all the work he had put in to secure the charter for Beckenham and there were no other nominations. Dr Bennett said he would treasure for many years all the kind things that had been said about him. Dr Bennett presented the Mayor's silver chain and gold enamelled badge to the new council. There followed the election of the Aldermen, four to serve until 1941 and four to 1938. Alderman James Crease was included and Mayor Bennett then appointed him Deputy Mayor.

Dr Bennett's practice was in the house where the Little Theatre is held today in Beckenham and is where his youngest granddaughter, Carol Walklin (Jeffries), was born. Dr Bennett then moved across the road to Corner Ways and eventually sold the practice to Edward Shipsey whose brother Maurice was the grandfather of Edward, the last baby to be born at Stonepark maternity home before its closure. Carol who lives today in Thornton Dene has many memorabilia of her grandfather, Mayor in 1935/36. The most striking is the silver salver that bears the signatures of the councillors at the time of the award of Freeman in 1955 to both Dr Bennett and Alderman Sampson. Carol also has the heavy bronze casket to the same design by Mr Robin Day and Mr Yabsley from the Beckenham Art School as was presented to Sir Winston Churchill. It contained a similar scroll although that is now framed on the wall.

Dr Bennett had served Beckenham for 25 years from when he was elected the member for Copers Cope in 1920. He held numerous posts and presided as chairman of the Library Committee at the formal opening of the Beckenham library on 4 March 1939 when his little granddaughter Carol presented flowers to both Mrs Healey the Mayoress and Mrs Bennett her grandmother!

In 1890, the brothers Charles and Frederick Adyes bought the freehold of the Cator Estate's King's Hall meadow and sold it on to the Brixton Amateurs. In 1904 it became the Cyphers CC. On 16 August that year, W G Grace's Champion London County side played Cyphers at King's Hall Rd (later Kingshall Rd).

Cyphers 145, WG Grace 5 for 57; London County 224 for 8, WG Grace 75.

On 30 May 1936 a new pavilion was opened at Cyphers in Kingshall Rd by Sir Edward Campbell, MP for Bromley. He was a keen sportsman and took two wickets in the celebratory cricket match against Surbiton although heavy rain prevented him showing his skill with the bat.

These cuff-links show the mysterious 'cypher' from which the club is named.

The pavilion became the envy of visiting teams with its long exterior balcony and capacious bar. It had been built by Holloway Bros mainly from donations as the club was very well known, occupying a central position among the numerous bank sports grounds. The housing estates in the developing suburb were bought by professional classes interested in cricket, tennis and bowls.

A hundred years later in 2004 the once proud pavilion was boarded up and the cricket pitch had returned to its original 'meadow' status but worse was to come. A fire broke out in the early hours of 4 February 2005 and the building now lies gutted with little to show for its former glory.

BECKENHAM'S FIRST MAYOR, DR J H BENNETT 1935/36

At Crease Park it was the turn of Barbara Pringle from Balgowan infants to present a bouquet to the Deputy Mayoress. Dr Edden of the Eden Park RA presented the key.

It was on Saturday 18 July 1936 that Kelsey Park was extended via the Wickham Rd entrance and the café opened. On the same day the Stanhope Grove ground and Crease Park were officially opened.

At the first ceremony, little Grace Hopkinson from Bromley Rd infants presented a bouquet to the Mayoress and when the 'Cedar Lawn' extension was opened Mr Charles Nickols of the Shortlands RA presented the Mayor with a silver key.

Dr Bennett had 40 years close interest in the Beckenham hospital and in 1914-1918 had served at Balgowan, the site in those days of the Military hospital. He would be pleased to know that his great granddaughter, Jane Walklin, is a successful film editor working for Yorkshire TV for programmes such as 'Heartbeat' and 'Lost for Words' with the late Thora Hird. Carol Jeffries as Nell Bennett produced an entertaining illustrated allotment diary in 1992 'All the Year Round' that recalls incidents from her childhood in the heart of Beckenham.

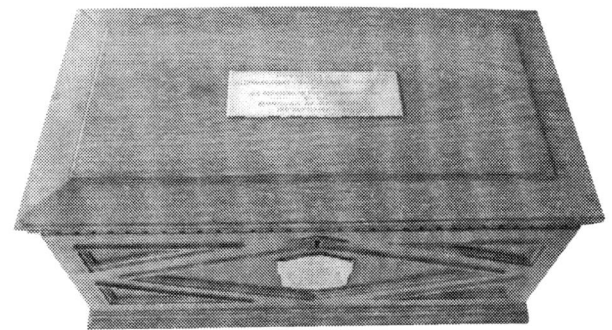

The James Crease casket is unique because although Sir Josiah Stamp also received his scroll in one, his casket was lost in 1941 when the Stamp home was destroyed by 3HE bombs and the family killed.

Here Mayoress Mrs Bennett wears the evening chain and badge that was given by Col. Chamberlain for Beckenham's Mayoress. The heavier chain for day wear was subscribed by the women of Beckenham.

The diamond wedding of Dr and Mrs Bennett was celebrated by a party at their home at the Knoll at the end of 1954. Of their four children, two sons and two daughters, one son had been killed in WWI and the other lived in Southern Rhodesia. One daughter lived in London and the other had married Sir Charles Jeffries.

As the Mayoral year ended, the Crystal Palace was sadly destroyed by fire on November 30 1936.

Three
Alderman Parker, Coronation Mayor 1936-1937

The year on which we are entering will I am sure be a memorable one in the history of our country. I know I can count on the citizens of Beckenham to take their full share in the great occasion to which we are looking forward so eagerly.

Mayor Parker's New Year message in 1937

Alderman Reginald Parker with his Deputy Alderman Healey was the Mayor in the exciting year of the Coronation of George VI arranged for May 12 1937. The Mayor's Chaplain was the Rev Guy King. A penny was put on the rates and £400 was put aside for the official decorations although they were hoping to recycle the Charter decorations

Ali Baba and the Naughty Thieves was an outstanding success for the Beckenham Dramatic Society, produced by local authoress Dorothy Carr and Victor Thornton. The twist was that the thieves entered the Beckenham Festival in order to steal the gold medal that was kept in a secret cave at the top of the Town Hall tower. Victor Thornton was the front of the horse, Horace, with Rob Johns at the back.

The separate parish of St John's Eden Park opened free from debt as the daughter church of Beckenham's Christ Church and two new clerics were welcomed; the Rev. Berry, formerly curate, became the first vicar of St John's in Eden Park Avenue and the Rev. Edward Laycock accepted the living of St Paul's in Brackley Rd. He was an architect who had worked on and off for twenty years in British Columbia until he returned for good in 1933. His skills as a trained architect served the parish well when he designed the new East window for the church after the war.

The Public Library site was decided upon near the Art School and Baths in Beckenham and the Wickham Common Infants School was opened by the Mayor at Coney Hall. Its architect, Mr Burgoine, had also designed Marian Vian, Hawes Down and Alexandra and had placed the new school facing South East so that the children would be spared the glare from afternoon sun.

However the prospect of war was becoming a reality. Sir Josiah Stamp entertained a full audience at Beckenham's Methodist church in February 1937 on 'Dictatorships' revealing his meetings with Adolf Hitler and other dictators like De Valera from Ireland. When asked for the best test for a dictator he said 'Quite simply, what he says goes'. He added that perhaps Town Clerks were the biggest dictators of all!

Councillor Sampson was the chairman of the Air Raid Precautions Committee and called for 1500 volunteers including 300 air raid wardens, 180 fire fighters and 140 manual workers for war damage repairs. Gas proof rooms and a gas mask depot were organised and a meeting at the Public Hall was filled to overflowing. The possibility of a gas attack generated the most questions. What would happen to babies, pets and small children?

We were told to put our dog into a gas proof lidless box in the house and to cover the top with a blanket soaked with a solution of washing soda.

Plans for the Coronation were well under way. Every baby born in the Borough on 12 May 1937 was to be given a christening cup. Decorations were organised for four points; Beckenham and West Wickham High Streets, Elmers End Green and the Borough boundary in Beckenham Rd; remember Penge was not part of Beckenham.

The best decorated road owed nothing to the efforts of the council. The residents of Churchfields Rd provided a wonderful display of festoons, bunting and flags forming a canopy over the road. The war memorial and the parks were floodlit and Frank Thornton organised the historical pageant.

Few photographs are available in the archives but the microfilm of the Beckenham Journal for May 1937 contains pictures of many of the floats in the processions from West Wickham and Beckenham. In the picture, we see part of the procession in Beckenham High St. Sadly there was heavy rain all day on the 12 May and Croydon Rd Recreation ground was waterlogged so that the parade was diverted up Whitmore Rd and Village Way. It was heartbreaking for the children with their decorated bicycles as the colours ran in the relentless downpour.

The children's celebration was postponed until Empire Day when the weather was glorious. Three thousand five hundred children gathered in the Elgood Playing Fields for community singing, gymnastic displays, country dancing and the March past taken by the Mayor and Mayoress in full regalia with the mace bearer and many other members of the Council. There were two Coronation day babies, baby girl Alcock from Links Way and baby boy Wilson from Acacia Rd. Alderman and Mrs Campbell also celebrated the birth of their granddaughter on Coronation Day. The picture shows schoolchildren dressed to represent people from different parts of the British Empire on Empire Day. West Wickham included their annual Fair and Flitch in the celebrations.

The winners in the Court of Married Happiness were Mr and Mrs Tom Smith, parents of two sons and three daughters all happily married. Mrs Smith brought to show the court a home baked cake, a pullover and a scarf that she knitted for her husband 40 years ago! They had met in 1897 when Tom was selling ice cream in a London Park and it was love at first sight. Tom was now a gardener and he was delighted to demonstrate the kiss he gave every morning to his wife as he left for work.

The dog show at the Fair & Flitch had 10 classes; tail waggers, most soulful eyes, cheekiest dog, longest tail, most obedient, shortest tail, largest dog, smallest dog, best marked and the loudest bark.

At least 1,200 trees were planted as Coronation avenues in the borough's streets. These included the horse chestnuts in Monks Orchard Rd and trees along St Mary's Avenue, Durban Rd, Highfield Drive, Oakwood and Stanley Avenues.

The third Dr Barnardo's fete to be held in Croydon Rd Recreation ground was opened by the Mayoress, Mrs Parker, when little Alita Morrison presented a beautiful bouquet. The ceremony was held beneath the trees near the 'Hippodrome.' The Mayor knocked off a coconut at the shy but he said it was only because the coconuts were especially loose. A few days later the Mayoress was equally successful at the St James's fete's coconut shy!

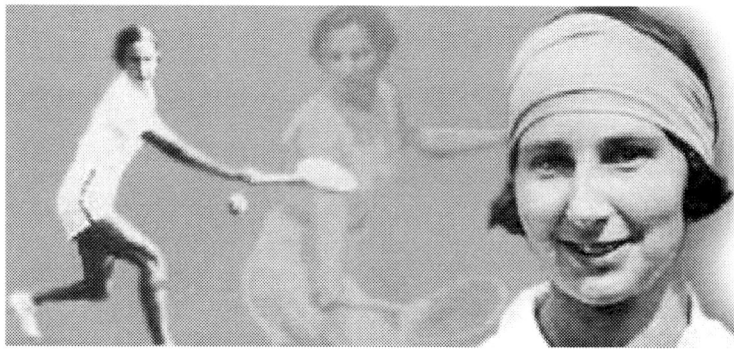

Beckenham Tennis Week had never been so popular. One of the well known players was the Great Britain 1934 Wimbledon Singles Champion, Dorothy Round. Although she was eliminated in the third round she went on to win again at Wimbledon. Since then we have had only three Ladies Champions, Angela Mortimer in 1961, Anne Jones in 1969 and Virginia Wade in 1976.

Dinah Craik (née Mulock), author, died on October 12 1887 and was buried in Hayes churchyard aged 61. Mr Southern from Crescent Rd was concerned in 1937 that the fiftieth anniversary of her death had passed unnoticed. Her book, 'John Halifax Gentleman' was translated into many languages. Where she lived at The Corner House, 114 Shortlands Rd is now one of the borough's listed buildings.

When we look at the present state of Beckenham as a shopping area, it is interesting to see that in 1937 the council were asking if there were too many shops in Beckenham. It was considered that no big business would dream of opening a shop in Beckenham because there was no shopping centre in the town in spite of its 900 shops.

Few of the old Beckenham shops remain today but Furley and Baker opposite Thornton's corner is a winner, taking over from the James Crease greengrocers shop in the late 1920's. The hairdresser Ruthen & Perkins (Hair) moved from Rectory Rd, now in Bromley Rd, and the bakery Lampards of Croydon Rd. are two more of the old Beckenham traders.

Four
Dr Edden from Eden Park is Mayor 1937/38

Is this a call to war? No, but to arm is the sole guarantee for peace, the finest and surest prospect of peace.

BBC radio broadcast to the USA by Winston Churchill 16 October 1938.

Dr Edden took over the duties of Mayor at a time when the conventional wisdom of the day was that Europe was just in theoretical conflict with Germany, but by the end of his Mayoralty, it was obvious that war was very likely.

Dr R. P. S. Edden lived in Eden Park Ave where he had his house built on a double site so that he could have his surgery at his house. Because his daughter Felicity was born that year, she had the honour of a civic christening at St George's church.

Dr Edden, known as 'Doc' to his friends, had numerous other interests apart from his family and his practice.

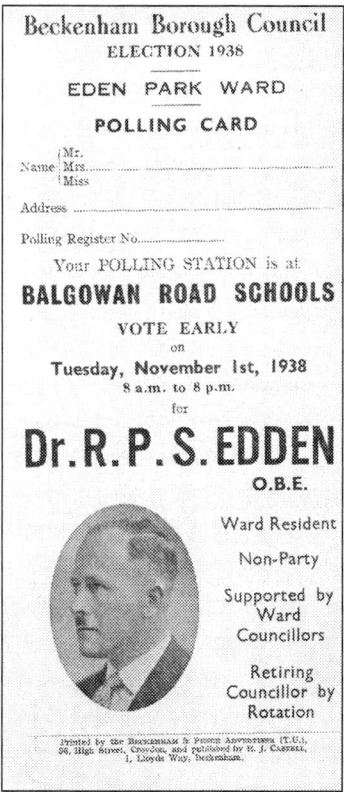

When he came to Eden Park he was sought out by the Residents Association in 1934 to be their first Chairman and was soon nominated as Independent candidate for the ward in the council elections. This culminated in his election to the office of Mayor for 1937/8 when he opened the new teaching pool at the Beckenham Baths.

He was a keen cricketer, a supporter of Beckenham Town FC of which he was a past President, an active member of the Beckenham Rotary Club of which he was President from 1940 to 1942 and President of the Beckenham Bowling Club for many years from its inauguration.

DR EDDEN FROM EDEN PARK IS MAYOR 1937/38

Here we see Dr Edden presenting the AFA Minor Cup to Jack Graham, captain of Beckenham FC A-team in May 1950.

During the war he ran the Mobility service to provide fast medical help wherever needed.

His name was included in those of the first six Beckenham mayors used for blocks of flats at the corner of Brackley and Southend Rds i.e. Stamp, Bennett, Parker, Edden, Healey and Jeff. In 1953 he was one of the 13 Beckenham mayors and 3 representatives who each planted an oak tree on 22 March beside the Petleys' house in Harvington to commemorate Coronation year.

Dr and Mrs Edden had two children, Michael and Felicity born eight years apart. Michael Edden spent most of his life in Zimbabwe but retired with his wife to make a new life in Australia with one of their four daughters.

Felicity Edden attended the Beckenham Grammar school for Girls and still has many friends from those days. She was in the train that crashed in the fog in November 1957 at Lewisham and walked out of the train unharmed. Felicity married the grandson Alan Boyden of the Maths teacher Mrs Boyden at Eden Park School. While taking care of her husband, son and twin boy grandchildren today she still managed in 2003 to win with her partner, Margaret Milne, the Doxford foursomes trophy, which all the lady golfers of the 'Wildernesse' club of Sevenoaks aspire to win.

Five
Alderman Frank William Healey is Mayor 1938/39 as war breaks out

'In the first month of war, Poland has been overrun, Russia's power has been asserted with the creation of the Eastern Front and the RN has hunted U-boats with zeal and not altogether without relish. It was for Hitler to say when war would begin but it will not be for him to say when it will end.'

Winston Churchill's broadcast over the BBC as First Lord of the Admiralty.

Born and educated in Croydon and appointed JP for Kent in 1936, Frank Healey was the first wartime Mayor 1938/39 and twice Deputy Mayor 1936/3 and 1939/40. He was a qualified photographer, keen gardener, amateur actor and enjoyed sketching.

He and his wife Amy had two sons and four daughters. It was Alderman Healey as Chairman of the Beckenham Urban District Council who cut the tape across the road at Justin Hall on 1 April 1934 to signify the union of Beckenham and West Wickham in preparation for becoming the Borough of Beckenham. He died at the end of 1954 at 42 Cator Rd and his funeral service was at Holy Trinity church in Lennard Rd.

Posters asking for help with evacuation of children from the city centres appeared but Beckenham was not considered in danger although over the boundary in Lower Sydenham and Lewisham plans to evacuate the children were well underway.

We were still not ready for a war. Most of the town's population had been issued with gasmasks but many more volunteers were needed for the ARP to total at least 1,200.

ALDERMAN FRANK WILLIAM HEALEY IS MAYOR 1938/39 AS WAR BREAKS OUT

Victor Thornton's pantomime, 'Dick Whittington' was much enjoyed but attendance was poor at Sir Aukland Geddes's meeting where he urged housewives to lay in stores gradually in preparation for the risk of war.

The first eight months of the year saw the fulfilment of many of Beckenham's hopes and dreams. Mr Dove, Mr Stock and Mr Scarr became the new Borough Engineer, Parks Superintendent and Education Officer respectively. The Central library was opened in Beckenham in March, the nurses' hospital extension opened by the Duchess of Gloucester on the 11 July, the West Wickham fire station on 15 July and the Odeon cinema one week before war broke out on 26 August

Sir Josiah Stamp escorted the Duchess of Gloucester through the guard of honour made up of VAD nurses, Civil Defence workers and Beckenham Bunnies. These were children who had been patients in Beckenham hospital and had recovered.

James Crease's granddaughter, Phyllis, is the Beckenham Bunny

A practice blackout was planned for the night of 9/10 August 1939 that in Beckenham started at 11.30 and continued until four in the morning. Most of the houses were already in darkness but where a window was illuminated, it showed up brilliantly. At the Technical Institute, ghostly stretcher parties moved about in silence with dim shadowy ARP members using the blackout to try out their procedures.

The AFS went further still, staging 'fires' in the Eden Park area. There were incidents in many of the roads; Cherry Tree Walk, Wellhouse Rd, Bramerton Rd, Eden Rd, Merlin grove, Lloyds Way, Goddard Rd, Crossways and the Royal Oak Laundry at Elmers End. Street lighting was dimmed as well there being no lights from any of the houses.

Tremendous public interest was shown at the opening of the Odeon cinema at Elmers End Green. It was a beautiful sunny evening at the end of August and a civic air was added to the occasion when the Mayor and Mayoress arrived with Sir Edward Campbell MP, the Deputy Mayor and several Aldermen and Councillors.

ALDERMAN FRANK WILLIAM HEALEY IS MAYOR 1938/39 AS WAR BREAKS OUT

We began to notice that many of the ambulance drivers were women. The Medical Officer informed us that a local garage had volunteered to instruct drivers on how to deal with engine troubles in the types of vehicles they would be driving. Many of the ARP wardens were women too. This was because although there was originally only to be one woman warden to five men, employers had moved the trained men wardens away, leaving the women to take over.

By the end of August filling sand bags was the order of the day and the Mayor was seen with Ald Bennett and Mr Welch, Chairman of the hospital working hard in the hot sun filling the hospital sandbags.

Blackout was for real from the 1 September while we waited for the expected announcement of war with Germany and the London children were evacuated although Beckenham was a 'neutral' zone.

Most of the children did not return to school before the end of November although there were Home Groups for nearly 3,000 children in close on 350 small groups. Many of their schools had been taken over by the ARP who at Hawes Down had appropriated the major part of it. Several ARP posts started off in the schools, like Marian Vian, St Christopher's and Woodbrook.

The Beckenham Food Committee, chaired by Ald. Jeff, enlisted volunteers to write ration books that were of three kinds, adults, children and adolescent boys. Up to forty men and women completed the work in 15 days, starting on Sunday 8 October ready for the beginning of rationing in the New Year.

WW2 food table at Penge library in 2005 showing oat cakes, spam and carrot cake

Six
Beckenham sees out the phoney war 1939/1940 with Mayor Ald Robert William Jeff

The battle of France is over, I expect the Battle of Britain is about to begin. Upon this battle depends the survival of Christian civilisation. Upon it depends our own British life. The whole fury and might of the enemy must soon be turned on us. Hitler knows that he will have to break us in this island or lose the war. If we can stand up to him, all Europe may be free but if we fail then the whole world will sink into the Abyss of a new Dark Age. Let us therefore brace ourselves that, if the British Empire and its Commonwealth last for a thousand years, men will still say 'This was their finest hour.'

Prime Minister Winston Churchill 18 June 1940

Beckenham's long awaited new Post Office was opened quietly on 4 December 1939 at the end of Rectory Rd to replace the one in Albemarle Rd, fortunately designed with air raid shelters for the staff. The Mayor and Deputy with other members of the Works committee visited informally at the invitation of the Head Postmaster although the war situation did not allow for a formal opening.

The ARP Concert Party presented their new show at the Public Hall with the usual Victor Thornton, Vernon Jones and Ida Pool ably supported in a burlesque pantomime.

The New Year started with the presentation of a silver cup to the parents of the first baby born at the new maternity hospital in Stone Park Ave. The inscription read

Presented with best wishes by the
Mayor of Beckenham Ald. R W Jeff
To Leslie Smith the first baby born
in the new Beckenham and Penge Joint Maternity Home
25 December 1939
Her parents came from 64 Langley Way, West Wickham.

It was a very cold winter and skating on the frozen lake in Kelsey Park was in full swing with the keepers working like Trojans sweeping the ice to give the most enjoyment to the skaters.

February brought the exciting news that HMS Cossack under the command of Captain Philip Vian had rescued nearly 300 British merchant officers and seamen from imprisonment on the Altmark (see left) in the Jossing fjord in Norway. They were prisoners from the scuttled pocket battleship Admiral Graf Spee. The second in command on HMS Cossack was Lt Commander Bradwell Talbot Turner whose grandparents lived in Overbury Avenue. He led the boarding party leaping 8ft from the Cossack to Altmark as he and his men swarmed aboard.

BECKENHAM SEES OUT THE PHONEY WAR 1939/1940 WITH MAYOR ALD ROBERT WILLIAM JEFF

The guards fled to high rocks ashore shooting blindly at the boarders but injuring just one in the shoulder. This was the subject of Winston Churchill's 'The Navy's here' speech at the Guildhall 23 February 1940 given to the 'brave officers and hardy tars' of the RN who had won the battle of the Graf Spee incident.

In May 1941 Captain Vian was involved in the search for the Bismark and as commander of the 15th cruiser squadron in the Mediterranean, Philip Vian distinguished himself in the relief of Malta. He took part in the assault landings in Sicily, Italy and Normandy. He was eventually Admiral of the Fleet and Knight Commander of the Order of Bath with many decorations including the Croix de Guerre. Nephew of the late Marian Vian with Aunt Charlotte and sister Claire living in Beckenham, Philip Vian and his wife Marjorie were used to dividing his leaves between Beckenham and Switzerland.

The papers were full of preparations for a long war: ration books, air raid shelters, enlistment of wardens, cultivation of sports fields like Sparrow's Den, clearing the lofts in case of incendiaries, salvage drives and the evacuation of children to Canada and America.

Beckenham's great salvage drive raised 200 tons of paper, 10 tons of aluminium, half a ton of bones, masses of iron, brass candlesticks and copper kettles. The Crystal Palace towers were to come down as their stability was in question and they would yield quantities of iron for the war effort but the Government wanted the North tower preserved.

We did not realise the salvage value of bones and threw away three quarters of them but they were 100% useful to the war effort. The bones that were imported to replace those thrown away were equivalent to the carrying capacity of one merchant ship each month. Three thousand tons of bones supplied 300 tons of grease for making explosives, soap and for lubrication, 450 tons of glue for paints and electrical goods and enough bonemeal to fertilise 108,000 tons of potatoes. We were told to put our bones into the garden to let the birds pick them clean and give them to the salvage collector when he called. Manufacture of table jellies was banned by 1942 because it was considered to waste gelatine and use up plant that could be more useful elsewhere.

A significant change was afoot in the local schools. One of the regulations was that women teachers should resign on marriage but most of the teachers on the supply list were married. Councillors were forced to agree to the temporary employment of married women teachers for the good of the education of the children. This ruling was never again brought into force. Subsequently there was disagreement over whether to allow married women teachers to have paid time off when their husbands came home on leave.

The phoney war came to an end with the retreat of the British Expeditionary Force and their rescue from Dunkirk in 'Operation Dynamo' that began 26 May 1940. We were especially aware of this in Beckenham as trains from the coast were passing through Beckenham Junction full of exhausted soldiers, many of them French and Belgian.

The Battle of Britain began in earnest on 10 July, reaching a climax on 15 August when all Fighter Command's resources in the South were in operation. The German attack became concentrated on the airfields, including of course our Biggin Hill. It was during his visits to the Kent airfields that Winston Churchill, who had been Prime Minister since 10 May 1940, coined the phrase 'Never in the field of human conflict was so much owed by so many to so few' in his speech to the House of Commons on 20 August .

One of the most patriotic ideas was to start a 'Spitfire Fund' to raise £5,000 for a Spitfire. Kent promised the Ministry of Aircraft Production to raise the money for a squadron of Spitfires. It became known as the Invicta Squadron 131 (County of Kent) and the aircraft were named chiefly after 22 towns of Kent like Beckenham, Bromley, Chislehurst & Sidcup and Bexley. In August 1942 the squadron gave vital cover during the allied attempt to seize Dieppe and it continued to serve until it was disbanded in December 1945.

BECKENHAM SEES OUT THE PHONEY WAR 1939/1940 WITH MAYOR ALD ROBERT WILLIAM JEFF

The 'Spitfire Fund' meeting on Thursday night 29 August at the Public Hall was followed a few hours later by bombs demolishing two houses on the corner of Clockhouse and Hampden Rds with three fatal casualties. Earlier in the week the Mayor's house had been damaged by the first bombs to fall on a London suburb. The Luftwaffe's main attack switched to night time bombing from September 6 and continued with little respite until 10 May 1941.

A terrible loss to the boys occurred when the headmaster of the Beckenham and Penge Grammar School, Sidney Gammon with his wife Olive and nineteen year old son David were killed by the only bomb to fall on North Beckenham that night 23 October 1940. Sidney Gammon came from Windsor Grammar School to Beckenham in 1930 and supervised the transfer of the school to the new buildings the following year. Under his guidance, Art, Music and Handicraft came to occupy as important a part in the curriculum as academic studies where the boys gained an increasing number of university scholarships particularly in Sidney's own subject, History. He spared no effort to foster international relationships by organising exchanges with France, Spain and Germany only to lose his life in a war he did everything to prevent.

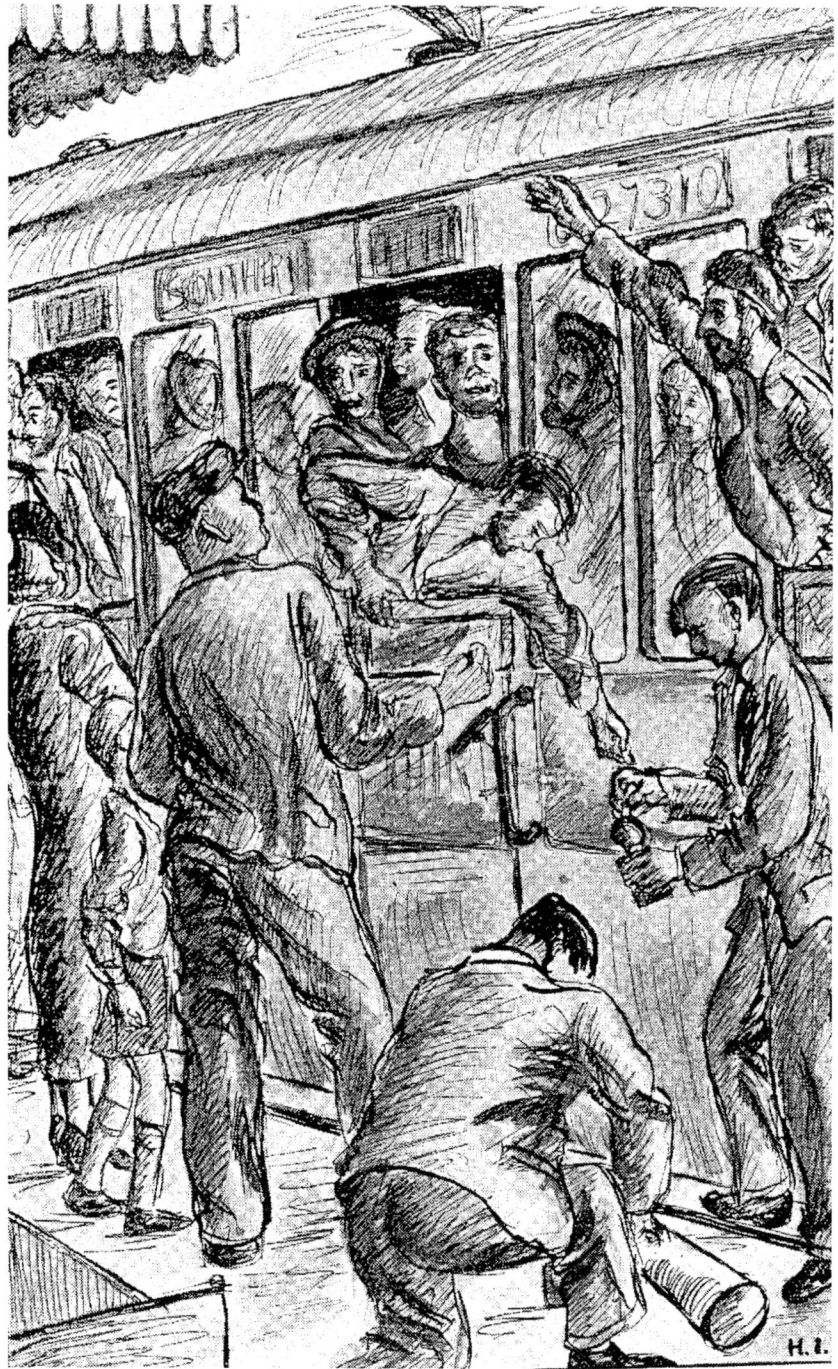

The Dunkirk soldiers at Kent House station

Boys from the Beckenham & Penge Grammar School for Boys will never forget the trains being held up at the signal gantry at the bottom of their field.

The Headmaster, opened up the tuckshop so that the boys could supply an assortment of sweets, biscuits and chocolates to the men, exchange souvenirs and practise their French.

Alan Dowsett, now living in Bristol, remembers taking a bucket of tea over to the train. He climbed into the carriages and will never forget the state of the wounded.

One of the Frenchmen scribbled a message on a card 'Cet acceuil si chalereux nous n'oublierons jamais' meaning 'never shall we forget such a warm welcome.' Further along the line, the trains passed by the cricket fields of Dulwich College and the soldiers cheered the boys, probably delighted to see the signs of normality after their dreadful experiences. The Rev. Michael Griffith was one of those boys, now living in Warwickshire, and he says he wished they had cheered the soldiers back!

BECKENHAM SEES OUT THE PHONEY WAR 1939/1940 WITH MAYOR ALD ROBERT WILLIAM JEFF

The diary 'Milestones' of Edward (Ted) James Burns of 65 Glanfield Rd provides an insight into the effect of the war on an ordinary family. Ted was a tea broker for S S Smith in the City. He writes:

> *'In the summer of 1939, life was very sweet, playing tennis, bowls and golf and taking hikes in the country but on 3 September 1939, Mr Chamberlain declared war on Germany. The tea trade was in a hopeless mess and I nearly joined up as a full time fireman. (He had enlisted part time in the AFS in 1938) We had to put up curtains to stop the light showing which was very depressing. Joan's school closed and the London children were evacuated. There were air raid shelters everywhere and buildings were sandbagged. Christmas was very quiet, rationing has been mentioned and our life is being put out of gear'.*
>
> *By January 1940 Ted was very depressed and he says 'This is a really bad month. The weather is the worst for a century. It has been very cold with fog, rain and heavy snow. Butter, bacon and sugar are rationed, coal is short, travelling awful and all you can do in the evening is listen to the wireless.'*

Later in the year, he saw his job go floating away down the gutters of docklands. Chests of tea were being washed away by the hoses of the AFS (including Ted) who were fighting the London dock fires.

At home, windows were broken and the ceilings had caved in because a bomb fell behind numbers 36 and 38 Glanfield Rd. Ted had a builder bring the Anderson shelter from the garden into the dining room where the family slept for years although his wife and daughter spent some time away in places like Bideford and Lingfield. The reader will be glad to know that after the war he returned to his old job and eventually fulfilled his ambition by being appointed to the Board having started as a tea boy at 13.

When Ted was a tea broker, two of his customers were the buyers and partners Torring and Edward Stockwell. Jack Cohen started out with a handcart selling the cheapest of their teas which he had bagged himself. Torring, Edward Stockwell, COhen spelled TESCO!

Of course, the children's view of the war was somewhat different. Although I was a very frightened eleven year old crouched with my dog Rover in the Morrison shelter when the bombs came screaming down, dare I say that it was also an exciting time? Tony Johns tells of his experiences after returning from Limpsfield to where his school, Aske's, had been evacuated.

> *'The Hurricane had crashed on to the Park Langley golf course. I raced up there on my bike to find the plane in flames with ammunition firing off in all directions, the pilot having escaped by parachute.*
>
> *I had a large souvenir collection including a fin from an incendiary bomb. We found nine or ten of these 18inch long incendiaries stuck in the sticky clay at Pickhurst. We strung them together through the rings on the fins and cycled home with them dangling from the handlebars like the onion men. The Home Guard father of my cousin Michael, who knew about such things, emptied out the thermite and we discharged the detonators by dropping the bombs from an upstairs window.*

Tony Johns in RAF 1946

Michael Clark in army 1944

BECKENHAM SEES OUT THE PHONEY WAR 1939/1940 WITH MAYOR ALD ROBERT WILLIAM JEFF

At my grandfather's house in Bromley Rd, a really large piece of shrapnel fell from the roof and we found that it weighed 2lb 9oz. We all collected shrapnel from the Battle of Britain dog-fights, often hot when we picked it up.

My collection also contained an incendiary bomb casing, the end plate from a shell cap, and a piece of parachute cord from the Greenways landmine. Many of the men were part time firemen like Reg Leeks, my father Rob Johns and Ted Nash.'

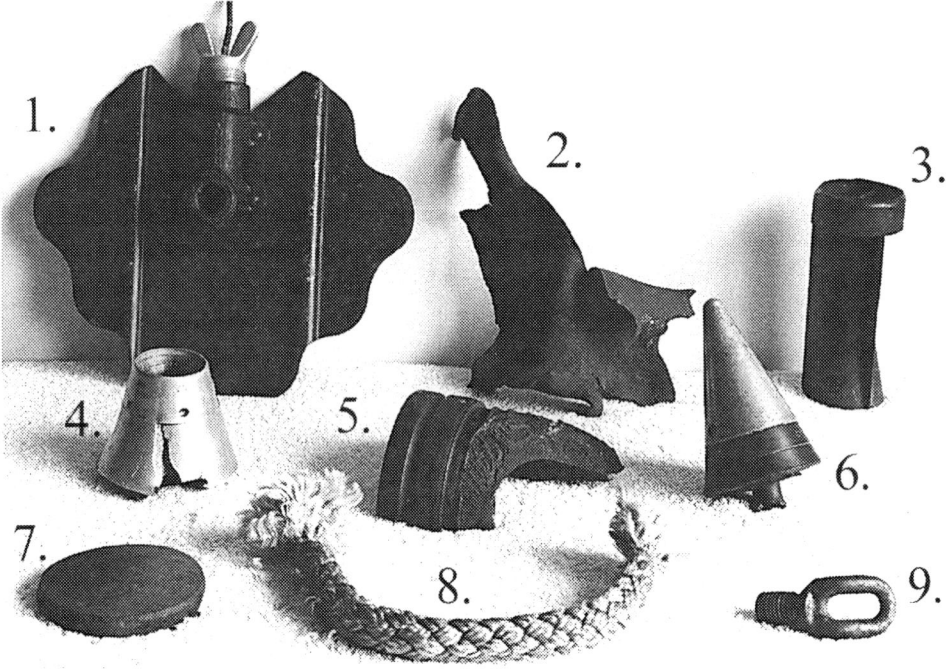

1. End plate from Incendiary Bomb canister
2. Piece of casing from Oil Bomb (Regal Cinema)
3. Incendiary Bomb fin (from Pickhurst)
4. & 6. Two Anti Aircraft Shell nose caps and
5. Piece of Anti Aircraft Shell shrapnel (from Grandparents (the Copelands) garden in Bromley Road)
7. Base cap from Anti Aircraft Shell
8. Piece of Cord from Parachute Mine (Greenways)
9. Ring from High Explosive Bomb (Pickhurst)

Above; some of Tony John's 'trophies'

Below; Tony Leeks and Tony Johns with the parachute of the Greenways mine.

Seven
Mayor Cllr W J Sampson comes with the blitz and stays 3 years 1940-1943

'Hitler took it for granted that when France gave in, we would give in. But we did not give in and Hitler had to think again. In order to win the war, Hitler must destroy Great Britain. We must be prepared for gas, parachute and glider attacks. Put your confidence in us. We shall not fail or falter. We shall not weaken nor tire. Give us the tools and we will finish the job.'
From Churchill's most passionate world broadcast appealing to President Roosevelt
9 February 1941

William Joseph Sampson was born in 1894 in Bristol. He served in WWI in the Gloucestershire Regiment Machine Gun Corps and by the end of the war held the rank of Captain in the Tank Corps. He was wounded three times.

He came to London in 1920 and moved to Beckenham in September 1930. His local service began when he successfully contested Shortlands in 1934. In 1935 he was elected Councillor in the new Beckenham Borough. In May 1941 he was elected an Alderman when the former Mayor R W Jeff was forced to resign because of ill health and held that office ever since. He was Mayor for three successive war years, from November 1940- October 1943, Deputy Mayor in 1951-52 and Mayor again in Coronation year. As Mayor Sampson took over from R W Jeff the blitz had started.

November 1940-November 1941

Brenda Wheatley, née Banks, was only three years old when a bomb fell on her house in Thayers Farm Rd over the long weekend of Saturday 14 September to Monday 16 September 1940. There was no 'All Clear' after the sirens sounded 'Warning.' Her father, who at 32 still had not been called up, was in the garden at lunchtime when he saw bombs dropping. He yelled for his wife and daughter to take shelter, throwing himself to the ground. Brenda and her mother rushed under the stairs and for years afterwards, Brenda had a recurring dream of an eerie whine and a yellow blur coming towards her. She believes this was the collapsing yellow wall of the hall. There were no fatalities but only the shared wall of the two houses and Brenda's staircase were left standing. They lost the dog, cat and rabbit and they were left homeless with nothing but their lives. They were housed temporarily above the shoe shop, Frost's, in Maple Rd and then to a requisitioned house in Forster Rd.

Beckenham's new post office was hit on 8 November 1940 barely a year after its opening and many people were bombed out from Rectory Rd.

At the Regal cinema, the audience stayed in their seats and saw the programme through to the end. Mickey Rooney and Judy Garland were appearing in 'Andy Hardy meets a debutante.'

MAYOR CLLR W J SAMPSON COMES WITH THE BLITZ AND STAYS 3 YEARS 1940-1943

Destruction at 63-72 Lennard Rd

The destructive force of parachute mines was shown when wardens from the ARP post near Holy Trinity church in Lennard Rd thought they saw a parachutist descending only to realise seconds later that the parachute was carrying a bomb. The explosion of 29 December 1940 destroyed from 68 to 72 Lennard Rd and killed an eleven year old girl.

Other parachute mines that had fallen on 15 November 1940 as a pair on Greenways and Merlin Grove caused even more widespread destruction, killing seven and injuring 16.

By the beginning of 1941, the Ministry of Health had decided to offer evacuation to Beckenham children but oddly only to those living west of the Mid Kent railway line. Some of the children went North and others to Teignmouth in Devon. On Sunday 2 January, three unexploded shells landed, one in the forecourt of the Coach & Horses, one in the first class swimming bath and the other on 25 Faversham Rd where the 10 month old David Putnam was killed. When a plane jettisoned its bomb load as it was caught in a barrage, several houses were struck and the occupants buried in rubble although all were saved by the swift action of the rescue squads. Prince, the dog of Mr & Mrs Wright, was blown from his chair in the dining room to the back garden, none the worse for his experience.

The blackout brought about a 40% increase in road deaths and a jingle was published to try to make people aware of the danger.

'When walking after dark at night
For safety's sake wear something white'

Beckenham's War Weapons week from February 22 to March 1 1941, cheered us up for a while as the mayors of Bromley and Beckenham had a friendly rivalry over the sum that would be raised in National Savings for the war effort. They were both aiming at £250,000 and agreed to donate National Savings certificates to all the babies born in their week, Bromley being the week before Beckenham. The Mayor with the highest total would present the certificates that the losing Mayor would buy! Bromley raised £440,730 but Beckenham triumphed with £603,968 so the 8 Beckenham mothers and 9 Bromley mothers were paid for by Mayor Alderman Lynch-Watson of Bromley. The Beckenham presentation by Mayor Sampson was on the stage of the Regal cinema while Reginald New played 'Ain't she sweet' on the organ.

MAYOR CLLR W J SAMPSON COMES WITH THE BLITZ AND STAYS 3 YEARS 1940-1943

There were 2,424 allotments in Beckenham but at least 100 applicants were on the waiting list. The size was reduced from 10 to 5 rods but still more sites were needed. More were provided in Blake's, Coney Hall and Croydon Recreation grounds, Overbury Avenue, Highfield Drive, Stanhope Grove and the Beckenham and Penge Boys Grammar School.

March, April and May were bad months for Beckenham. Thirty auxiliary firemen were killed in three incidents; the five who were killed on 19 March at Plaistow Rd, West Ham were buried at St John the Baptist West Wickham on 23 April. The procession with the five flower-covered hearses stretched from the top of Corkscrew Hill down the road to the church. Denis Fitzgerald had been bellringer, Sunday school teacher and church council member of St John's. Charles Drew was on duty at the Coney Hall substation two nights out of three. Leslie Palmer's coffin was borne by his four brothers, one an auxiliary fireman and the other three in the Home Guard. Frederick Moore, a coach builder, was the first of the five to join the AFS. Stanley Short, the eldest at 36, left two children.

Four men were killed in Court Downs Rd on 16 April, three outright and one died subsequently from terrible injuries. They were R Beacon, D H Chalmers, S R Hudders and J Maynard. The driver, 29 year old Carl Taylor, was awarded the George Medal for returning to the blazing pump to drag out the injured Maynard who died later. A high explosive bomb had fallen 20 feet away from the vehicle in Court Downs Rd and as fragments pierced the petrol tank, the pump had burst into flames. Carl was the owner of the hairdressing business 'Maison Carl' in Beckenham Rd. Gerald Crease was injured at the same time as he crossed Wickham Rd from the house opposite. He was living at the family house of his father, James Crease, 30 Wickham Rd and had been helping the residents opposite remove incendiaries from an outhouse roof. A piece from the pump severed his left leg below the knee and shrapnel broke the femur of his right leg.

Three days later 21 firemen died at Old Palace School, Leonard St, Poplar, which was made a sub fire station since the children had all been evacuated. Ironically four crews had been ordered from Woodside where things had eased, to the old four storey LCC Board School in Bromley by Bow where the situation was getting worse. Arriving at 1.30am on 20 April they were all killed by the landmine that fell on the school at 1.53am. The mine on a parachute penetrated the building and came down the stairs where it exploded killing two women outright. One was only recognised by the piece of blue crochet she was making. The firemen were all killed by the blast.

Stephanie Maltman, a campaigner for firemen to be accorded the same recognition as the armed forces, interviewed relatives who were able to relate the sad details.

On the 25 April the firemen were buried in a mass grave at the Beckenham cemetery after a memorial service at the parish church of St George by Canon Boyd and a solemn procession through the town. The grave was dug entirely by their comrades and was softened by masses of daffodils. After the bodies had been placed in the grave, posies and bunches of flowers were dropped in and there were 350 wreaths.

Two firemen, Norman Mountjoy and Ernest Beadle, the husband and brother of Olive Mountjoy, both killed with the other 19 at Old Palace School in Bow, were buried the previous day beside those at West Wickham. Olive Beadle and Norman Mountjoy had married at Christchurch on Saturday June 15 1940 just ten months before the tragic incident.

The memorial stone at the Elmers End cemetery was unveiled seven months later by Mayor Sampson on Saturday 13 December 1941. Among those present with the widows and close relatives were Sir Edward Campbell MP, the Town Clerk Mr C Eric Staddon, Councillors of Beckenham and Kent County and officers from the police and fire service. After a short service by Canon Boyd, trumpeters of the London Fire Brigade sounded the Last Post.

MAYOR CLLR W J SAMPSON COMES WITH THE BLITZ AND STAYS 3 YEARS 1940-1943

The men lost were P C Aitchison, Ron M Bailey, A C Barber, Kenneth J Bowles, H J Carden, R J Deans, F J Endean, C Farley, G J J Hall, L T Healey, A V Kite, A E Minter, F G Parcell, M C Parfett, W C Plant, L Roots, E W Vick, W J Woodland and H C Wotton.

The remains of the school were demolished in 1948 and a new school was built on the site in 1952.

Mayor Sampson unveiled the memorial on 13 December 1941

William Somerville was a member of the Millborne school sub firestation but he was on leave that night and survived the war. His son Frank Somerville, who was born after the war, organised a memorial plaque at the school to be unveiled on Saturday 19 April 1997, exactly 56 years later, dedicated to the 36 who lost their lives in the incident with the greatest loss of life in the history of the Fire Brigade.

One of the original firemen who attended the unveiling was Alfred Breck who lived with his brothers and sister in Eden Rd Beckenham until his father was killed in WWI and his mother died prematurely leaving the children orphans when he was 12. They were taken into care and he lost contact with his sister Lydia who became a nurse. She died in a hospital ship when Newhaven was bombed. He joined the Penge AFS in 1938, although being an electrician he was in a reserved occupation. The AFS was nationalised in 1941 to help standardise the equipment so that different groups could work together with unified couplings etc. Beckenham and Penge were in area 37. Alfred served at Lloyd's Bank Sports ground in Copers Cope Rd where the AFS occupied the whole of the pavilion. It was the substations that were manned by the AFS members who were regarded as civilians.

Alfred had married in 1940 and eventually there were three boys and two girls in the family. One of his interests was in art and he acted as a steward to an exhibition of the work of the war artist Kingsley Sutton. He also remembers the explosives expert Charles Hards who lived with his wife Dorothy in Eden Rd until his luck ran out while defusing an unexploded bomb at Woolwich. As a child he had attended St James's school and recalls the massive elm trees in the grounds. He also remembers the boys of Craven College from the building now the Elmer Lodge. WWI brought about the end of Craven College as the boys became service men.

The St James's stream that flowed into the lakes there contained fingerling trout that the boys would catch where the river passed down the side of Upper Elmers End Rd.

MAYOR CLLR W J SAMPSON COMES WITH THE BLITZ AND STAYS 3 YEARS 1940-1943

Now Alfred Breck lives with his daughter at Whitstable where he muses over the unjust treatment of the AFS at the end of the war.

No demob suits awaited them at their discharge and no special medal or national memorial until the Queen Mother stepped in. What do you think of the card of safety pins handed out in exchange for the buttons off their clothes as they walked away in what was left of their tired old uniforms to their lives back in civvy street?

The death of the Charter Mayor, the first Baron Josiah Stamp, was among the tragedies that occurred. His house, Tantallon at 4 Park Hill Rd, Shortlands was razed to the ground on the night of 16 April 1941. His wife Baroness Olive Jessie Stamp and eldest son the Hon Wilfred Carlyle Stamp died with him with three of the four maids. Elsie Unwin was the only survivor in the cellars of the house which received a direct hit from one of three 500lb bombs to fall in the same area. They were survived by the Rt Hon Trevor Charles Stamp, the third Baron, the Hon Arthur Maxwell Stamp, Captain in H M army and Wilfred's widow the Hon Katharine Mary Stamp of Farringleys, Shortlands. The area has been redeveloped and renumbered so we can only guess where the houses were. The Lord and Lady Stamp Beckenham Hospital Memorial Fund had raised £1088 6s 2d by the end of the year.

Fire watching in schools and businesses, offers of tin hats for 5s 6d and stirrup pumps for £1 and practice gas attacks in Penge High St were ways of coping with the blitz of 1941. Rationing became more severe and the meat allowance to schools was cut to 1s 2d for every 7 dinners served. Steel indoor table-like Morrison shelters had been promised but the nuts and bolts were not delivered until the summer!

There were many remarkable escapes. From the ruins of one house, six people were rescued. Mrs Brackley was sitting by the fire in an upstairs room with her sister when the room went dark and she grabbed at the last thing she had seen which was the mantelpiece. She felt herself falling down, down, down until, half buried, she looked up to see several flares in the sky although she was protected by a beam. The rest of the family were all buried but rescued with very little harm done. Mrs Rainger saw a parachute descending and rushed into the house to tell everyone to get out. Then when nothing happened they discovered the parachute with four red hot flare canisters attached. There must have been 40 yards of silk and they thought it might raise money in the next War Weapons Week!

The residents of 76 to 80 Churchfields Rd were not so lucky. All the Watts family was killed at number 80 although their dog was unhurt. Mr Keen searching through the debris at number 76 found his wife's engagement ring and their canary alive in its cage but his wife was dead. Mrs White and her new born daughter were rescued from the wreckage but 35 year old Mr White was killed when he dropped by next door to see Mr Cowland at number 78. However by the middle of June things had quietened down although Winston Churchill's speech 22 June 1941, hours after Hitler attacked Russia, showed that he believed invasion was still a possibility.

> *'We have seen three intense turning points in the war. France fell under the German hammer and we had to face the storm alone. The RAF beat the Hun raiders out of the daylight hours while we were still ill prepared. The USA passed the Lease & Lend Act for 200 million pounds sterling. Now we have the fourth climacteric as Hitler has invaded Russia, his ally. This is a prelude to invasion of Britain and subjugation of the Western hemisphere.*

But now there was time for ARP parades at Croydon Rd Recreation ground and in West Wickham. To entertain us in August, Victor Thornton, playing the part of Sir Andrew Aguecheek, produced 'Twelfth Night' in the garden of Mr & Mrs Percy Jones, Looe Rocks, at 39 Manor Way. The garden incorporated part of the terrace of the old mansion Kelsey Manor which was used as the stage for the comedy. Janet Drysdale who had toured with the Shakespean actor, Donald Wolfit, played Viola.

MAYOR CLLR W J SAMPSON COMES WITH THE BLITZ AND STAYS 3 YEARS 1940-1943

Alderman Sampson was unanimously elected Mayor for the second term at the meeting on 10 November 1941 described as having 'the cheerfulness of a lark, the fearlessness of an eagle, the peacefulness of a dove and the sagacity of an owl.' Thus we went into third year of the war.

November 1941-November 1942

Two local vicars died in December 1941. The Rev. Llewellyn- Davies, vicar of St Barnabas, collapsed and died on the platform of Beckenham Junction station on 10 December. The recently retired Rev. Caleb Jackson Ritson from St James's church died aged 76 in London on 7 December. Originally a science master of Manchester Grammar School, he had been a priest in Beckenham for 33 years.

The war quietened down on the home front in William Sampson's second year as Mayor and we had no raids in Beckenham from July 1941 until the beginning of 1943. Efforts were concentrated on making the best of things. Recipes using potatoes that we could grow in abundance included potato pastry and double sugar rations (one pound per person per week instead of half a pound) were issued for two summer weeks to encourage us to make plum jam from the particularly good plum crop. There was a campaign for collecting and drying foxglove leaves that could be used for extracting drugs for treating heart disease. Books for paper salvage were collected as a mile of books; one mile was from the Park Langley garage to Shortlands station and another was a circuit from Kent House station and back via the Beckenham County School for Girls in Lennard Rd. Families were encouraged to exchange Wellingtons and gym shoes as rubber for the home market was in short supply and the children had no gym shoes. The council even considered supplying children with them as mothers were reluctant to use up clothing coupons on gym shoes but the idea was turned down as it would cost £400. I had a friend who spent all her school years playing lacrosse in two left boots as that was all was left in the shop, Frost's in Maple Rd.

One of the most exciting local projects was Warship Week in February 1942. It had been decided to raise between £350,000 and £700,000 to adopt the destroyer HMS Sikh. Processions in Beckenham and West Wickham consisted of models of the ships Golden Hind, the Victory, HMS Sikh, a pirate frigate, a Viking ship and a 'Heath Robinson' ship all built by Civil Defence personnel. Dances, fairs, demonstrations of unarmed combat and bayonet fighting, naval and military bands, comic football and children's modelling competitions were among the events on the great day. A mock quarter deck was built in Croydon Rd recreation ground with a plaque of the Beckenham coat of arms sliding along a mast to show how much money had been invested in Government Securities towards the destroyer. By the end of the week the grand total was £595,177.

HMS Sikh was an elderly destroyer but already had a connection with Beckenham because it was part of the fleet serving in Norway with Captain Philip Vian on the Cossack. Her captain considered Captain Vian one of the finest leaders produced by the war when HMS Sikh was one of the fleet chasing the Bismark. Then the Sikh moved to the Mediterranean for the defence of Malta and was eventually sunk off Tobruk in 1942 where the crew was taken prisoner by the Italians. They were repatriated in June 1943, 37 men being lost from a complement of 250. Captain Stokes who had been in charge of the ship in Norwegian waters came to Beckenham to present the badge of HMS Sikh in November 1942 and to be given a plaque in return that was to have been placed on her quarter deck. Since she was no more, the plaque was retained by the council in her memory. 'To commemorate the adoption of HMS Sikh by the citizens of Beckenham, Warship Week, February 1942.' She was certainly not forgotten because the Beckenham Sea Cadets named their training ship in Copers Cope Rd after her and the Sikh Comforts Fund continued to support her crew.

As the coast of Kent and Sussex was closed to the public in 1942, the council devised a 'Holidays at Home' scheme with displays, fairs, picnics and sports days in the parks. At an inter-firm sports contest in the Standard Bank of South Africa ground (now Amida) the Deputy Mayor gave the Jackson Challenge Cup, won that year by Wellcomes. Competitors included Twinlocks, Small Electric Motors who won the tug o' war final against the Aerograph and Muirheads.

Mr and Mrs Percy Jones put their garden, Looe Rocks, 39 Manor Way, at the disposal of Victor Thornton's Shakespeare Company in August with the proceeds going to Beckenham Hospital. The production of The Merchant of Venice was well up to their usual standards and Victor's Shylock was considered a superb piece of work.

William Joseph Sampson was unanimously elected for his third term when he chose the same Deputy, Cllr Jackson, as he had worked with for the previous two years.

November 1942 / October 1943

I have never promised other than blood, tears, toil and sweat but now we have a victory in Egypt as Rommel's army is routed. This is not the end. It's not the beginning of the end but it is perhaps the end of the beginning.
Winston Churchill at the Lord Mayor's luncheon 10 November 1942

Towards the end of January 1943, we were unpleasantly woken up to the fact that Beckenham was still in the Front Line. Tony Johns reports as follows:

'During my brief evacuation to Limpsfield in Surrey, my family had moved from our house in Forest Ridge to a much larger house at 18 Bromley Rd on the opposite corner of Bevington Rd to the Methodist church. My bedroom was on the top floor with two windows, one facing the church and the other facing Manor Rd. On 20 January 1943, a Fokkerwulf 190 bombed and machine-gunned Sandhurst School at Catford, I had been home in bed for a few days with flu when I heard the sound of low flying aircraft. I jumped out of bed just in time to see an ME 109 with a Spitfire on its tail fly between our house and the Methodist church. I could see both pilots clearly. Moving to the other window, I saw both aircraft climb to avoid the trees of Kelsey Park. I believe the German was shot down over open countryside.'

Raiders had penetrated the Thames defences on 'scalded cat' raids but seven were destroyed, four ME 109s and three FW 190s.

Mayor Sampson directed his zeal and enthusiasm to all branches in the local authority but particularly the Works Committee, which he chaired for 16 years. Other committees of special interest were the Fire Brigade, Air Raid Precautions and Civil Defence Emergency. He enrolled as a warden in 1937 and became a Post Warden, Incident Officer and Honorary Chief Warden. In his dual role as Mayor and Chairman of the Civil Defence Committee he responded to all the calls made upon him and helped maintain the townspeople's morale. He resigned his position as Mayor in October 1943 as he was required by the AMGOT (Allied Military Government Occupied Territories) to be prepared to use his unique experience of local administration abroad at any time. In the spring of 1944, Alderman Sampson was released to work with the Allied Control Commission in Southern Italy until September 1945. When the Civil Defence was revived in 1949, Alderman Sampson was one of the first to enrol and was again Honorary Chief Warden in 1950.

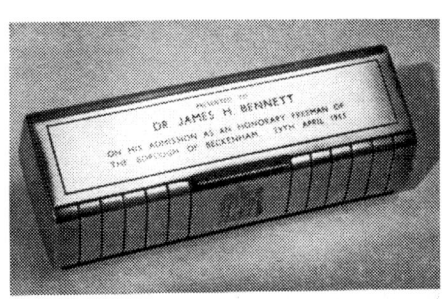

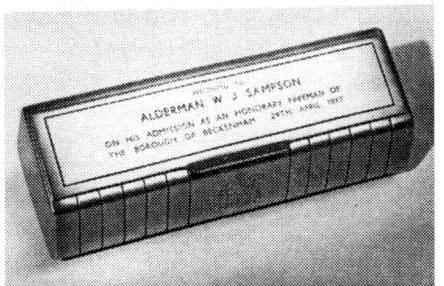

His sound judgement and wealth of experience on all kinds of bodies like the Parochial Charities, Hospital management, Rents Tribunal and Mayor's Fund as well as the Council could only be recognised by the grant of Honorary Freeman of the Borough on 29 April 1955 in the Council Chamber by Cllr C B Curtis, the Mayor. He was awarded the sealed scroll of Freedom in a bronze casket on which was engraved Alderman W J Sampson. In addition he received a green fine leather programme of events with his initials in gold at one corner. It was a dual ceremony with Dr James Henry Bennett receiving the Freeman at the same time.

MAYOR CLLR W J SAMPSON COMES WITH THE BLITZ AND STAYS 3 YEARS 1940-1943

Mayor Sampson was a keen philatelist. At a meeting of the Beckenham Philatelic Society in March 1954, he displayed his twentieth century Swiss mint and used stamps and was elected a member of the society.

When he died at the Middlesex hospital on Monday 13 April 1959, a civic funeral was organised for the following Friday at St George's church. It was described on the front page of the Beckenham Journal as follows:

'A double file guard of honour composed of men and women from the Civil Defence and the Council's Works Dept stretched from the lych gate to the church door. Preceded by the Mace Bearer, the Mayor, Councillor Kathleen Moore, Deputy Mayor and Town Clerk, fully robed, walked in procession with the rest of the councillors from the Town Hall in Church Avenue. The coffin was draped in the Borough flag and local vicars accompanied the Rector the Rev. Hammond and the Rural Dean, Canon Howden to meet the coffin at the lych gate. The flags on the Town Hall and the St George's tower were at half mast. In his address the Rector said that Alderman Sampson brought to Beckenham something of the same influence that another Freeman of the Borough had brought so richly to the nation as a whole. (He was of course referring to Sir Winston Churchill!)'

William and his wife Agnes who died in November 1971 were cremated and their ashes scattered in the Beckenham cemetery rose garden, plot P4 F11/5.

William and Agnes had three children, Geoffrey, Derek and Margaret. Sadly Margaret was the victim of a horrific attack while walking her dog in Epping Forest on 24 November 1975. She left two daughters, Pat aged 24 and Sue. Margaret's husband Roy Lightfoot eventually remarried and went to live in Bristol. Pat Lightfoot became Pat Angel living in Brentwood and her sister lives in Wales. They possess a remarkable scrapbook about their grandfather William Sampson that contains many photographs not known elsewhere. Mrs Eileen Sampson, Derek's widow, lives in Beckenham and possesses the family's entire Mayor's memorabilia including a signed silver cigarette box and the bronze casket of the Freeman's award.

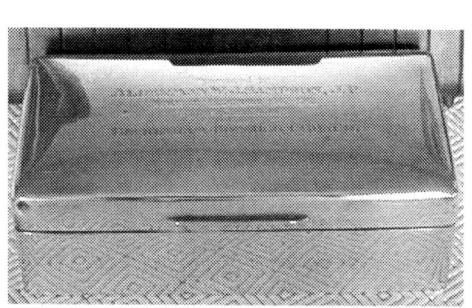

A most respected Mayor, Joseph William Sampson, and his silver cigarette box

Eight
Alderman C A Campbell is Mayor during the year of the doodlebug 1943/44

The siren had sounded and at the same time, dozens of bombers were passing overhead. Suddenly above the drone of the bombers we heard the dreaded sound of a doodlebug. It appeared end on through the clouds surrounded by a glare that lit up its stubby wings. We threw ourselves to the ground as it hit the factory opposite and we were blown through the archway of Muirheads covered in plaster and brick dust.

Tony Johns

The New Year started with the news of a world shortage of butter. We depended upon Australia to maintain our 2oz per week ration of butter but there had been disastrous bush fires in Victoria.

Another shortage that perhaps we did not appreciate was of the flax needed for parachute harnesses, wing fabric, hosepipes and even army boots. Formerly it came from the Netherlands but now Scotland produced it.

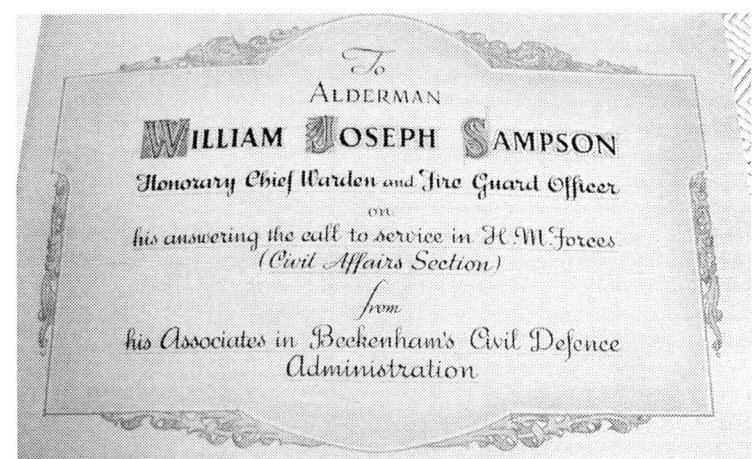

Alderman Sampson was still with us but a leaving party was provided for him at the beginning of February. Marie Slade made him a cake of the wardens' post

'Under New Management,'

He was presented with a boomerang inscribed (from Itma)
'I go — — I come back.'

Previously Alderman Sampson had unveiled the Sikh tablet in the vestibule of the Town Hall as a permanent link between Beckenham and its adopted destroyer.

Beckenham Swimming Club continued to provide entertainment with galas such as one against the RAF. A pilot instructor jumped off the top board to demonstrate dinghy drill. A book-sized packet turned into a rubber boat with hood, paddles and flag within a few seconds. It was the type that had saved hundreds of our pilots. The 'Salute the Soldiers' gala was held on 1 April as a contribution to the £400,000 target. The final figure raised was £501,239 9s 3d. Other matches were held with the RN and the Uxbridge Fire Service.

The Headmistress of the Beckenham County School for Girls, Miss Fox, enjoyed greatly the concert given in honour of her retirement. She was given a silver cigarette case and cheques for her to please herself. The concert arranged by Nancy Wiseman was a rousing success especially the Yorkshire Symphony by the kitchen staff. It was scored for tin pans, glass bottles and bazookas with help from the piano and the choir. Miss Fox asked for the money collected for her by the school should be invested as a school prize which became known as the Miss E M Fox Prize for Creative Work.

ALDERMAN C A CAMPBELL IS MAYOR DURING THE YEAR OF THE DOODLEBUG 1943/44

In April the west wing of the old Abbey School in Park Rd was burnt out in an early morning blaze.
Dry old timbers blazed furiously especially when fanned by the wind leaving charred rafters standing out starkly against the sky, in imminent danger of falling in. Seven pumps directed by Column Officer Jameson could not quell the fire.

When Mayor Jackson took up his year of office, the RAF and USAAF had been bombing the launching sites for the doodlebugs in France since August 1943, delaying Hitler's attack until June 1944.
The beginning of the year 1944 saw resumption of some of the bombing with HE and incendiaries dropped from piloted enemy planes with the accompanying damage from unexploded shells from the intensive barrage put up by our own guns. Two churches collapsed in seas of flame. As the raids faded away in April, the council agreed on summer entertainment in the parks by putting aside £300 for this purpose. Little did we know at the time that Anderson shelters would provide the most used facility in the summer months.

The night of the 12/13 June was a German range-finding exercise of ten bombs accompanied by a spotter plane, Junkers 88. By this time, our defence was well planned. Fighters over the coast were the first line of defence, with AA guns concentrated over Sevenoaks to Rochester and a balloon barrage round London. A Tempest squadron was established at Newchurch in Kent to lead the battle in the air and Beckenham was the target in the early hours of 16 June 1944 for its first three flying bombs. One dropped on the previous parachute mine scene of devastation at Merlin Grove, until recently occupied by Italian POWs, but caused no fatalities. Another killed Luke Morgan at the Evening Standard Sports ground in Eden Way and the third fell on the ARP post in Tootswood Rd, killing wardens Reginald and Florence Seath and George Ripley.

Later in the morning of the same day, six of the Heavy Rescue crew who had attended the Tootswood Rd incident were killed by a direct hit at Links Rd, West Wickham with Fred Goodchild dying at number 10. The next day, an RAF Lt interviewed by the BBC called these pilotless planes 'doodlebugs.'

The Germans were told that these new weapons would end the war within three months but a change in our defence moved all the guns to the coast where they brought down some two thousand flybombs. The balloons destroyed about 300 and the RAF fighters shot down or turned round another 2,000. By September 16, all V1 sites had been overrun but mysterious 'gas explosions' were occurring from 8 September. A month later, the government admitted to the V2, a rocket that struck out of the blue with no warning although none landed in Beckenham until 1945.

For the 80 days of the doodlebug bombardment, the newspapers were restricted in their reporting but at the end of September details were released and appeared in the Beckenham Journal.

Readers can find summaries of the casualties and roads affected by the blitz and the flying bombs in 'Beckenham the Home Front' published in June 2005. Perhaps the most serious of the V1 attacks occurred on 2 August 1944 when 44 people were killed at Mrs Richard's restaurant in Beckenham Rd just past Clockhouse station. This was London's heaviest day with 97 bombs falling in the 24hrs of 2/3 August. There were several narrow escapes such as Pamela Johns cycling from her friend, Christine Smith's house at 174 Beckenham Rd, reaching safety at the public shelter near the library seconds before the V1 fell. Beckenham Swimming Club member, Arthur Frazer, was even closer as he was cycling in the opposite direction, towards the explosion. As he dived for cover, he lost his trousers! Lil Field was buried in debris in the garden of 1 Churchfields Rd, almost at the site of the explosion but she lived to tell the tale.

ALDERMAN C A CAMPBELL IS MAYOR DURING THE YEAR OF THE DOODLEBUG 1943/44

Some wartime teenagers recollect evacuation in 1944

It was not the doodlebugs that sent us to Yorkshire on 3 July 1944. When the notice went up on the board, we thought it would be an adventure for the holidays. How wrong we were! Eight hours on the train to Doncaster followed by bus to Bolton, delivered us to the pits and slag heaps of Goldthorpe, Thurnscoe and Wath-on-Dearne instead of the Yorkshire dales of our dreams. It was just as much a shock for the people of Yorkshire. They were expecting dear little five-year-olds, not complaining teenagers unused to going back to school in the middle of August, and a co-ed school at that! The boys did not like us much in Science. They were accustomed to the girls sitting at the back watching the boys doing the experiments. We intended to do the work ourselves.

On Saturdays we were expected to make ourselves scarce. We had already tried helping with the harvest, pea-picking. Useless! The women just pulled up the whole plant and stripped off the pods in an instant while we were still picking them off one by one. So instead we caught the bus to Doncaster and went swimming all the morning. Since we had little money, afternoons were spent in the pictures seeing the programme round twice from the cheap front stalls. One afternoon, our idol, Dennis Morgan was starring in the 'Desert Song' but 'Fanny by Gaslight' was up the road so we dashed in the rain from one cinema to the other. Was it always raining in Yorkshire? Did we play a game called 'stoolball,' using a round wooden bat held up in front of a square notice board?

I don't think we ate much at least not at first. Yorkshire pudding all crisp from the oven was unknown. Instead it was a flat round cake drenched in gravy, quite ruined. Chips seemed to be the norm and what were mushy peas?

So who were we? Beryl and Pamela Robbins, Valerie Curtis, Pat Ridler, Phyll Curtis with her younger brother and her friend Thelma Gyi with Miss King and Miss Rabson. Briefly Miss Henshaw, the new Headmistress, borrowed one of our bikes and was last seen riding off into the sunset. Val and Pat came back to Beckenham within about six weeks, preferring Hitler's V weapons to slag heaps, mushy peas and boys from co-ed schools. They had discovered that the school certificate syllabus was with a different board and that they needed to come back for the London syllabus. Others stayed for longer, returning for Christmas like Thelma, or even seeing out the rest of the war in Yorkshire, like Phyll and Beryl. Sister Pamela and brother had to put up with it. There was more to those boys after all!

St. Mary's Vicarage destroyed July 1944 by a V1

Nine
A most eventful year with Cllr Richard Steven Jackson 1944/45

The siren sounded for the last time on Wednesday 28 March with the arrival of a doodlebug at Scadbury Park, Chislehurst, the last one of the war to cause casualties. From then on, the fight for peacetime began.

On 5 January 1945 a doodlebug launched from a Heinkel bomber over the North Sea dropped at the junction of Burnhill and Fairfield Rds causing 13 deaths and devastation to Christ Church, a very bad start to the year. Jean Hunter's story is typical of the trauma caused by this unexpected blow to Beckenham so late in the war. Jean Hunter (nee Radford) was bombed out of 19 Balmoral Ave early in the blitz and the family managed to find a flat in Kelsey Park Rd. Ultimately this was a bad move because when Jean was fifteen, her father and uncle were killed by the doodlebug that fell in the Christ Church area that winter evening. They were of a party of four who were leaving the Liberal Club in Fairfield Rd. Two turned down to the High St and escaped the bomb but John Radford and his wife's brother, Fred Bunting, turned up the road to go to Fred's house in Burnhill Rd. They walked straight into the V1. Jean's mother looked for her husband and brother frantically, ending up at the Town Hall's ARP post where her husband was the ARP controller. That was where she was given the sad news.

In the same month, the Mayor, Cllr Jackson was injured and later in the year he lost his eldest son. Another Heinkel-launched V1 fell on the National Provincial Bank sports ground in Copers Cope Rd causing damage to houses but no fatalities.

Out of the 517 rockets that fell on London, only five fell on Beckenham. Travelling at four times the speed of sound, a V2 caused a double boom as it broke the sound barrier. Midland Bank Sports ground in Lennard Rd was hit on 2 January at 12.15 pm and Cyphers indoor bowling green received a V2 a week later at 10.50 in the morning. On 21 February at 11.21 a V2 fell behind St John's church in the Harvington estate. Fortunately the only fatal casualties were two cows and a chicken! Then just after midnight on 10 March a V2 fell near Marian Vian school in Shirley Crescent Our final V2 destroyed numbers 73 and 75 Crystal Palace Park Rd causing nine deaths on 15 March 1945.

The parish church of St George's reopened on 7 April 1945 after the congregation had repaired the damage suffered by the second of two doodlebugs that fell in the vicinity on 2 and 28 July 1944. The first falling on 3-5 Albemarle Rd caused some damage to the church but the second landed on the houses in Church Rd, seriously damaging the East end of the church. Plans were submitted for the reconstruction of the Railway Hotel but it was twenty years before it was decided what to do with the area that is now Beckenham Green.

We had a quiet VE Day mainly celebrated by evening bonfire parties that the children had been collecting together for days while we waited for the declaration of the end of the war.

The picture shows the mayor at 'Stand down'

Over the next few days there were many street parties and the air raid wardens made their farewells all over the borough. There had been some 60 ARP posts, many based near schools. Post 28 was based at Vaile's garage in Elmers End. The pig club that had been at Hawes Down was wound up in June.

The wartime roles of Beckenham's light industry were revealed. SEM (Small Electric Motors) was commissioned by the Admiralty to make ventilation fans, hand-driven generators for life boats and aircraft generators for heating clothing with a workforce predominantly women. The Aerograph near Lower Sydenham station supplied spray guns to paint thousands of parts. Detonators by the million were made by Percy Jones's Twinlocks at Elmers End with much else besides. Among the thousands of loose-leaf notebooks for the forces were Fleet Air Arm code book covers bound with lead so that they would sink at sea. Also there were tools for the aircraft industry and parts especially for the Mosquito. In peacetime, J B Pillin Ltd on Church Hill made greasing units for car service stations but during the war the firm produced hydraulic jacks, each made of some thirty parts. These were installed in Lancaster bombers to open the bomb doors and in Typhoons and Mosquitos to operate the wing flaps. Dowsings in Southend Rd was another firm converted for war work, making heated clothing and boots for airmen with muffs for guns and cameras to stop them freezing.

Oranges from South Africa appeared briefly in the shops with 1lb on each ration book. Sardines in olive oil at 1s per tin came from Spain and Portugal. Apples were delivered from Canada and as the milk ration was increased to two pints a week there was an increased supply of custard powder to go with it.

A young man called Ron Stedman became the toast of the Beckenham Swimming Club when he was invited to swim in Paris against the Swimming Clubs de Paris. No one could catch him as he sprinted up the pool or scored half the team's goals in water polo. He was to represent Britain in the 1948 Olympics.

News filtered through of the needs of the Europeans and among the requests for help were clothes and blankets for the babies being born in Holland.

Schools were due for reorganisation following the Education Act of 1944 and Modern schools were planned. The Speech Day of the Girls County School brought back the first Headmistress Miss Fox to award the prizes but Miss Rose the Deputy Head had to present the Headmistress's report because the new Head, Miss Henshaw, was seriously ill in March 1945. Beckenham had lost two stalwart supporters earlier in the year when Sir Edward Campbell MP and Alderman Elgood both died. Sir Edward Campbell, MP since 1930, was re-elected in the General Election held on 5 July 1945 but he died on 21 July before the results were announced five days later.

A MOST EVENTFUL YEAR WITH CLLR RICHARD STEVEN JACKSON 1944/45

Harvest camp at Brenchley for some Beckenham County School Girls meant travel in the back of a lorry, grated apple sandwiches for lunch when we'd picked apples all the morning and our first experience of life under canvas in 8 man tents.

Harold Macmillan who had lost his seat at Stockton was supported by Winston Churchill in the following by-election that he won in November. When they toured the constituency on 10 November, Churchill was handed the dress sword of Josef Kramer, the Commandant of Belsen concentration camp, by Bill Field.

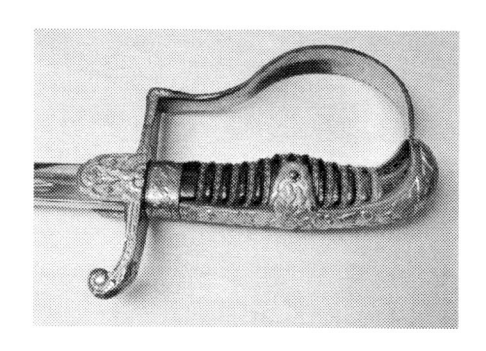

L to R top row: Elise Beeton, Pat Duplock; middle row Elizabeth Evans, Ann Hurford, Jeanine Warman, Thelma Gyi; front row, Sheila Thompson, ?, Margaret Jay.

Bill was the ambulance driver who had taken the sword from Kramer's office when he was driving survivors away in his Red Cross ambulance. The sword is kept in the archives at Chartwell.

Alderman Elgood worked for education throughout his service on the council. The playing fields between Village Way and Manor Way were named after him and he was always more than welcome at the Girls County School. Every year he presented a cricket bat to the most promising member of the cricket team, giving it at the beginning of the summer term so that the recipient would have the pleasure of using it during the season. The awards at Speech Day included the Mrs C A Elgood prize for Special Service.

The school cook at harvest camp.

We still enjoyed the pictures and Deanna Durbin was a favourite with 'Can't Help Singing' showing at the Odeons of Elmers End and Penge.

Born in Winnipeg, Canada, Edna Mae Durbin, in 1921, she rivalled Judy Garland and was an option for Dorothy in the Wizard of Oz. Although she retired from public life in 1949, you can still find websites and fanclubs devoted to her. She was Winston Churchill and Anne Frank's favourite and Winston would often watch her film 'One Hundred Men and a Girl' during WWII to celebrate British victories.

Jasmine Records 1995 brought out a CD of many of her best songs including 'Can't Help Singing.'

So ended a year of change and stress that the Mayor and his Deputy Cllr Boyd Boyd would never forget.

Ten
Alderman Guy Brook
the post-war mayor 1945/6

We left Beckenham just four weeks ago and boarded the SS Suecia at Tilbury Docks. Of the sea voyage the less said the better for in many cases we were not good sailors although we kept to channels marked by buoys as free from mines. We landed at Gothenburg after nearly 48 hours and proceeded by train to an almost regal reception at Stockholm.

Mavis Leeks writing of the school visit to Sweden 1946

Alderman Brook was elected the first Mayor for six years to be free from the dread of war with Cllr Maynard as his Deputy and we were reminded of his slogan in Shortlands many years before

'Vote for Sampson the strong man
And Brook no interference'

He had been an independent councillor since 1934 and earned the Freeman of Beckenham in 1964. His daughter Wendy Ascoli was for many years the secretary to the Bromley Mayors. He had many responsible posts starting with General Manager of the National Benzol Co from which he retired in 1956. He was the first Life President of the Norwood Bowling Club until 1974 and 12 years President of the Hayes Horticultural Society. He was an officer with West Wickham's Royal British Legion and a Governor of the Maudsley Hospital. He lived to the grand age of 83 and in addition to his daughter he left two sons, Don and Colin. So back to the challenge he faced in November 1945 as the men and women returned from war and wanted a new world.

The year finished with a return of Judy Garland in the Wizard of Oz, shown on Christmas Day at 3.00pm at the Regal ——- a suitably triumphant ending to a year that began so badly.

The diary of the Mayor and Mayoress was full of parties: the Beckenham Electricity Dept, Wickleaf the newly formed West Wickham Firemen's club, children's party at the Shortlands Working Men's Club, cocktail party at the Tallow Chandlers Hall, 'Welcome' at the General Assembly of UN at the Albert Hall, gifts for the Beckenham Hospital, West Wickham Red Cross Youth and the children of Post 34 Fire Guards' party gives some idea of the range of their assignments.

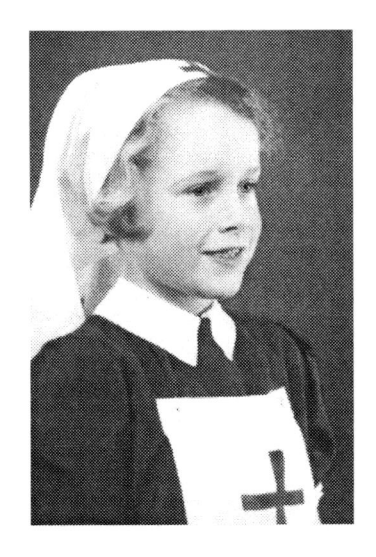

There was also the fancy dress party at the Mansion House where their daughter Wendy Brook and Felicity Edden, daughter of 1937/8 Mayor Dr Edden, were in attendance with other children of former Mayors. Wendy was dressed as a red devil but she envied Felicity's nurse's outfit. It was an exact replica of a nursing sister's uniform made by the matron of the Beckenham Maternity Hospital, Dorothy Beard. Sometimes Felicity was allowed in to the nursery to help bath the babies when Senior Sister Lomax was also very kind to her. Wendy became a physiotherapist and worked for a time at the Bethlem Royal Hospital.

There were to be many problems ahead, none greater than the overwhelming application for council housing that exceeded 200 families unsatisfied and waiting as the year went on. Replacement housing was very slow.

The bungalows were erected but could not be occupied because they lacked the promised fittings although by May the Mayor was able to hand the key to former service man Mr Blackham for the hundredth completed bungalow.

The council introduced a points scheme which included points for war service, disablement from the war, having been bombed out and those having to share accommodation but it did not make any more homes available. Mr Blackham was well qualified because his own family's house in Burnhill Rd had been hit by Beckenham's last doodlebug when he was away in the forces.

Then there was the need for a car to be provided for the Mayor. Mayor Brooks spoke of the indignity of arriving at a function with the Mayoress, both in their regalia, when he would have to drop off his wife and then drive off to find somewhere to park his car! In March it was estimated that it would cost £350 pa to run an official car but at the next meeting the cost had risen to £443. It was adopted by 15 votes to 13 and the Mayor had a chauffeur driven Daimler to take him about.

The congregation of St Michael's church which was destroyed by incendiaries in March 1944 returned to their own parish in a tiny church that they had built themselves in February 1946. So many houses had been destroyed during the war that the Council were overwhelmed with applications for council housing.

Looking on the bright side, Margaret Wellington, aged 18, of Beckenham Ladies, was filmed for the new Pathé Pictorial to show her swimming technique. Showing at the Kings hall, Penge was 'The Wicked Lady' with Margaret Lockwood, James Mason, Patricia Roc and Michael Rennie. The Eden Park Hotel was again the venue when the AFS held a reunion dinner for 200 people dancing to the music of Billy Mole's Orchestra. They were hoping to keep their members together for many years to come by asking those not invited to contact the organisers.

It was the year of the development of the Secondary Modern schools. As yet there were no new buildings but reorganisation was underway at least with the names. There were Open Days in April for Churchfields, Alexandra and Bromley Rd Modern Schools so that parents could see how they were working. Because the school leaving age was being raised, the schools faced a shortage of teachers.

The Beckenham Planning Group proposed a Beckenham Art Centre with a Concert Hall, Auditorium and Restaurant but it never materialised and can only be seen in the 27 April 1946 edition of the Beckenham Journal! There were protests over the long vacated Italian POW camp in Merlin Grove being taken over for Germans when the owners of the property wanted their land returned.

On a happier note, Mayor Brook entertained, with past Mayors, representatives of Beckenham's industries for lunch at the Eden Park Hotel reflecting that much of their output for the past 6/7 years had been highly secret. Speakers included Dr Trevan from Wellcome, Mr Franks of the Wayne Tank Co and Mr Foll of Muirheads. There was also the opening of the first Drama Festival for 6 years, won by 'Down to the seas' by Stuart Ready from Shirley.

Another controversial matter was whether to celebrate Victory Day on Saturday June 8th at a cost of £1,000. It was decided to give the day over to the children with sports and entertainments at four of the open spaces, Alexandra, Croydon Rd Recreation ground, Blake's and Coney Hall but it rained hard all day. At West Wickham they ran the races in the rain but the former AFS running the Croydon Rd event promised the sports for the next Saturday and took the children to the Regal ballroom.

A member of staff sat down at the piano to play any tune called for until the conjuror and Punch and Judy man arrived. The rain ceased for the evening bonfires and community singing. The one at Shortlands had an effigy of Hitler in the centre with fireworks that blew him to eternity.

The weather did not immediately improve because the entrants for the Miss Business House Beauty Queen shivered through the Whitsun Parade held at the Standard Bank ground. Mayor Guy Brook had the pleasure of handing sash, bouquet and bronze statuette to Joan Dibley the winner from Small Electric Motors.

From 21 July, flour, bread and cakes were rationed. The normal adult allowance was 9BU's/wk that would buy a 3lb bag of flour or two large loaves and cakes weighing 1/2lb. An adolescent had 12 BUs and a manual worker 15BUs.

This hardly worried a group of 28 girls from the Beckenham County School who spent August in Sweden escorted by Headmistress Miss Henshaw and her friend Miss Trost.

Here you see from the left Isabel Reid, Dorothy Percy, Mavis Leeks, Doreen Chambers and Thelma Flack.

Among visits to Stockholm sampling the cream cakes, they visited a chocolate factory and ate more than their monthly sweet ration in an afternoon. Mavis Leeks of Forest Ridge wrote an account for the Beckenham Journal at the end of August.

Arrival at railway station. L to R Pamela Sands, S,S, Joan Burns, S, Pat Ridler, S, Thelma Flack, Felicia Panton, Betty Morrison, Audrey Colthorpe, Mary Goodison. (S=Swedish girl)

'We left Beckenham just four weeks ago and boarded the SS Suecia at Tilbury Docks. Of the sea voyage the less said the better for in many cases we were not good sailors although we kept to channels marked by buoys as free from mines. We landed at Gothenburg after nearly 48 hours and proceeded by train to an almost regal reception at Stockholm.

We arrived at Vigbyholmsskolan, one of Sweden's four public schools, on Monday night and stayed there for the next three weeks. Each of us had a Swedish girl as a room mate and there was never a dull moment. The school was beside a lake in pinewoods where we could swim and look for blueberries in the woods. The girls lent us bicycles to explore the country around. We were always going off on official visits, several times in Stockholm to go shopping. At first we wanted to buy everything but gradually got used to it and made our limited cash go a long way. One evening we gave a condensed performance of the Mikado and gave a spirited rendering in clothes ranging from real kimonos from the Swedish girls to bath robes and bedspreads. We also sang well known Swedish songs just as lustily with no idea of what the words meant. We shall none of us ever forget the kindness shown to us all the time we were in Sweden.'

There was a great deal to be done to clear away the signs of war in Beckenham and the army came to help the clearance of 150 wartime shelters, wardens posts and static water tanks.

ALDERMAN GUY BROOK THE POST-WAR MAYOR 1945/6

The Beckenham Journal of 5 October describes how a 500lb unexploded bomb was dug up, defused and exploded on the waste ground at the back of 154 and 156 Pickhurst Rise, West Wickham. Warden Mr Samuel of post 55 said he remembered one of a stick of bombs that fell in October 1940 failed to explode and he was able to locate its position to a few yards. Capt Frake and Cpl Timms of Bomb Disposal defused and exploded it at the bottom of the shaft dug to find it. The paper has pictures on pages 1 and 5 of the brave men who made the bomb safe.

Winston Churchill accepts the Freedom of Beckenham from Mayor Brook and the Town Clerk

It was a happy personal thought of the Mayor to suggest to the Council that it invites the Rt Hon Winston Leonard Spencer Churchill to become a Freeman of the Borough. The ceremony took place at Chartwell on Monday 28 October.

Among the words spoken when the resolution was passed to honour the Rt Hon Mr Churchill MP were these:

> 'When the danger was greatest and there seemed little if any ground for hope that we could possibly survive the ordeal, then it was that Mr Churchill constantly rallied and supported us and the rest of the nation by his words and strength of purpose.
> By his staunchness, determination and confidence, however dark the prospect, he gave us hope and encouragement, inspiring us to carry on to meet our ordeal with courage and patience and to unite in doing what little we could in the common cause of liberty.'

The scroll was designed by Mr Sindall a wartime Civil Defence Staff Officer and sealed in a bronze casket made by the Beckenham foundry, Butler-Jones (nameplates) Ltd. The delegation, which was introduced by the Rt Hon Harold MacMillan MP for Bromley, included the present and three past Mayors who had played positive roles during the war. In his speech acknowledging the honour, Mr Churchill said

> 'Beckenham is not far from my home in the heart of beautiful Kent. It stands in the well known track of "Bomb Alley" and I fear that many marks of those ordeals still remain among you.'

Readers may be interested in some figures from that time. There were 1,201 alerts, 1 crashed enemy aircraft, 973 HE bombs of which 143 were unexploded, 13 parachute mines with 2 unexploded, at least 9,000 incendiaries, 73 flying bombs and 5 V2s. People killed numbered 351, which included the Charter Mayor, 602 grievously injured and 1,151 less so. At least 20,000 properties were destroyed or seriously damaged. At the end of October, it fell to the Mayor to unveil the headstone to the 5 Wardens and 7 Heavy Rescue men who had died in the war. It was next to that of the AFS in the Elmers End cemetery.

The Mayor and Mayoress revived the custom of the Civic Dinner held for the first time since 1938. All previous Mayors except of course the late Sir Josiah Stamp, were present at the Eden Park Hotel with Mr Staddon the Town Clerk and the Mayor Elect, Cllr J H Atkins. Much of the social life of the town had been revived during this Mayoralty and Alderman Guy Brook was commended as he retired for his outstanding services as Mayor.

Eleven
The Auxiliary Fire Service 1938-1945

I think we were all aware of the danger the firemen faced. The bombs fell virtually every night and the men were constantly on duty tackling fires, saving people. Beckenham was directly on the flight path to London and the planes used to fly over all the time.

Mollie Bowles, widow of fireman Ken Bowles.

It was in 1875 that a Public Health Act was formulated to make local authorities provide Fire Hydrants for the fighting of fires. This was not a problem for districts like Croydon and Middlesborough with their own water works but the cost involved was too much for at least half the country's local authorities.

Beckenham was one of the richer districts and by 1938 Beckenham's Fire Brigade was considered efficient and modern. This was when the Fire Brigade Act of July 1938 demanded the recruitment of an auxiliary fire service as part as the country's Civil Defence Force. In the event of war the pay would be £3 per week for men and £2 for women.

Beckenham's AFS practising in Kelsey Park

THE AUXILIARY FIRE SERVICE 1938-1945

Although the Auxiliary Fire Service only lasted three years before it was unified nationwide as the NFS (National Fire service), the men served their country during the time of the Luftwaffe's most severe attacks on London in the blitz of 1940/41 and continued until they were disbanded in 1945. Oddly they were always considered civilians.

Beckenham's original old fire station was erected on behalf of Francis Tress Barry of the Clock House who had organised a volunteer fire brigade and contributed generously to building Christ Church. He became Sir Francis Tress Barry of Clewer, Berkshire when he received a baronetcy in 1899. Peter Hoare adapted the building at the corner of Kelsey Square in December 1869 for the fire engine. After many years as a green-grocer's shop run by an Italian family, it survives today as a hairdresser.

The first horse drawn fire engine was in charge of the Superintendent, Captain Charles Purvis, who was the tenant of Foxgrove farm where the fireman practised. They also carried out their pumping practice in Kelsey grounds or at Brook Place at the bottom of the High St providing free amusement for the locals. Tilling's the bus company had two fresh horses always available and the crews were summoned by bell. This was replaced by a maroon until a shell damaged the church roof! Eventually the bell went to Kelsey Park to signal closure at the end of each day. The local authority took charge in 1882 and the fire station moved to Bromley Rd using the old Manor House stables. Until 1913 when they were provided with motorised fire engines, there were substations at Birkbeck, Shortlands and Lawrie Park to speed up response over the rough roads. The successors to Charles Purvis were in order Messrs Griffin, Davies, Gear, Evans and Netherwood who was the Chief Officer by WWII. Council houses for the firemen were built at the rear of the fire station in 1929 and firemen also used the houses in Church Rd that were destroyed by a flying bomb in July 1944.

The main Beckenham fire station in Bromley Rd had five substations, each manned by one regular fire service commanding officer and AFS members. These were sited at
1. The Standard Bank of South Africa ground in Stanhope Grove (now Amida)
2. The Midland Bank ground in Lennard Rd
3. Elmers End bus garage
4. Barclay Perkins* sports pavilion between South Eden Park Rd and Wickham Way
5. Burnham's factory in Kangley Bridge Rd.

*Barclay and Perkins was a brewery originating from the Anchor Alehouse established in 1616. When Henry Thrale sold the business to David Barclay, his manager Perkins went into partnership to form Barclay & Perkins Co. Another substation was located later in Copers Cope Rd at the Lloyd's Bank sports ground which replaced the Midland Bank when that was bombed.

The West Wickham fire station, only opened in 1939 had a single substation in Coney Hall at Gates Green Rd. There were also 36 Action stations in private houses where a trailer pump would be stored, often by a taxi driver/part time fireman. Residents would provide nightly accommodation for the crews. Beckenham included ambulances in their service although this was by no means usual.

The regular firemen and the auxiliaries worked together with one accord for the success of the service as a whole but many of the regular firemen were territorials from the army and navy and so were called up for the armed services. Beckenham was part of the outer London area K which included Erith, Crayford, Bexley, Chislehurst and Sidcup, Orpington and Petts Wood, Bromley, Beckenham and Penge. Croydon was in area L, the other southern outer London group.

It was during the blitz of 1940/41 that Beckenham's fire service showed its worth and expertise but ironically it was victim of the greatest loss of the lives of firemen in a single incident. Thirty firemen died in March and April 1941 in three incidents as you can read in chapter seven. Houses named after the firemen victims are shown in the table.

THE AUXILIARY FIRE SERVICE 1938-1945

Housing blocks named after firemen casualties

No and incident	Surname of fireman	Site of housing block
1 Old Palace School	Aitchison	Churchfields Road, BR3
2 Old Palace School	Bailey	Bailey Place SE 26
3 Old Palace School	Barber	Westbourne Rd, SE26
4 Court Downs	Beacon	Border Crescent SE26
5 Old Palace School	Beadle	Westbourne Rd, SE26
6 Old Palace School	Bowles	Westbourne Rd, SE26
7 Old Palace School	Carden	Newlands Park, SE26
8 Court Downs	Chalmers	Border Crescent, SE26
9 Old Palace School	Deans	Newlands Park, SE26
10 Plaistow Rd	Drew	Oakwood Ave, BR3
11 Old Palace School	Endean	Seward Rd, BR3
12 Old Palace School	Farley	Seward Rd, BR3
13 Plaistow Rd	Fitzgerald	Oakwood Ave, BR3
14 Old Palace School	Hall	Bailey Place, SE26
15 Old Palace School	Healey	Bailey Place, SE26
16 Court Downs	Hudders	Churchfields Road, BR3
17 Old Palace School	Kite	Bailey Place, SE26
18 Court Downs	Maynard	Churchfields Road
19 Old Palace School	Minter	Bailey Place, SE26
20 Plaistow Rd	Moore	Oakwood Ave, BR3
21 Old Palace School	Mountjoy	Bailey Place, SE26
22 Plaistow Rd	Palmer	Perth Rd, BR3
23 Old Palace School	Parcell	Newlands Park, SE26
24 Old Palace School	Parfett	Seward Rd, BR3
25 Old Palace School	Plant	Newlands Park, SE26
26 Old Palace School	Roots	Seward Rd, BR3
27 Plaistow Rd	Short	Perth Rd, BR3
28 Old Palace School	Vick	Lennard Rd, SE26
29 Old Palace School	Woodland	Lennard Rd, SE26
30 Old Palace School	Wotton	Lennard Rd, SE26

There are other names among those of the firemen that have been used to name houses. On the Chulsa Estate with the houses of the firemen Beacon and Chalmers are houses called Agate, Bailey, Browne, Burton, George, Hay, Hurst, Lathwood, Ripley, Seath and Wingham. Leslie Frederick Hurst and Gladys Muriel Blinkhorn-Hay were Air Raid Wardens killed at the Wardens Post 40 in Queen Anne Avenue on 4 December 1940. Post 42 in Tootswood Rd was hit by a flying bomb on the early morning of 16 June 1944, killing Florence and Reginald Seath and George Ripley. Ernest Stanley Agate, Henry Bailey, Harold Browne, Frank Burton, Ernest Stanley Lathwood and George Wingham were killed as members of the Heavy Rescue at Links Rd, West Wickham on the same morning, having just come from the Post 42 incident.

Leonard George was a long serving member of the Heavy Rescue who died after nearly five years service at the Elmers End Bus Garage when it was hit by a flying bomb on 18 July 1944.

As long ago as November 1940 he was making the news, tunnelling under the wreckage of bombed houses to bring out people trapped among the debris. He described working with a penknife from the relative safety beneath a table to remove a brick from a wall so that he could insert an oxygen tube through to a woman who was suffocating beneath a thick blanket. Then he found she was trapped beneath a piano where she and her husband were tangled among the keys and wires. Eventually he was able to take the weight of the piano while the others in the rescue party pulled her out. When he lost his life beneath a collapsing wall at the bus garage he had not been on duty but came to help since he lived nearby.

THE AUXILIARY FIRE SERVICE 1938-1945

Although Beckenham's fire service was as up-to-date as any in the country, the bombing revealed the shortcomings of many poorer outlying districts. When fire brigades were required to work together this was frequently found to be inefficient as their equipment was not compatible. Beckenham had operated closely with the other London areas and the men were good companions. They doubted that the NFS would serve as well as its former combination of AFS and regular firemen but by August 1941, it was obvious that the Government intended to unify all the fire brigades in the near future. Perhaps the greatest loss to Beckenham was the transfer to Leicester of the Chief Officer, A. N. Netherwood. The Mayor pointed out that it was a great honour and reflected the Beckenham firemen's superiority.

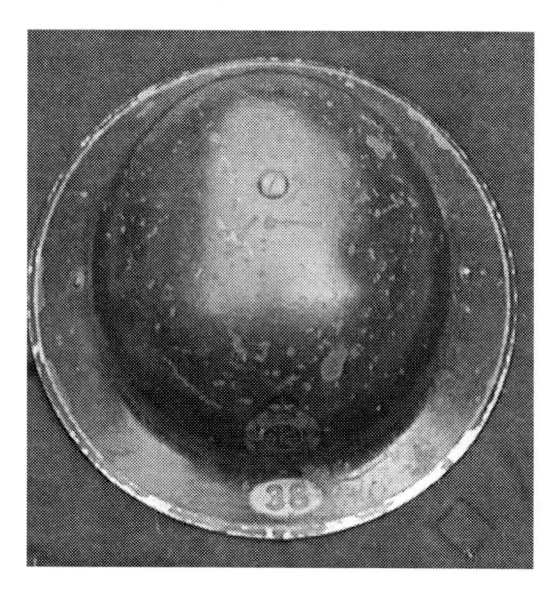

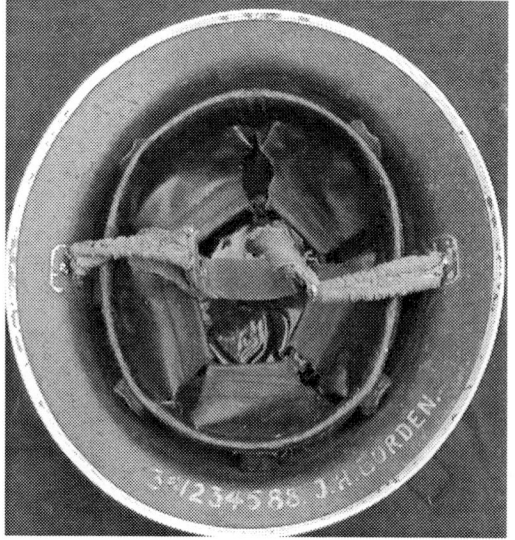

There were only 32 Fire Force Commanders appointed and Mr Netherwood was one of them. Second Officer Jameson was appointed in a temporary capacity as Beckenham's Chief Officer. By 1945, F.F.C.Netherwood had returned to be in charge of London's area 38. The helmet above belonged to the father of former Beckenham mounted policeman, Ray Burden. You can see that the helmet was clearly marked with the fireman's name and number for identification if the man was lost. The man's axe also bore his name for the same reason.

By November 1941, other key men from Beckenham were being transferred by Government order to posts in the NFS where their expertise was needed. The Beckenham fire service took this badly particularly after their manpower losses earlier in the year in the blitz. The loss of the men in the Poplar school incident was the biggest single loss of the war.

Some Lighter Moments

By the middle of June 1941 the worst of the blitz was over and there was time for parades at Croydon Rd Recreation ground and in West Wickham. In July and August, there was a contest for the AFS to find the fastest team to finish a trailer pump course. This involved knocking down targets with the pump as well as completing the course. The fastest team out of 14 in the preliminary contest at the West Wickham fire station, finished in one minute 53 seconds and were the only team to get below two minutes. The team of Leading Fireman Oldfield with auxiliary firemen Sawyer, Clapp, Biswell and Masters was coached by PO Forsyth. It went on to represent Beckenham at the local stage, which Beckenham won in one minute 44 seconds, beating Orpington by two seconds. Both went forward to the regional finals which Hampstead won.

At the Civil Defence Sports Meeting at the Midland Bank ground in Lennard Rd in August the AFS triumphed with 42 points. Their nearest rivals were Depots B and A with 25 and 22 points respectively.

Another contest was for the Sampson Cricket Challenge Cup with the AFS team playing and beating C depot Casualty Services.

THE AUXILIARY FIRE SERVICE 1938-1945

The final match was played at the Foxgrove cricket ground on Wednesday 10 September 1941.

The AFS team for the Sampson Challenge Cup in the Cricket Competition at the Foxgrove Ground in 1941
Back row L to R: L T Ralph (D depot umpire), T F Knight (Sec 5), P M Kedward (Sec 6), F G Cole (Sec 2), C F Harris (Sec 4), G F Lewis (Sec 4), S A Keen (Sec 4), M Goode (Engs Dep), C I Rose (Sec 2 Umpire), scorer.
Front row L to R: S H Moore (Sec 2), G P Burnham (Sec 8), Mayor Sampson, C A Burt, Captain (Sec 2), the Controller C Eric Staddon, C J R Woods (Sec 5), R B Farmer (Sec 5).

The Civil Defence Swimming Gala on Sunday afternoon at the end of September was NOT won by the firemen although the best all round man was E. Stratton of the NFS for his back and breast stroke first places. The event was won by Control with 27 points, the Wardens and the NFS sharing second place with 16.5 points each.

One other victory for the Beckenham firemen was in the tennis at Queen's Club in September. Former Kent player G. Mountain beat the title holder W. Bennitt from the London station B66 by 4-6, 6-2, 9-7. They had both played and won their quarter and semi finals during the morning!

In February 1945, the London Region NFS was presented with the savings plaque for collecting £447,208 during the 'Salute the Soldier' campaign. Of this sum, area 37, represented by Leading Fireman Cordy and Fireman Cooper, had made the biggest contribution with £187,255.

In quiet times, some firemen spent their time making toys for children. Many of them were expert carpenters and had talents for making models. Bryan Wotton received several cleverly crafted reproductions of naval vessels.

Near the lake of Crystal Palace Park was a dump of materials from bomb damaged houses that the firemen were allowed to use. A full size Wendy House was made using wood from the dump. The metal from 7lb food cans was used to concoct saucepans and frying pans etc. Balsa wood made fruit and vegetables that looked real once they were painted.

THE AUXILIARY FIRE SERVICE 1938-1945

The firemen also helped the war effort from September 1942 to April 1945 with different stations tackling the various jobs. Soldering was the speciality of the firemen of RR3 station in Copers Cope Rd where 175,764 condensers and terminals passed through their hands. Firewoman Trixie Rich from Orpington earned the distinction for being the fastest incendiary parachute stitcher in the London area. The men improvised their own workshops to be on hand for fire calls and put in over 302,368 man-hours assembling equipment like mine detectors and cockpit lamps.

In February 1945, Beckenham Fireman Strong was chosen for the contingent of the NFS despatched for fire fighting abroad with the American Army in Western Europe.

The part-timers of Hawthorndene

The Action stations were closed with the advent of the NFS and a central station was opened in Beckenham Place off Southend Rd for part-time firemen of area 37, known as C2W. This Beckenham station was run by Company Officers Morgan, Bagg and Warner.

During quiet times the part time firemen did voluntary work such as the redecoration of the children's ward at the Cottage Hospital led by Leading Firemen Harris, McKibben and Weeks with 60 men. They also gave 100 consecutive days service to make damaged houses habitable.

On arrival of the V-bombs, the part time service was immediately in action putting out fires and attending rescue operations.

Here we see Reg Leeks with Ernest Gowers at the Hyde Park 'Stand Down.'

The service certificate of Reg Leeks shows that the local fire brigade was transferred to the National Fire Service in August 1941

THE AUXILIARY FIRE SERVICE 1938-1945

On the occasion of their 'Stand-down' in March 1945, there was a picture of the firemen of Hawthorndene across the front page of the Beckenham Journal of 10.3.1945. Their celebration dinner had been held at the Regal Ballroom on Thursday 22 February when 150 men had attended. Guests of Honour were Assistant FFC Leeks, Divisional Officer Gordon Smith, Senior Chief Officer Vernon Jones and Chief Officers Jack Morgan, Jameson, Frewer, Bagg and Warner.

They were able to give a cheque for £400 to Beckenham Hospital from excess balance from the dinner and this went towards naming a bed. The service did not cease with the 'Stand-down' but remained 'On call.' A parade of 5000 part-timers was held in Hyde Park in March 1945.

Who can we find today who are relatives of the firemen?

Being over 60 years ago, it is not easy to find the descendants of these men but several relatives have been traced. Local historian Cliff Watkins, is second cousin to Ron Bailey.

Shirley Morris of the NW Kent FHS is second cousin to William Plant who was only four years old when his father died. William and Shirley share their great grandparents as Shirley's grandfather Thomas Richard Burtonshaw and William's grandmother, Laura Elizabeth Proud (nee Burtonshaw), were brother and sister.

Closer relatives include Olive Hamer (formerly Mountjoy, nee Beadle) the wife of Norman Mountjoy and sister of Ernest Beadle. Olive remarried Stanley Hamer the dispensing chemist of Upper Elmers End Rd and today lives in Altyre Way.

Anne and Alfred Minter's daughter Eileen married Stan Kelly although she is no longer alive.

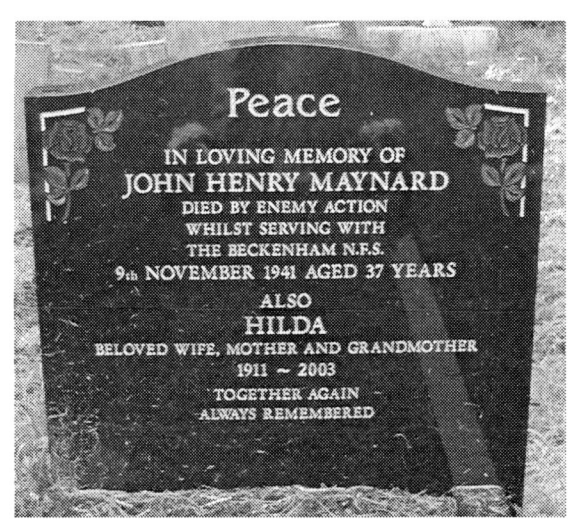

The grave of John and Hilda Maynard in the Beckenham cemetery shows that John's widow, Hilda, was 92 when she died in 2003. The original grave was of the type shown here to the firemen Hudders and Chalmers but when Hilda died, her daughters had this new shiny black gravestone erected.

THE AUXILIARY FIRE SERVICE 1938-1945

Bryan Wotton, Herbert (Bert) and Irene (Rene)'s son, lives at Rustington, West Sussex. His father came from Bermondsey and worked for a chain of butchers but he wanted to open his own business and to that end moved to Elmers End to work as manager for Bill Hazelton, a fatal move as it turned out! He was a skilled carpenter and added certain 'luxury' touches to their air raid shelter, including a special shelf for their Parkinson's humbugs. When his father was killed, Bryan was five years old and lived at 78 Upper Elmers End Rd at the corner of Adams Rd. His mother would tell him that she remembers his father waving to them as he went through the snicket on his way to the sub station in the Standard Bank ground on that last day, 19 April 1941.

Bryan remembers other firemen's families as the regular firemen used to arrange great parties for all the children at the main Beckenham Fire Station in Bromley Rd and Stanhope Grove. Bryan recollects that Albert Kite's son and daughter went to the parties. Raymond Farley went to Hawes Down School and his mother was a dinner lady there. Daisy Endean and Ann Minter were his mother's friends.

Bryan went to Marian Vian and at the age of five felt quite old enough to go to school on his own. There was the offer from the fire service to go to a boarding school but he was glad his mother rejected it. His mother was a qualified butcher and had to work very hard for six days a week. An ungrateful Government awarded widows a miserly pension far below that of an army widow. He would be left in the care of Doris Hazelton from the hardware shop at Elmers End. She would make tasty pies on the 'parlour's pine table for sale at their butcher's shop under conditions that would not be allowed today! This arrangement landed Bryan in Beckenham Hospital recovering from burns caused by a spirit stove exploding when Alan (Banger) Hazelton was soldering a Dinky toy. Alan's older brother John was about to join the Merchant Navy as a butcher and took over the lease of the hardware shop as a butcher when he left the sea. Bryan's uncle, his father's younger brother, was an errand boy for Hazelton's.

The remains of Old Palace School, Poplar after 20th April 1941

If you read between the lines of Bryan's story, you can see the sacrifices made by those young firemen, their widows and children. Of course it was just the same for those in the forces but the difference is that the losses of the firemen were not recognised by the Government. Their widows were left to struggle on a pittance and life was particularly hard. The Annual Remembrance Parade at the firemen's church of St Giles in September each year has really come too late for surviving firemen in their nineties and for the last two years has not been held at St Giles. Their families resent the back seat they are expected to play in a parade of young, representatives of the present. Each year there are fewer and fewer AFS members present from the service disbanded in 1948 with Princess Anne as the patron. During the firemen's time of service from 1938 to 1945 there was no branch of the forces that could be depended upon more to help their fellows in every possible way.

John Maynard

Bert Wotton

A remarkable coincidence is that Bryan Wotton's step daughter-in-law is Xandra Frances Tress Barry, descendant of the family that inaugurated the fire brigade in Beckenham in 1869. She is the third daughter of the 4th Baronet Sir Rupert Rodney Francis Tress Barry's second marriage and she married Major Simon John Cox who is Bryan's stepson.

Kenneth Bowles

Twleve
A year of construction for Mayor Cllr James Hilton Atkins 1946/47

'We now move on to what may be a more normal year in which we must address ourselves to sober realities and day to day responsibilities. How much is done will depend on you.'

From Mayor Cllr J H Atkins speech when elected 10 November 1946

The Mayor described himself as being educated at evening classes and by listening to other people. He served in the Merchant Navy from 1910 to 1915 and then joined the RAMC for the rest of the war. He entered the LCC in 1921 moving to Beckenham 10 years later. He was Independent member for Eden Park from 1935 and apart from his hobbies of bowls and reading, his main interest was in the education of the young to become responsible citizens. It was wholly appropriate that the Council had instituted a new custom to recognise Good Citizenship in young people to take place as the new Mayor took over. Sixteen year old Boy Scout, Noel Robert Couldrey, received recognition as the Heavyweight Boxing Champion in the Scouts and David Osborne aged fifteen for his outstanding performance in his technical examinations.

The death of nineteen year old Victor Gosling on 21 November 1946 at the Ministry of Pensions Hospital at Aylesbury recalled another award given in May 1945. During an air raid in May 1941, his parents had been killed and he had been blown into a tree at their home in Pickhurst Rise. He was paralysed from the hips down and was awarded the Scout's Cornwell badge four years later in recognition of his bravery and amazing cheerfulness during his long stay in hospital. He was a member of the first West Wickham Scouts and this award was their equivalent of the VC.

As the New Year began, Dove, the Borough Engineer revealed a plan he had drawn out on the back of an envelope when the first bombs fell by the Railway Hotel near Beckenham Junction station. The main feature of the plan was a large roundabout at the end of Rectory Rd which would be a real asset to the traffic today. There were many objections to the plan which was to make the area Beckenham's Civic Centre. Mr Jutton the chemist and Mr Andrews of Andy's cycles wanted to know if they would be offered alternative accommodation at the same rent elsewhere. Miss Vian and Vernon Chalk commented that we should not be pulling down houses at such a time of shortage and that those bombed out from St George's Rd needed their houses back. The old Bromley Rd School would disappear in the plan. The discussion went on throughout the year but nothing came of it!

One of the coldest winters was underway and many of the side roads were to remain frozen into icy ruts until the spring. Sports fixtures were abandoned. Voltage reduction and electricity cuts became the norm with domestic power cut between 9 and 12 in the morning and 2 and 4 in the afternoons and with voltage reductions at other times. Local industries were hard hit. Muirhead's could work as usual because it generated its own electricity but others like the Aerograph, Twinlocks and Pillin's ceased all work except for cleaning and maintenance. Kohnstamm Randak's tannery was allowed sufficient power to prevent the skins rotting but could not produce the leather uppers for shoes.

In March it was announced that the British Restaurants at Elmers Green and the Yew Tree must close although St George's would be allowed another year if it did not make a loss.

A YEAR OF CONSTRUCTION FOR MAYOR CLLR JAMES HILTON ATKINS 1946/47

The Beckenham branch of Barnardos helpers could not hold their fete in their usual Oaklands because its owner was ill, but Miss Petley offered the Harvington house and garden for the purpose. This was especially popular as she offered pony rides to the children as well as all the games, competitions and stalls. Victor Thornton's daughter, Valerie, presented the bouquet to Secretary Anne Tynan at the opening of the fete.

Alderman Simon Fitzmary, Sheriff of the City of London, gave land in Bishopsgate Without for building a Priory, now the site of Liverpool Station. His name is perpetuated at Beckenham's Royal Bethlem Hospital in Fitzmary House, one of the buildings opened by Her Majesty Queen Mary in July 1930. In July 1947, the Queen came to Beckenham to celebrate the seven hundredth anniversary of Bethlem's founding. Of course after a fine morning she arrived with the rain but after tea she was able to play her part in planting a copper beech opposite Fitzmary House.

Dick Barton's Snowy White conducted a quiz in Croydon Rd Recreation ground on Beckenham's Safety Day.

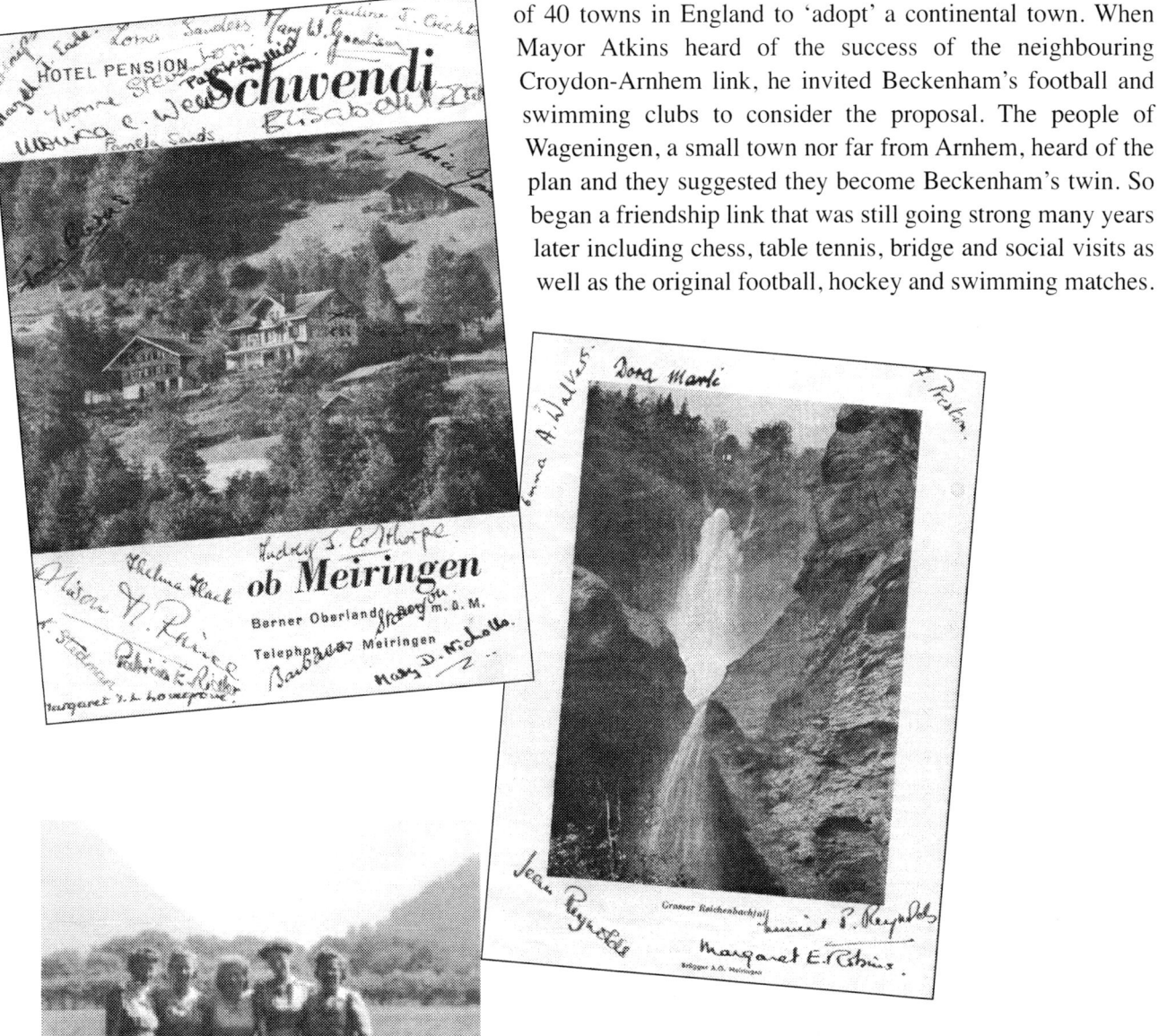

It was at the end of July 1947 that Beckenham became one of 40 towns in England to 'adopt' a continental town. When Mayor Atkins heard of the success of the neighbouring Croydon-Arnhem link, he invited Beckenham's football and swimming clubs to consider the proposal. The people of Wageningen, a small town nor far from Arnhem, heard of the plan and they suggested they become Beckenham's twin. So began a friendship link that was still going strong many years later including chess, table tennis, bridge and social visits as well as the original football, hockey and swimming matches.

The girls of the Beckenham County School who went on this trip in 1947 will never forget the trek up the mountainside to the Pension, the Jungfrau, Interlaken, the Rhone glacier, the clean, clean countryside and all the treasures in the shops of neutral Switzerland.

We like to think that the staff (signed here) enjoyed it as much as we did. This waterfall dominated the view from the Pension.

A YEAR OF CONSTRUCTION FOR MAYOR CLLR JAMES HILTON ATKINS 1946/47

The Mayor was well known for his support of the young especially on the sports field. He disagreed with those who held that every succeeding generation was worse than the last. Sixteen youth organisations took part at the Toc H athletic meeting at Coney Hall in May 1947 where Sydney Wooderson presented the trophies after winning his own two mile race at Dartford. The winners were Wickham Court with Penge Pioneers the runners up but the Mayor commended the fitness and comradeship of all the competitors.

A wonderful piece of news reached the papers in August when Percy John Conway, blinded by the explosion of an incendiary bomb that fell at his house in Cherry Tree Walk on 16 April 1941, began to regain his sight. Few skaters at Streatham and Purley ice skating rinks realised that the tall young skater dashing round the rink was blind but now he was able to see colours and could look forward to his career as a physiotherapist. Another victim of the war was Beryl Player who was seriously injured in June 1944 when a V1 fell on her grandmother's house. Her grandmother was killed and Beryl lost her right arm. After two years in hospital she learned to swim with Balgowan School and gained her Royal Life Savings Award at Beckenham Baths.

A house in Venner Rd used by two young men to preserve the history of the English stage was reported in the local paper in August 1947. They were Raymond Maunder and Joe Mitchenson. Raymond started the collection with a set of theatre programmes when he was about ten years old. It grew to include memorabilia from film, ballet, opera, Music Hall, London's lost theatres, gramophone records, old books and radio programmes but much of their collection was still uncatalogued. There were china figures of players from the past in their characteristic poses and actors would call at the house to check details of period dress and hair styles. The film world used them for play bills and photographs likely to be hanging in the vestibule of an old theatre, say, for 'The Mark of Cain' in 1906. Mander and Mitchenson hoped for a fairy godfather to provide a permanent museum for the collection where it could become a centre for research. After finding a home at Beckenham Place Mansion for twenty years, their dream came true in the twenty first century when it was housed in the Jerwood Library in the Old Royal Naval College, Greenwich.

Joe Mitchenson (left) and Raymond Mander (right) at the National Theatre Opening Ceremony 18 February 1981. Joe died 1992 and Raymond in 1983. Photo permission of the M&M Theatre Collection, Jerwood Library

The Cyphers Memorial Board to those killed in the two world wars was unveiled at the end of September by Mayor Cllr Atkins and dedicated by his chaplain, the Rev. Berry. There were also memorial benches round the grounds. Some like G A Wardle, Second Lieutenant George Radcliffe of the Royal Irish Fusiliers and Henry Charles Stembridge of the London Rifle Brigade were casualties of WWI but most died in the Second World War. Some were civilian victims of the doodlebugs, like Frank Snazell from Lennard Rd 16.8.1944, William Hazelgrove of 58 Kingshall Rd 2.7.1944 and Graham Baker only 18 who died in Beckenham hospital after being injured 22.6.1944 in Crampton Rd. He had been at home in the kitchen when he heard the flybomb approaching but reached the Morrison shelter too late to avoid injury. He was a promising pupil at the Beckenham & Penge Grammar School for Boys and was sitting his Higher School Certificate expecting a State Scholarship.

Frank Albert Snazell was for many years the captain of the Cyphers bowls section and lived with his wife Frances May at 112 Lennard Rd. On the fatal day in August, he had taken his daughter Mrs Elsie Oswald for treatment at a London hospital and they were on their way to Herne Bay on the Margate Express. Overhead, a fighter pilot was after a doodlebug to turn it away from London.

After he tipped its wing, the V1 crashed at Newington near Sittingbourne and exploded beneath the railway bridge over Oak Lane. Seconds later, the Margate Express reached the bridge. The engine jumped the gap but the first two coaches plunged into the chasm and were burnt by the fuel from the doodlebug. Eight people were killed including Frank Snazell although his daughter survived until recently.

There were several young men who were lost when on active service in the RAF. Pilot Officer Jack Lynn of 149 Squadron was the first to join up and the first to lose his life. He had been a member of Cyphers cricket since 1933 and became one of the club's leading run makers. Flying Officer Charles Rodgers is remembered on the Alamein memorial, died aged 33 on 30 October 1942. Flying Officer Peter Chappell of 247 Squadron died aged 23 on 5 October 1943. His name is on the Jonkerbos War Cemetery.

Flight Lt Kenneth Banks last played for the club in 1941 and was killed in a flying accident just after the end of the war on 29 May 1945 when he was 21. The fighter plane was seen to emerge from the clouds to crash in a field breaking a window in the nearby church. The plane had been repaired by the manufacturers after a serious crash but it appears that it had an undiscovered fault that caused the tragedy. His grave is at the Beckenham cemetery with his sister Nancy Tonkin (née Banks). Nancy is well known as the co-author of the book 'Beckenham' with the late Eric Inman. Nancy and Bill Tonkin's elder daughter, Susan Bonell (née Tonkin), is a Wing Commander in the RAF.

Flight Lt Kenneth Banks

This is Ken's last letter home written the day before he died

A YEAR OF CONSTRUCTION FOR MAYOR CLLR JAMES HILTON ATKINS 1946/47

Not on the memorial board but a member who played for just one season in 1938 was Flying Officer W Humphries who was killed on 11 June 1940.

Birkbeck and West Wickham branches of the Townswomen's Guilds were joined by Cator in November and at the inaugural meeting a month later there were forty members. The branch continues to meet to this day and has taken part in so many local activities over the years.

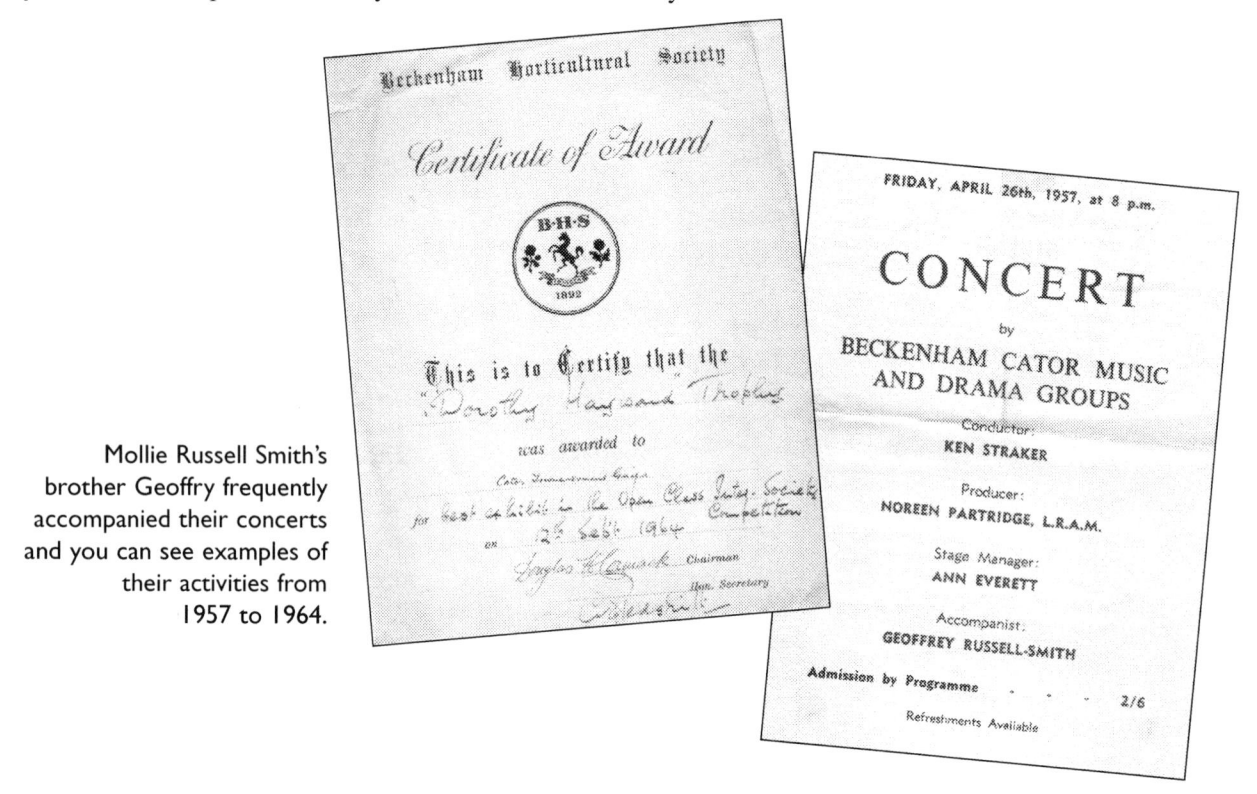

Mollie Russell Smith's brother Geoffry frequently accompanied their concerts and you can see examples of their activities from 1957 to 1964.

In November, the retiring Mayor Cllr Atkins presented the Young Citizens certificates awarded by the Civic Recognition Custom started last year. Eric Thomas was an exceptional Art student, Ian Boniface saved the arm of a fellow scout by applying a tourniquet after an accident, Cadet West was chosen for the foil fencing at the Royal Tournament and Barbara Tovey won the first Queen's Guide award in the Beckenham Division.

Thirteen
Mayor Thomas Boyd Boyd serves from November 1947 to May 1949

'King George VI had said that a leader must possess three qualities; personality, sympathy and idealism and Cllr Boyd Boyd possesses these in unquestionable degree. A man of few words, they are words of wisdom and judgement.'

            Cllr White's introduction to Cllr Boyd Boyd as Mayor in November 1947

Cllr Thomas Boyd Boyd deserved election for the extended period of 18 months because he had served on every committee and never shunned any duty since he had joined the council in November 1937. He was a Liveryman and Freeman of the City of London and Managing Director of a firm of Shipping Agents. He chose Alderman Jackson as his Deputy and the Rev. Hughes from St James's Elmers End was his chaplain.

His time as Mayor saw many outstanding events starting with the marriage of Princess Elizabeth to Prince Philip on 20 November 1947. This is how Margaret Parsons described the event in the Beckenham County School for Girls' magazine.

> *'I was tremendously excited when the ticket arrived which was to admit me to Buckingham Palace to see the wedding procession of Princess Elizabeth and Lt. Philip Mountbatten.*
>
> *When we arrived at the palace at 9.30 am, thousands of people were already standing along the route but our tickets acted like a charm and the police readily let us pass through the palace gates. We stood on one of the balconies overlooking the quadrangle round which the palace was built. When about forty cars containing wedding guests had set off for Westminster Abbey, two hundred soldiers of the Guards regiments marched into the quadrangle with their band and the Glass Coach drew up at the State Entrance. The Queen and Princess Margaret took their places and with three other coaches containing the Kings and Queens of Europe they all set off to the strains of the National Anthem. Then the Irish Coach arrived and Princess Elizabeth, a striking figure in her beautiful wedding gown, walked down the steps with her father. The scarlet and gold coach drawn by the Windsor Greys gleamed and the scarlet livery of the coachmen and footmen lent a splash of colour to the dull November morning.*
>
> *As they left, we were taken to the reception rooms. The Picture gallery was filled with the scent from bowls of white carnations and mimosa. The Ball Supper Room was set out with individual round tables each laid for about eight people. The tiers of the wedding cake were decorated with the badges of the various organisations with which the bridal couple had been associated. The icing was like filigree work and two white ribbons in a bow at the top fell either side of the cake to where white roses were arranged on a silver stand. On a table nearby were eleven other cakes; one was in Wedgewood blue, another in pink and yet another like a church.*
>
> *A page hastily ran a vacuum cleaner over the red carpet and the photographers were busy setting up their cameras.*

MAYOR THOMAS BOYD BOYD SERVES FROM NOVEMBER 1947 TO MAY 1949

We hurried back to the balcony to see the captain's escort of the Household Cavalry in their red and white ceremonial uniforms and with silver and gold helmets ride into the quadrangle on magnificent black horses. They were followed by the Glass Coach with Elizabeth and Philip. As Elizabeth stepped from the coach, Philip held up the delicate train of her dress. The guests soon arrived to be greeted by Earl Mountbatten at the top of the steps.

After lunch we went into the forecourt as the Royal Family came out on to the balcony. The Duke of Gloucester held up little Prince Richard who was waving vigorously. Prince William was reluctant to go back inside and had to be rescued by the Duke of Gloucester. As Elizabeth and Philip set out for the station, the guests showered them with pink and white rose petals. We had a perfect view of the Queen who wore an apricot and gold lamÈ dress with diamond earrings and necklace. The Duchess of Kent wore a dress figured in silver and the palest pink while Princess Margaret was a most dainty figure in her white bridesmaid's dress.

As we left the Palace the crowds still waited and shouted for the King and Queen but for me the excitement was over. I was left with a picture in my mind of a wedding I shall never forget.'

In the New Year the proposed closure of the Penge Fire Station provoked a furious argument in the Penge Council Chamber with a petition of 4,625 against. Cllr Emery wanted to know what right the council had to say it had no objection to the plan of the Kent County Council to close it. Why should Penge with its many factories, nursing homes, theatres and shops be deprived of its fire station and need to rely on Beckenham, Woodside or Perry Vale? Beckenham considered it should have at least as good a fire service as before the war and was concerned that its services were being taken away to the Kent County Council.

Bob Monkhouse, a 19 year old cartoonist, broadcast in 'Beginners Please' on the Light Programme in February. Writing all his own material, he said that he was seriously thinking of taking up entertainment as a career when he left the services!

Among the many dances attended by the Mayor and Mayoress, was the 'Leap Year' dance held by the Hairdressers Trade organisation. The entertainment included new look coiffures created on models by local hair dressers. Then the Burgomaster, Den Herr Klassesz, from Holland and his party was officially welcomed by the Mayor on the first visit of Dutch people from Wageningen. They brought white tulips to place on the Beckenham Memorial and a photograph of their town in exchange for a plaque of the Beckenham Arms made by the Beckenham School of Art.

A family memorial tablet to Sir Josiah Stamp with his wife and son was dedicated at the Beckenham Methodist church on Sunday 4 April and unveiled by Trevor, the current Lord Stamp of Shortlands. Civic acknowledgement was displayed by the attendance in their robes of the Mayor and Town Clerk with the Mace that had been presented to the new Borough of Beckenham when Sir Josiah Stamp was the Charter Mayor.

Deputy Mayor and Mrs Jackson started a mile of pennies with 600 coins in Beckenham's High St outside the Greyhound. After 6 hours they had to give up at 262 yds but they had collected 7,869 coins representing £32 15s 9d for the Lord Mayor's Children's Fund.

In April, little Vera Eileen Barrett from Overbrae was playing a game of Hide and Seek when she spotted an old fashioned milk churn, the kind with a narrow neck and tapering sides. Of course, she became stuck with her head and hands in the neck. Two fire engines and an ambulance came within minutes and the firemen were soon able to release her, none the worse for her experience.

MAYOR THOMAS BOYD BOYD SERVES FROM NOVEMBER 1947 TO MAY 1949

Fifteen year old Petula Clark sang to a large audience at the Anerley Town Hall in order to open Penge Youth Week. In her current film, she was playing as the youngest daughter of Jack Warner in the 'Huggett Family.' Among her songs were 'Dear Old Donegal,' 'Beautiful Dreamer' and 'One Meat Ball.' Presented with a bouquet of pink roses and surrounded by autograph hunters, she signed her way out. Her career started when she was 9 years old and she became Britain's 'Shirley Temple.' Here in 1946 she plays with Sid Field in 'London Town.'

Sadly, the third event involved the death of Keston Scout, Alfred Swallow, on 12 May when a 20mm RAF cannon shell exploded while he was playing with it. His father said at the inquest that it was time that the authorities cleared the fields round Layhams Farm that had been used by the Home Guard. A resident from Wickham Court Cottages, Cornelius Driscoll, agreed as he had picked up bullets and bombs with fins on many occasions.

The London Olympic Games were the highlight of the summer of 1948. Beckenham had five representatives. T H Christie and A S F Butcher of the Thames Rowing Club participated in the 4s and 8s. Arthur Gordon Pilbrow captained the sabre team for the second time, the first being in Berlin 1936. He had been the British champion in 1932, 1935 and in 1938. He lived in Rectory Rd and had been a part time fireman during the war. Two Beckenham swimmers took part in the freestyle events, Ronnie Stedman the 100m freestyle and Margaret Wellington the 100m and 400m freestyle. Margaret was the fastest woman swimmer in all England and Ronnie was the first Englishman officially to break the minute for the 100m freestyle. This he did at Odense, Denmark in 59.1 seconds.

John Mann, well known as 'Snowy White' from 'Dick Barton Special Agent' was in the news again in July, signing autographs at a fair at Thornton House. The last week of July had been the hottest week in Beckenham since 1911 but when the weather broke it rained off the West Wickham Conservative Fete and there was the worst flooding for years from the River Chaffinch. The Beckenham historian, Geoffrey Tookey, with his son Richard, was rescued in a gale in the channel off Shoreham when his friend's yacht was pounded to pieces at Seaford beach. The 18 ton yacht 'Gull' belonged to the Sudbury Recorder George Pollock. By September the weather had settled again and the Beckenham Horticultural Society held their September show at the Croydon Rd Recreation ground for the first time in their history and had a perfect day.

The Games Wardens Scheme for local parks was well underway. It was the idea of the Parks' Superintendent, Mr C Stock with the Chief Games Warden, Mr F W Fry. They hoped to change the attitude of the children so that instead of running away, they actively sought the wardens out. Football Leagues for both juniors and 15-18 years were set up with netball for the girls. The ex-parachutist instructor at Churchfields organised football, netball, volleyball, boxing, weight lifting and sprinting. He set the 'toughies' to paint the corner posts of the boxing ring, a job they were proud to do.

The Beckenham Baths was in regular use for all kinds of activities in the winter when the first class bath was boarded over and called the Grand Hall. Every Wednesday was the Old Times Ball. The late Chrysanthemum Show had more than 450 entries and was opened by the Mayoress Mrs Thomas Boyd Boyd. The Beckenham Canine Association held two shows there a year and the Old Blues Dramatic Society presented G B Shaw's 'Arms and the Man.' It became the regular venue for the 5-a-side championships of the teams from the parks.

MAYOR THOMAS BOYD BOYD SERVES FROM NOVEMBER 1947 TO MAY 1949

The matches were played on a Friday night to a packed gallery. The team in the picture came from 1962. The boarded-over swimming bath used to amplify the sound of the players running and the atmosphere was fantastic. Wrestling was transmitted live on Saturday afternoons by commentator Kent Walton. As the years passed by stars like Jackie Palo, Big Daddy and Mick McManus wrestled at Beckenham.

The parachute on a landmine delayed the explosion so that it caused the maximum damage. This is what happened when a landmine fell close to St Paul's church in Brackley Rd on 17 November 1940. It blew out all the windows, shattered the roofs, smashed the altar and reredos and wrenched in the doors. This was the first of the Beckenham churches to be damaged. On 31 October 1948, the new East window was unveiled, the design of Canon Laycock who briefly explained its features. The white Christ was interceding for all mankind as Adam and Eve portray the world's sorrow and conflict. The two saints St George and St Paul were shown with the angels and archangels and the entire window was directing thoughts upwards— —-in Adam was death, in Christ renewal.

West Wickham ex-fireman Archibald Blakemore made a playhouse for the infant Prince Charles with two others, Jack Brown and C M Parkes. In 1942 he had been the area organiser for the London fire force wartime nurses scheme making toys for wartime nurseries.

The playhouse stood ten feet high with two lower floor rooms and an attic bedroom with a flight of stairs. Mr Blakemore's two sons, Bernard 4 and Philip 2 thoroughly enjoyed exploring inside as did hundreds of other children at the Quality Fair where it was a feature of the exhibition. It was offered to the Royal couple for their son and the Princess accepted.

In February 1949, a meeting in the vestry at the parish church of St George's was disturbed by a man rolling up the altar carpet, worth about £100. The thief ran away was never seen again!

The picture shows the temporary repair to the East window of St. Paul's

April saw the hottest Easter on record and more than 1,000 queued every day for a twenty minute splash in the swimming baths. Sweets came off the ration and within a fortnight the sweetshops were empty as everything had been sold.

As the end of the Mayor's time in office came to a close, he and the Mayoress were presented with an illuminated address by nearly sixty local organisations in recognition of the conspicuous public spirited services rendered during their extended period of office. It was executed by Mr Redman the Art Master at Hawes Down. Cllr Waylett reminded everyone of the numerous football matches kicked off by the Mayor, his interest in the teams from Wageningen and the joint interest with his wife in all youth and horticultural projects. The Mayoress was presented with a very handsome mirror and a beautiful vase of flowers.

Fourteen
Getting back to normal with Cllr Thomas Mallett 1949/50

'He has a most happy disposition and one cannot help liking him. He is well known all over Beckenham for his interest in bowls. To be on the same rink with him is more than a game; it is an education in patience, and imperturbility, admirable qualities in a Mayor.'

Alderman Atkins proposing Tom Mallett as Mayor

Formerly a Marine Engineer, Tom Mallett had been a councillor for Lawrie Park without a break since first elected in 1935. The Rev. Brett of Holy Trinity church, Lennard Rd was his chaplain and he chose Cllr George White from Copers Cope Rd as his Deputy.

Whit Monday 11 June 1949 saw the revival of the West Wickham Fair and Flitch at Hawes Down. Mrs Chamberlain, wife of Col. F W Chamberlain, crowned Audrey Handy the Queen of the Fair. Audrey's dress of filé lace over white satin was made by her mother and aunt and her train bearers were Jean Wood and Christine Payne.

Beryl Mountford was the crown bearer and there were six attendants, Janet Wynne, Doreen Prosnall, Ina Edwards, June Lee, N Footner and H M Godfrey.

GETTING BACK TO NORMAL WITH CLLR THOMAS MALLETT 1949/50

One of Bob Pack's 'Roman Baths' at Langley

Do any of you recall the 'Roman baths' on the site of the Langley Park Mansion, where the Beckenham Grammar School for Girls (now Langley Park) was opened in 1959? It was a favourite playground of Bob Pack from the flats over the United Dairies shop at the corner of Eden Park Avenue. There was a smaller bath usually covered with duckweed and a larger one among the trees. This 'bath' was about 12 ft deep and full of water. The boys would lash wood to oil drums and try to float across the water as two gangs while throwing bricks to make the biggest possible splashes. They would all go home soaked late in the evening.

In those days, if they were lucky, boys had airguns. They would practise by taking aim at the cut off trunk of an enormous tree at the end of the lane and loved the ping sounds of the ricochets. On Sundays, the older boys would run cycle races on the old tennis courts that made a wonderful dirt track.

Close by was the Edenbeck Sports ground where on 9 July a crowd of over 600 attended their sports day. After the serious races of the day like the Ladies 220yds, there were mainly novelty races, many for the children who had to be run in heats, such were their numbers for the egg and spoon, three-legged and cycle races. Miss Hutchinson won the Ladies Ankle competition and the secretary, Dr Sam Wilkinson, was the popular winner of the Knobbly Knees.

There was a Mammoth Fair in Croydon Rd Recreation ground and the Bank holiday was celebrated with a carnival procession. The West Wickham Conservative Fete on the Oak Lodge Estate had 10,000 visitors. Of the 1000s of balloons launched into the air, some hundred were returned, the further reaching Frinton in Essex as most of them were lost at sea. This hardly compares with the balloons that reached Belarus as Oak Lodge School held parties for its fiftieth anniversary in 2004.

Two snippets of news from the 'crazy season' were that two hundredweight of dead fish were hauled out of Kelsey lakes. They died from lack of oxygen as flood water washed silt into the lakes that absorbed it all. The other was that oats were harvested in Beckenham on the Royal Bethlem Hospital ground, previously leased to the Evening Standard as a sports ground. This was once Monks Orchard Field belonging to a landowner called Munke in the 1550s and had not been cropped for a hundred years.

Grand Swimming Aquacades were regularly held at the Beckenham Baths in aid of the Mayor's Fund for distressed people in the borough. There were always comedy acts like impossible dives, aquatic tug-o'-war and enormous policemen being ducked and saved by impossibly small children.

GETTING BACK TO NORMAL WITH CLLR THOMAS MALLETT 1949/50

L to R (white shirts) Top row: Jennifer Jennings, Doreen Chambers, Pat King, Middle row, Christine Bridges, Barbara Mitchell, Marjorie Akehurst, Kathleen Stedman. Front row: Evelyn Andrews, Sylvia Jane, Pat Ridler, Pamela Preston, The Dutch team wore red shirts

GETTING BACK TO NORMAL WITH CLLR THOMAS MALLETT 1949/50

A memorial plaque to the twenty Beckenham staff killed in WW2 was unveiled by the Mayor in the vestibule of the Town Hall. It had been made by Mr Keen from the borough engineer's dept and was dedicated by the Mayor's chaplain, the Rev. George Brett from Holy Trinity. Among the twenty names were F J Bunting and J F Radford who had been killed by the V1 that fell on the Christ Church area in 1945.

Over the past five years Christ Church had been restored at a cost of £25,202 16s 4d raised by the congregation. Hundreds of people could not gain admission to the thanksgiving service on January 12 1950 taken by Dr Chavasse with the Mayor, Cllr Mallett, Deputy Mayor Cllr White and C Eric Staddon, the Town Clerk.

Front page news in February 1950 was the problem of housing Beckenham's triplets. Mr and Mrs Price already had three children when their triplets were born early in December. They lived in a 3 roomed flat in Churchfields Rd but even so they were eighth on the council's list for a three bedroomed house. There was nowhere in the flat to dry the babies's clothes and six days after leaving Farnborough hospital the smallest baby, Christine, died. She was nearly 8 lbs with a birth weight of 3lb 12 oz and at 10 weeks she had seemed healthy. The couple were left with 5 little boys, babies Alan and Anthony with David 2, Terry 3 and John 5, still in their first floor 3 roomed flat.

But when Mr. Tom Mallett appeared in a Panama hat for Penge Constitutional Club against the Beckenham Club on Saturday not only did winter close down with a slam, but people within a 2-miles radius developed prickly heat

Snowy White was again in the news on Christmas Eve when he entertained 700 youngsters at the Regal to present the prizes to the winners of the Minor's Club Painting Competition. He found that they remembered more of Dick Barton's adventures than he did!

There was thought to be no hope for the 1,000 on the housing list and even the 60 desperate families had been waiting since 1947.

In March 1950, Princess Elizabeth accepted a bed designed by Frank Guille from the Beckenham Art School for Prince Charles. Made of long lengths of slatted yew, it was 3ft broad and 5ft long. Animals decorated the outside and inside were silver escutcheons.

On Easter Monday, 8 April 1950, the Old Girls of the Beckenham County School played a Ladies Hockey Team from Wageningen when the score was a 4-4 draw. At their AGM in May, it was decided to call the association 'Adremians' a name derived from the school motto, Ad Rem Mox Nox.

The last official engagement of Mayor Mallett's term was the unveiling of the tablets inscribed with the names of Beckenham's WW2 dead on the memorial at the bottom of the High St. A long procession of men, women and children with wreaths, crosses and small bunches of flowers passed by the new bronze tablets searching for the name of their lost loved one. The memorial bears the names of 312 Forces, 42 Civil Defence and 288 Borough residents.

The retiring Mayor had attended some 180 social functions and 90 Council Meetings. He was remembered for his activity in the realm of sport, laying out pitches and tidying up the open spaces. 'Our Tom,' with his characteristic beaming smile, played himself out at the opening of the Coney Hall Putting Green on 20 May, holing the first ball in three!

Fifteen
Things were looking up for Cllr Edward Charles Dixon 1950/51

'When I consider the activities of my predecessors, I know only too well the standard I must live up to. Only my best will be good enough for Beckenham.'

Cllr Dixon at the start of his Mayoralty

Cllr Dixon, elected for Park Langley in 1935, was the first Mayor from the Langley area when he took up office on 22 May 1950. Alderman Atkins was his Deputy and his Chaplain was the Rev. C H Faulkes, vicar of St Barnabas.

Who remembers the glamorous tennis player, Gertrude Gorgeous Gussie Moran, appearing in all her finery at the Beckenham tennis week from 3 June? Gussie was an American tennis star who played at Wimbledon in 1949 and wished to play in a coloured dress but anything except pure white was forbidden. Gertrude's answer was a short tennis dress with ruffled lace-trimmed knickers designed by Teddy Tingling, former tennis player turned fashion designer. She was a huge draw because of her frillies and Beckenham was delighted to welcome her at the tournament.

Diana Dors was among the judges of the Queen of Penge Jubilee Gala week when Ivy Godwin of Twinlocks was elected Queen. This was not a surprise as she was already both 'Miss Twinlock' and 'Miss Beckenham Business Houses'!

There was a fair in Betts Park but of course it rained.

The Queen of West Wickham's Fair & Flitch was Gay Fisher being crowned here by the previous Queen, Audrey Handy.

There was a meeting of the Beckenham Amateur sports Association following the success of the Games Wardens in the local parks where the Mens Open Tennis Tournament was doing well. Harvington was suggested for a Sports Arena and election of the officers included many local sportmen. Cllr Boyd Boyd who had been the Mayor in the Olympic year 1948, accepted the Presidency. Supporters came from associations as diverse as Penge Boxing Club, the Invicta Rifle Club, Beckenhan Ladies Swimming Club and Beckenham Football League.

THINGS WERE LOOKING UP FOR CLLR EDWARD CHARLES DIXON 1950/51

Ladies from the Eden Park TG on one of their visits in 1956

The North West Kent Federation of Townswomens Guilds was flourishing and the Eden Park branch was started in 1950 with great enthusiasm. The expertise of these ladies, supported wonderfully by sons and husbands, carried the TG through to the late 1980s. They had outings to industries like the Express Dairies and Wilkinson Sword, wine and cheese evenings and four celebrations through the year with the Spring sausage and mash or fish and chips in the church hall of St John's church. Summer would involve a Garden Party in a member's garden, September would be a Ploughman's lunch and of course there would be the Christmas Party. Choir, started in 1961 by Polly Perkins, and drama came together to produce colourful shows like Hi de Hi, Cats, Our Fair Lady, Annie Get Your Gun, Mum's Army and Summer Holiday, gathering new talent all the time. They peaked with the Queen's Silver Jubilee in 1977 with 'The Two Queen Elizabeths.' Young women are far too involved in career and children to need the TG today although meetings still take place. With sight failing her, the 97 year old pianist, Kay Walker, had to retire recently from accompanying after decades of service.

The principals of Woodbrook School, Miss Mead and Miss Elvin, retired for the first time after 22 years together. They met at Stratford House School and started Woodbrook in September 1928. One of their pupils in the thirties was Julie Andrews and, by 1938, they proudly extended the school with a large hall. By 1950 there were 170 pupils and the school was expanding all the time. The sports commentator, Rob Bonnet attended the kindergarten there in the 1950s. As Miss Mead was presented with a tea set and Miss Elvin an upholstered stool, the school was taken over by Mrs Douglas. However they shortly returned to take up the reins again for a few more years yet.

Perhaps you may wonder about the origin of the flocks of parakeets that scream overhead and colonise Beckenham's tall trees. Mr Gray had an aviary at 30 Manor Park Close in West Wickham where he discovered that parakeets reared their young more easily if they were allowed to live all the year round in open air cages. If it were snowing, the green-grey babies would become little snowballs but wake up for food. He had 200 rare bird breeds and among the British species he had a chaffinch that was fifteen years old. They were due to move to Burgess Hill with their birds and Great Dane 'Danté' but maybe they were the source of Kent's parakeets.

THINGS WERE LOOKING UP FOR CLLR EDWARD CHARLES DIXON 1950/51

August saw the dedication of a stained glass window in St John's church, Eden Park Avenue in memory of Bertrand and Florence Petley of Harvington. It was given in memory of their parents by their children Hugh, Philip and Dorothy Petley. The name Harvington was given to the large house by the Petleys. They became engaged in the village of Harvington, near Kidderminster, and thereafter they took the name for their house wherever they lived, including Burma. Mrs Petley ran a farm at Harvington from 1919 to 1946 when she died after becoming dispirited by the compulsory purchase of some of her land for prefabs by the council.

In Kelsey Park, the lake had been drained, leaving a depth of liquid mud up to 10ft deep. Eight year old Joan Rayner's dog 'Simon' became stuck in the mud and it was thought all was lost. Then two firemen, Sub Officer Magrath and Fireman Stone worked in the darkness to make a bridge of ladders and branches to save the mongrel from the mud which was as dangerous as quicksand. The two men were honoured by the Mayor at a special ceremony at the Regal in March 1951.

The new season of Arts and Music saw Maurice Denham conducting 'Twenty Questions.' Dressed immaculately in morning suit with a flaming red carnation in his buttonhole he introduced the subjects nutcracker, henpecked husbands, ingrowing toenail, saveloy and blood orange to the two opposing teams, one all men and the other all women. Two well known local ladies on the team were Mrs Longhurst from the Junior Library and Nancy Wiseman of the Grammar school.

Harvington

Valerie curtseys at Barnardo's Fete held at Harvington, with Dorothy Petley second from the left.

Two mystery fires occurred in October. The first was at the Three Tuns in Beckenham. It started in the cellar and funnelled up the stairway trapping Freda Banwell, child nurse, and her charge, 18 month old Gillian, upstairs. Station Officer Clapson and Fireman Day rescued them from two storeys up. The child's great grandmother, Mrs Morley, sat by a window lower down with Fireman Biddle until the fire was extinguished when he was able to help her down the charred staircase. The licensee, Mr Morley, was on holiday with his wife and the child's parents. He was the President of the Beckenham Canine Association and bulldog breeder. Mrs Marjorie Clarke, Secretary of the Association was also in the Three Tuns. She escaped by climbing down a drainpipe but fell down the last few feet!

The other fire destroyed the remains of the Crystal Palace with a big blaze that lit up the sky and took two hours to control with ten pumps. The only car allowed on Anerley Hill was carrying Winston Churchill on his way home to Westerham.

THINGS WERE LOOKING UP FOR CLLR EDWARD CHARLES DIXON 1950/51

Julie Andrews, the star of 'Educating Archie' at the time, was made very welcome at Christ Church to sing at the children's concert. She had lived in Cromwell Rd with her parents, entertainers Ted and Barbara Andrews until 1946.

It was time to say goodbye to Miss Hayes of Marian Vian School. She was presented with a walnut standard lamp by the Head Prefect, Sheila Goodman. She lived a very lively retirement until she was 104 years old. Usually the school was visited by Charlotte Vian but snow had settled in and we were in for a bitter, very wet winter. A new use was suggested for the football pitches in Cator Park as a boating lake. In such games as they tried to play, the ball would just stop dead in a great puddle.

Activities moved indoors, especially the pantomimes in the Grand Hall of the swimming baths. The Grove Dancing and Dramatic Club produced 'Sing a song of sixpence' in Mary Cheshire's extravaganza where every child had a dressing-up part. There were demons, fairies, blackbirds, flowers, gypsies, bubbles, cobwebs, bees, jockeys, ponies and baby dolls. This was followed by the first pantomime of the Beckenham Children's Theatre, 'Bluebeard.' There was again a large cast and wonderful catchy tunes like 'Meet me at Myrtles Milk Bar' and 'Blood, blood, gallons of blood.'

The 24th Drama Festival was held at the Grand Hall where Beckenham author, Gerald Stanwell, received the trophy from Maurice Denham for 'Comrades in Tibet.' Produced and acted by Victor Thornton, the play for six players lent itself to a small theatre.

Mayor Dixon and the Mayoress both enjoyed the annual dinner of the Beckenham Swimming Club. The Mayor referred to the success of Ronnie Stedman and the opportunities provided by the borough's swimming scholarships.

Beckenham Arts & Music were pleased to have Brian Johnston to talk about 'Looking for Thrills.' He spoke of his first broadcast on 'In Town tonight' where he was expected to stay all night in the Chamber of Horrors sitting with Crippen, the brides in the bath man. He said models were wearing the genuine clothes of the criminals and their eyes followed you everywhere. He stayed from 5 to 11 and by then, frightened of his own voice, he left. Other memorable occasions were when he was bowled at by Compton and Edrich, suspended from a harness in the ballet and tested the ejector set of a jet aircraft.

As Cllr Dixon's Mayoralty came to a close, preparations for the 1951 Festival of Britain were well underway for Cllr Christie to take over.

Sixteen
Cllr Charles Percy Christie is the Festival of Britain Mayor 1951/52

The ninth of June 1951 was the magic date for Mayor and Mayoress Christie as Beckenham's own Festival exhibition was opened at the Croydon Rd Recreation ground. As the Mayor said in his opening speech, the exhibition was intended to be a tribute to the skill and workmanship of British craftsmen.

For the ten days of the exhibition, a charming old couple from Blandford Rd had been chosen as 'Mr and Mrs Beckenham.' Mr and Mrs Sidney Cowper had both been born in Beckenham and after attending Alexandra school, Sidney had been a baker and confectioner all his life.

An army of five hundred workmen had toiled all the week to set up the miniature 'Ideal Home' of local traders in the three giant marquees.

The first of the giant marquees housed the Civic and Clean Food exhibition which included the bottle washing plant of three local dairies, George Bowyer, Express and United, Lyons model choc-ice making plant and Sainsbury's ideal food counters.

At the entrance to the B marquee was the George Green Ltd display, a firm established in Beckenham only five years after the original 1851 exhibition. There was also Dunn's oak reproduction furniture, the luxury and comfort of Cedars House Furnishings, Olby's with their latest Hoovers and a wonderful demonstration bathroom. Lighting was displayed by Robertsons of Beckenham High St. and the newest office equipment was shown by Twinlocks of Elmers End.

A flower garden with a pond and cascade by Holdaway Nurseries of Park Langley drew visitors to the most popular displays in the C marquee. A miniature car race provided by Lyons had remote controlled Cadby Hall vans that could be steered round an obstacle track, inviting queues of those wanting to try. We could watch Kenneth Ross of Elmers End as he fascinated the spectators with his skill at throwing pots and admire the cut crystal and glassware of his display. Pretty girls soon had an admiring audience as they made buttons, brooches, bowls and clay figures for sale. Rowley Studios showed off their photography, Stanmar Products their hand made shoes and Tremaynes of Beckenham had raffles for pairs of nylons. Peggy Foy's Studio from West Wickham made pottery souvenirs and Evelyn Paget attracted a large audience of ladies to the hair dressing displays.

CLLR CHARLES PERCY CHRISTIE IS THE FESTIVAL OF BRITAIN MAYOR 1951/52

Outside attractions included children's fashion shows organised by Babydom, trailer homes from the Park Langley Garage an excellent playground that was always in use and demonstrations from Prestcold refrigerators. If today, these displays appear ordinary, the reader must appreciate that food and clothing were still rationed, furniture solely available in the Utility range and only the wealthiest would own a refrigerator or a Hoover.

The Mayor attended the fiftieth anniversary of the opening of Beckenham Baths in 1901. To mark that event, the Chairman of the Baths Committee, historian Robert Borrowman, had taken a header from the diving board.

The Mayoress unveiled the plaque of the Training Ship Sikh at the Beckenham & Penge HQ in Croydon Rd, Penge. Since they had been bombed out of their original HQ in Copers Cope Rd, they had met at Minshull House School in Park Rd, Bromley Rd School air raid shelter and the Elgood Playing Fields sports pavilion.

This year also saw the eighth centenary commemorative service at the parish church of St George to which the Rector Canon Boyd welcomed not only Dr Chavasse the Bishop of Rochester but also Princess Alice, Countess of Athlone.

The Bishop commented on the changes of the past 100 years that with the coming of the railways had engulfed Beckenham's dreaming woods and pastures, country seats, farms and parklands in a wave of building. The picture shows Kent House Rd in the early 1920s.

We were still worried about the prospect of war with Russia and the blitz was vividly recalled when there was a full scale Civil Defence exercise with its centre on the V1 bomb site between Churchfields and Sidney Rds. Although not visualised as an atomic explosion, a shower of missiles on the Anerley Town Hall was imagined as causing damage to a similar area to an atom bomb. We currently had only 280 CD personnel whereas they would need 1,140 to be effective

One morning the residents of Pickhurst Green where Pickhurst Rise meets Pickhurst Lane woke early to a loud hissing noise like a steam engine. A sixty foot fountain rising above the houses and trees was rising from a burst water main. Water was cut off until 10 o'clock and the unprepared householders said they could not even make a cup of tea.

The church council of St Paul's church was making plans for a vicarage and a new church hall. David Baxter thought the proposed Georgian style house to be built facing the church tower had a beauty of line that would be appreciated as the years went by and that in fifty years time, people would say they had done well. Now that those fifty years have passed, what do you think of the red brick vicarage of St Paul's, Brackley Rd?

Miss Henshaw is the 4th lady from the left.

The month of May saw the inaugural dinner of the Beckenham Soroptimists at the Public Hall. Girls Grammar School Headmistress, Kathleen Henshaw, accepted the Charter as Vice President in the absence of the President, Miss Hourston, who was ill. Mayor Christie wished them every success and his wife the Mayoress said she had thoroughly enjoyed the evening as their Chairman. It was the first occasion that she had been Chairman of anything and she thanked everyone for asking her.

Seventeen
Cllr George Charles William White prepares the way for the Coronation of Queen Elizabeth 1952/53

Described as 'a bundle of energy and a glutton for work,' Cllr White was the ideal choice of Mayor for a year which would involve clearance of bomb sites and preparation for the Coronation on 2 June 1953 by which time he would no longer be Mayor.

Cllr William Duncan

A founder member of the Copers Cope Ward Ratepayers Association, Cllr White had represented the Copers Cope Rd Ward before he became the Mayor and both he and his wife Gladys served the area in the Civil Defence in the war. He was a Senior Fire Guard at Post 7. It was no surprise that he asked the Rev. Donald Knight to be his Chaplain. The Mayor's Civic Service was held at St Paul's church in Brackley Rd on 15 June. The church was beautifully decorated by the Beckenham Horticultural Society of which the Mayor had been the Deputy President. Well known for his quotations from the bible, the vicar chose Hebrews 11, v 10 saying 'Our great mistake is that we try to build on crumbling ruins of old civilisations.' The Deputy Mayor was Cllr George Montagu Rochfort Lord JP.

The memorial service to the late Reginald Leeks was held at St George's church on Tuesday evening 3 June 1952 attended by the Mayor, councillors and Civil Defence representatives of all kinds from Kent and London. He had been the Assistant Fire Force Officer of Beckenham's AFS during the war. The lesson was read by Victor Thornton who said, 'We have lost a great friend and a very gallant officer, a man of fine moral quality.'

Beckenham's Diamond Jubilee Flower Show was opened in Croydon Rd Recreation ground by the Mayoress with two large marquees on the bandstand lawn. The 541 entries were the best in living memory. The Council's exhibit of fuchsias and coloured leaf plants won a special gold award and the Mayoress said that she thought they were better than the Chelsea Flower Show. Kingfisheries exhibited wonderful tropical aquaria with fish including neon tetras and swordtails and the Bolton Bros Super Funfair had rivals for the attention of the children in the Fancy Dress parade and Tiny Tots races.

The corporation's third new bowling green to be laid since the end of the war was opened by the Mayor at the Churchfields Recreation Ground on 5 July with Alderman Guy Brook who was Chairman of the Parks Committee and Mr Stock, the Parks Superintendent. The Mayor threw the first jack and wood and the jack was mounted as an ash tray and presented to the Mayor as a reminder of a happy afternoon.

St Christopher's School put on a Beckenham History Pageant with the help of local historian, Geoffrey Tookey, a scene from which is shown hers in the school grounds.

CLLR GEORGE CHARLES WILLIAM WHITE
PREPARES THE WAY FOR THE CORONATION OF QUEEN ELIZABETH 1952/53

Car racing tests were being held on the two miles of twisting track in the Crystal Palace grounds using midget 500cc cars. Occasionally Mike Hawthorn driving a 2.5 litre Bristol Cooper would join in investigating the possible noise nuisance of racing on the track.

Mindful of the need to get well ahead with the planning for the coronation, the Mayor set about inviting 78 organisations for their ideas. On behalf of the West Wickham Community Council, Geoffrey Sarjeant said that it had already drafted a plan for three weeks of celebrations but he was urged to pool ideas and to not be too parochial. They would start with the Fair & Flitch, with street teas, a costume pageant, bonfires, fireworks and dancing on Coronation day itself. In addition a Coronation Ball, a Merry England Production and a special Shopping Week were suggested. It was decided on a limit of an expenditure of £4,000.

When the Coronations Celebrations Committee revealed their proposed programme the rest of the council thought it was uninspiring. Whereas West Wickham was thinking of celebrating for three weeks, Beckenham was suggesting an 8 day programme only, with no pageant or souvenir programme. They would floodlight the two parish churches and the Town Hall but the tradesmen and residents would decorate the streets and houses themselves. Street parties would be allowed but no financial assistance would be available. Cllr Price said that Beckenham had forgotten to enjoy itself but there had been so many changes since the celebrations of the 1930s and it was true that people would be watching TV on Coronation Day itself. At least the Council decided to buy souvenir Coronation spoons and beakers for the schoolchildren.

Radio Rentals, by 1952, was the largest company in the television rental business. Since the picture on your TV was likely to start revolving or disappearing without notice, it was comforting to be able to call out the repair man to make it work again within a few hours.

A wonderful piece of news for four societies was that an anonymous donor had decided to provide them with a hall for their meetings at the corner of Croydon and Shrewsbury Rds, the Azelia Hall. It was to be built at once for the Blind Club, Infantile Paralysis Fellowship, Darby & Joan Club and Veterans Club.

November saw a first in the world of bird watching when local naturalist, Geoffrey Manser, noticed a cormorant alight on the north side of the upper lake in Kelsey Park on Sunday 2 November 1952. The bird watchers did not think it would enjoy a Kelsey Park lake diet for long but half a century later, cormorants are a common sight on our lakes, diving for fish and hanging out their wings to dry. Perhaps this is because the lake in the South Norwood Country Park near Elmers End station has encouraged them since 1990.

The weather was turning against us. The Queen Mother's visit to Biggin Hill with Winston Churchill was held in drenching rain although while they were lunching at Chartwell, the sun came out. They were Honorary Air Commodores of the City of London squadron 600 and the 615 Surrey squadron but the day was saved by holding the ceremonies in giant marquees.

A week later a 90 mph gale inflicted severe damage on mature trees like the old Stone Pine in Kelsey Park, a tall elm in the garden of Lavender Cottage and the 1,000 year old Cedar at 'Cedar Lawn' in Wickham Rd. Frederick Coleman driving in the early hours had a narrow escape in Cumberland Rd when a tree fell across the front of his car. When the roof was blown off Mrs Peacock's aviary in Elwill Way, all her birds escaped. Many shop windows shattered in the High St and in Vera Frances the dresses were ripped by the broken glass.

CLLR GEORGE CHARLES WILLIAM WHITE
PREPARES THE WAY FOR THE CORONATION OF QUEEN ELIZABETH 1952/53

Early on 5 December, cold still air became trapped near to the ground. Smoke billowing from chimneys as people tried to keep warm thickened into a pea soup fog of soot, sticky tar, sulphur dioxide that turned into sulphuric acid, hydrochloric acid and fluorine. Deaths three times normal were not noticed until the florists ran out of flowers and the undertakers had no coffins left. The smog lasted for five days until welcome west winds blew it into the North sea. The choking smog was believed to have contributed to the sudden deaths from asphyxiation and heart failure of at least 4,000 people in the London area at this time and possibly as many as 12,000. While two thirds were over 65, twice as many babies died as normal. A well known local figure, Percy Jones, died in January. Return of the smog for four days in 1991 from 12 to 15 December was due to nitrogen oxides produced in car exhausts and there were relatively fewer extra deaths because we recognised what was happening and remained indoors.

On the 31 January 1953, another tragedy began as the east coast of England suffered one of the worst floods in living memory. Throughout the evening, freak winds and a swelling tide pushed the sea to dangerous levels and flood defences were breached by huge waves. Over 300 people lost their lives, 24,000 houses were flooded and 40,000 people were evacuated, many sitting on their rooftops in the freezing cold night awaiting rescue. Thirty minutes after midnight, Canvey Island defences were overwhelmed, the whole island was underwater, every house evacuated and 11,500 made homeless. Fifty eight people died. The waters reached as near as West Ham where 3,000 were marooned in their bedrooms. The Mayor of Beckenham initiated a special collection for the victims which quickly raised £900.

The Beckenham Journal's Christmas Crossword 1952 had a local flavour

Across
1. Ape newly for a Penge bus stop (8)
5. One of these goes before a house in Beckenham (6)
9. These looked back over the years. (6)
10. Missing in the exchange, the amenity open space has gone from West Wickham to 1 down; better wind up what's left for 5 across. (6)
11. Ran backward in the act of loan for a Beckenham Rd and a Wickham avenue. (7)
12. Losing its head lay in the upset hen becoming another Beckenham Rd (5)
14, 16. Second word in the borough's motto (5)
17. Did the Bath beau rusticate here at West Wickham (4,4)
21. Remember thee! —-, from the table of my memory I'll wipe away all trivial fond records. (3)
22. Yacht! Leg before the Parish Church. (4,4)
24. Little Diana mixed up at Ely, had better give it up. (5)
26. Country seat in Beckenham? (4, 5)
28. Receptacles for 28 down. (7)
29. Lord, man! It's a road off 11 across. (7)
30. Before it was a UDC, Penge was this Shakespearian Prince. (6)
31. Only three in the borough are so named on the sign; two of them are high. (6)

Down
1. The missing part of 10 across appears before and disturbs Gay Nell (11)
2. Fabrics usually are. (5)
3. Len gave it for moral uplift. (9)
4. Absence of swank ends the game at Balmoral Avenue or Twickenham. (2,4)
6. Poplar, cherry and almond conceal another tree. (5)
7. Change of address when Peter Rabbit took over from Toad? (5,4)
8. Indifferent by half? Just! (2)
10. And kiss me Kate; we will be married o' — — — — - (6)
13. It's made me slender. (6,3)
15. Sounds as though we might invite visitors to the borough thus. (9)
18. 20 follows this for Penge and part of Beckenham. (2)
19. A bird before the wooded hillock seems to have lost its way in West Wickham. (9)
20. Hold these for a bet. (6)
23. Time is the — — — — (6)
25. You can go for one in the The One in Beckenham but you don't have to have a car to live there. (5)
27. This comes from agues. (5)
28. Tree refuse? (3)

CLLR GEORGE CHARLES WILLIAM WHITE
PREPARES THE WAY FOR THE CORONATION OF QUEEN ELIZABETH 1952/53

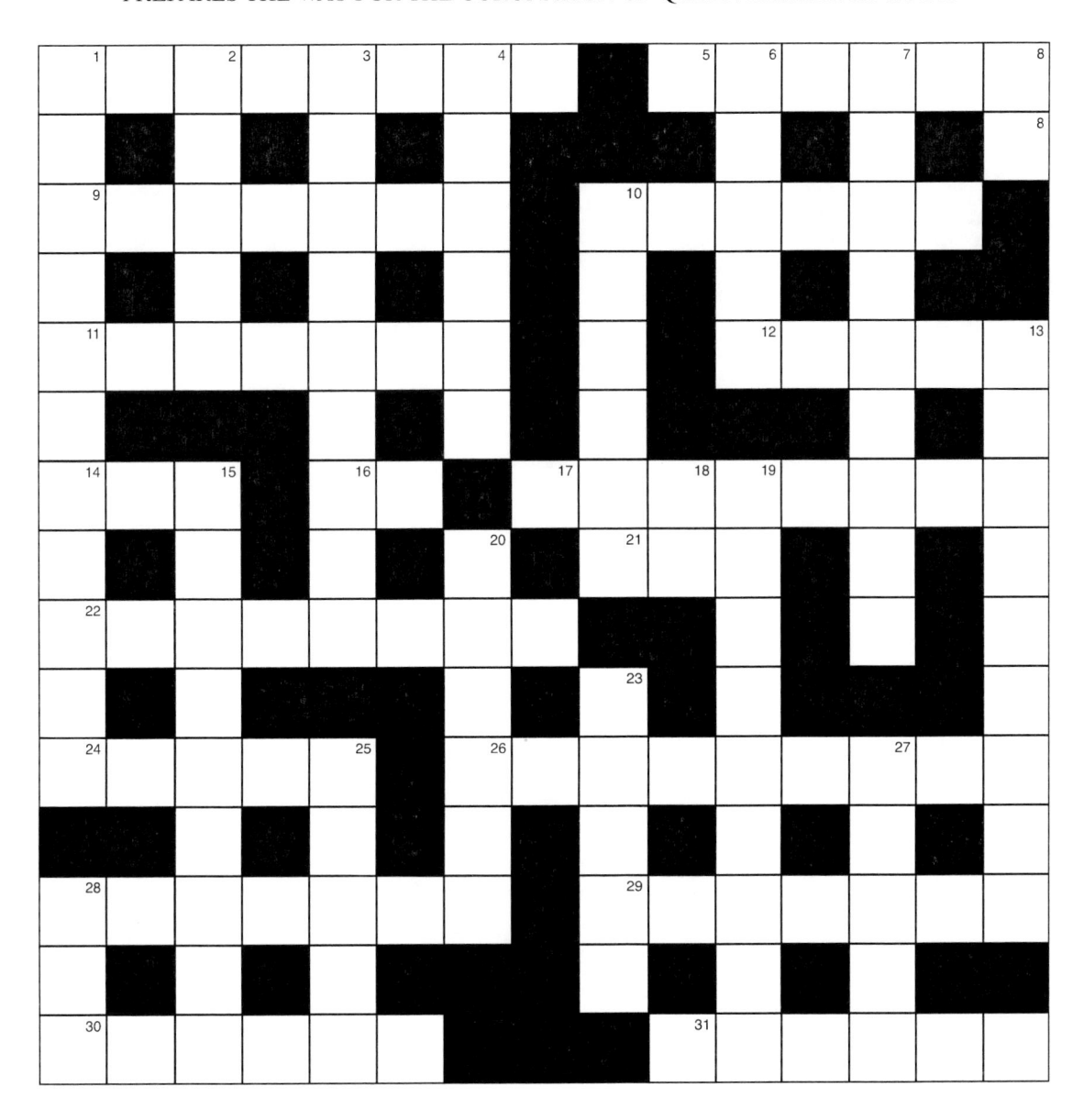

Solution on page 135

Eighteen
Alderman Sampson returns for the Queen's coronation 1953/54

The whole day was a triumphant success in spite of bitterly cold winds and drenching showers. It was a day of great rejoicing and heartfelt gratitude for the gift of Her Majesty.

Mayor Sampson, the Mayoress and the Mace Bearer went everywhere on Coronation Day and saw everything. They managed to visit all the street parties for the children although the miserable weather sent them indoors to church halls, work canteens and drill halls. One party took place in the street in Aylesford Avenue where canopies had been erected over the tables and Mrs Baldwin of the lower end of Ravenscroft Rd emptied her front room of furniture to make room for 50 children and their party. The residents of Churchfields Rd had painted the kerb stones red, white and blue. As the weather cleared up in the evening there was Dancing in the Damp in the Croydon Rd Recreation ground and fireworks.

There were two Coronation babies born within 20 minutes of each other; a boy was born to Mr & Mrs Dixon of Queensway, West Wickham and a girl to Mr & Mrs Gale of Eden Rd, Elmers End. The Mayor gave them National Saving Certificates.

Mayor Sampson does his rounds

There were two special supplements issued by the Beckenham Journal on the 6 June 1953. One is full of photographs of street parties and the other was the Coronation issue showing the crowds in Beckenham High St at the Fair organised by the Copers Cope Rd Ratepayers and Residents Association. The Mayor is shown bidding goodbye to one of the nine coachloads of the Darby and Joan Club off to see the decorations along the Royal Route in London.

Dancing in the Damp

ALDERMAN SAMPSON RETURNS FOR THE QUEEN'S CORONATION 1953/54

Crowds in Beckenham High St facing towards Thornton's corner

Looking up the High St towards Verneys the coffee shop and ice cream parlour

ALDERMAN SAMPSON RETURNS FOR THE QUEEN'S CORONATION 1953/54

Beckenham tennis also was victim to bad weather. New Zealand's George Worthington beat America's top player, Gardnar Mulloy in the Men's singles. The winner of the women's singles was 'Little Mo' otherwise Maureen Conolly. Opponents never found a way to beat Little Mo. She won all nine Grand Slam tournaments that she entered from 1951 to 1954 and in this year, 1953, she was to win them all. Sadly, a riding accident in July 1954 finished her tennis career and she died, aged 34, from ovarian cancer in 1969.

Perhaps 1953 was the most glorious of the post-war years for the Cyphers CC. During the war, two teams still ran for most of the time although matches were cancelled in September 1940 at the start of the blitz and when the flying bombs were at their most threatening in the summer of 1944. From 1940 an RAF crew had occupied the pavilion while operating a barrage balloon on the front cricket pitch, narrowly missing being killed when an anti-aircraft shell penetrated the roof over the sleeping quarters. The cricket teams played on the pitch at the back and used a horse to pull the mower to cut the grass when fuel was unobtainable. In January 1945, a V2 demolished the indoor bowls rink built on the outfield near to the balloon crew's dugout. This was still out of action in 1953 but Cyphers was enjoyed by a growing army of tennis players on the grass courts, outdoor bowls enthusiasts and above all competent cricketers. A new generation of post-war leading batsmen included Ted Purnell who became Cypher's most distinguished captain for 13 years. He had supported the club as a youngster and collected autographs of the leading players.

Rupert Holloway leads out his men against Beckenham. L to R Ted Purnell, 'Wis' Wisdon, Jimmy Black, Frank Kelsh, DJ Wardle, 'Briggy' Brigden, Jim Crawford, Willie Wardle, Rupert Holloway, Tom Jenner, RP Brook.

Left; Young Ted Purnell goes autograph hunting at Frank Woolley's benefit match in 1948.

ALDERMAN SAMPSON RETURNS FOR THE QUEEN'S CORONATION 1953/54

The actor Trevor Howard, front row extreme left, brought an MCC XI to Cyphers in July 1951

The other thrilling event of Coronation year was the ascent of Everest by Hillary and Tensing. St Christopher's School was honoured by a visit at the end of the summer term by Hillary and Lowe. There had been five climbers in the final assault as well as the support party but we only remember the two who reached the top. The St Christopher's girls know better as there were also Mr Lowe who did much of the step cutting, Sherpa Angnima and Mr Gregory from Blackpool. It was just luck that Hillary and Tensing attempted the last climb, inching their way up a narrow crack which took them to the top.

The opening of the Azelia Hall was delayed for six weeks until the middle of September due to a hold up in the supply of bricks. Given by local resident, Mr Parker, another £2,000 in addition to the original donation of £15,000 was being collected for furnishings. It has been in much demand ever since.

It fell to Mayor Sampson to unveil on 25 October 1953 the new memorial at West Wickham to the five fireman killed in March 1941 at Plaistow Rd. The small grave to its left is in memory of two firemen killed at the Poplar School on the night of the 19/20 April 1941, Ernest Beadle and Norman Mountjoy.

ALDERMAN SAMPSON RETURNS FOR THE QUEEN'S CORONATION 1953/54

Christmas brought the present of a television to the patients of the Stilwell ward at Beckenham hospital given by the Friends of the Hospital to cheer those unfortunate enough to be there over the holiday.

Worsley Bridge School opened ahead of schedule at the start of the Spring term 1954, the year in which two more schools were opened, Alexandra Juniors and Oak Lodge.

This was the fourth year for the scouts Bob a Job Week. It was mainly the older Cubs who gave their time as the scouts were either too shy or too busy at school. Alan Thomas, 11 year old scout of Christchurch said he only collected 16 shillings for nine jobs and was getting very tired.

Cub Don Boadella aged 10 had found the largest number of jobs for £1 9s. Derek Crush aged 9 said he was given a blunt pair of shears to cut the grass and also cleaned two prams. The scout leaders asked us to please pay the rate for the job as the boys were doing their best, cleaning windows, shopping, sowing grass seed, picking up stones from allotments etc.

As Mayor Samson's fourth year came to an end, he awarded a civic recognition certificate to Cadet Flt Sgt Crafter for proficiency at rifle shooting. While representing the ATC at small bore rifle shooting he scored 195 out of 200. Appropriately, Cllr Curtis became the next Mayor on Empire Day for which he had a fervent belief.

As usual, the people of Beckenham were able to depend on Victor Thornton for something special in the form of 'The Merry Wives of Windsor in Kelsey Park. Victor took the part of Abraham Slender and Vernon Jones was Sir Hugh Evans, a Welsh parson. Nancy Wiseman, music teacher from the Girls Grammar School could be seen among the singers and Victor's daughter, Valerie, was one of the servants.

Nineteen
'Ben' Curtis, Mayor 1954/55, a name to be remembered

A Beckenham Mayor who will not be forgotten is kept alive in Bencurtis Park where the Glebe Housing Association in West Wickham has provided housing for the elderly. Originally the home of High Sheriff, Francis Walter Chamberlain, solicitor and Sector Commander of the Home Guard during the war, Glebe House was bequeathed to provide housing for retired people by his wife Mrs Chamberlain.

Unsurprisingly Christopher Benjamin Richard John Bean Curtis was known as Ben to his friends. He came from a long established local family whose grandparents had owned the furniture shop Dunns. One time Beckenham swimming Club member and squadron leader during the war, he also became a keen golf player. He married Beckenham County School girl Phyllis Wauchope-Watson in the summer of 1932. He had been elected Mayor in his eighth year of serving on the council and as an auctioneer and surveyor, he had a particular interest in housing. He traded at 257 Croydon Rd as the estate agents C B Curtis & Sons and was chairman of the council's Housing Committee. The business is still there today as Curtis Haines, being purchased by Richard Haines in 1979 when Ben Curtis retired to Shoreham by Sea, Sussex.

It was particularly appropriate that he should be Mayor in 1954 because the housing situation in Beckenham was critical. A total of 1,827 families awaited proper housing and before his appointment as Mayor, Cllr Curtis had been concerned about the 'slum' conditions of other houses in Limes Rd and Chancery Lane. A vigorous program of building large estates would have meant a complete change in the character of Beckenham such as the use of the Harvington Estate for 366 new houses. The alternative was to rejuvenate areas described as slums and to build blocks of flats on small sites. The Beckenham Labour party was bitterly opposed to the council's attitude and tried to insist that every site should be used to meet the need. Fifty years later, both small and large sites are being used as witness the 500 dwellings on the late Wellcome estate and all the Closes constructed in the gardens of large Victorian houses. The figures for new houses finished in Beckenham by the end of June 1954 were 419 council houses and 506 private houses. Fortunately the houses in Chancery Lane that date from 1840 remain and are part of a Conservation Area.

One of the first ceremonies attended by the new Mayor and Mayoress was West Wickham's 21st Fair and Flitch on 12 June. The event was summed up as 'Procession started 2.30, rain started 2.31!' However Mayor Curtis declared that he and the Mayoress had considered entering for the Flitch Trial and then the Mayoress crowned Vivien Barrett Queen of the Fair out of the rain in the marquee. They also stayed to see ten-year-old David Bray's dachshund, Fritz, win 'best-kept dog of the show.'

Although the Mayor admitted at the flower and vegetable shows that gardening was not his strong point, he and his wife attended shows all over the borough and spent a lot of time looking at the exhibits. The roses had a good year because of the rainfall but the vegetables suffered.

The Mayor's chaplain was the Rev. Bernard Hughes from St James Church. At the civic service on 10 July we who read his address today are reminded of the shadow of the threat of the hydrogen bomb to civilisation and the disillusionment of the post war years.

'BEN' CURTIS, MAYOR 1954/55, A NAME TO BE REMEMBERED

Barry Curtis at the wheel of his sports car in Beckenham High St The men standing are from L to R Olly Oldfield, Dave Crickenden, Bob Pack, Ken Kitchener.

Then two weeks later Mayor Curtis and his wife opened St David's College Sports Day where he congratulated the headmaster, Mr Schove on obtaining his master's degree in science during the year.

Their sons Barry and Clive had attended the school and the Mayor's message to the pupils was to concentrate in their early years so that they could reach really high standards later on.

Soon after the end of the Mayor's year, Barry, aged 21, with his brother-in-law Alan Watson, ran aground on the Goodwin Sands. They were sailing back from Calais in a 2-ton yacht, 'Bob Sante' but were blown off course when the motor failed. After six hours on the sands, the Walmer lifeboat towed them off. Not a bit discouraged, Barry ran a sailing business at Shoreham Beach until his death aged 64 in August 1997, while his brother worked in Hong Kong.

Perhaps the highlight of this mayoralty was the end of sweet rationing in July 1954 so that we really felt that the war was well and truly over.

Three new Primary Schools were ready in 1954, Alexandria and Worsley Bridge Juniors and Oak Lodge Primary for Infants and Juniors. The opening ceremony for Oak Lodge on 10 July was performed by Col F W Chamberlain after whom the new road Chamberlain Crescent was named. Col Chamberlain was a founder member of the West Wickham Residents Association in 1929 and had been the Chief ARP warden for area south in the war as well as the Home Guard Commander. The school's architect, Mr Hugh Pite, had designed the building for 240 children without corridors using the assembly hall for circulation.

Beckenham won the interclub events against Croydon, Sutton and Cheam in the Mayor's Aquacade in aid of the Mayor's Fund for the elderly. The Triton Diving Goons with their crazy dives included sawing off the end of the diving board while sitting on it and the Beckenham Swimming Clubs in pyjamas and nighties had a goodnight race holding lighted candles. Two notable local swimmers with Kent titles were Valerie Thornton, granddaughter of TW Thornton of Beckenham Journal fame and Chris Walkden the eventual Olympic breaststroker.

'BEN' CURTIS, MAYOR 1954/55, A NAME TO BE REMEMBERED

Beckenham's adopted ship, HMS Constance, docked at Chatham in October 1954 after 8 years absence. Sitting on the hatch cover in the bows was the ship's mascot, a little brown dog called Trixie. She had been saved by the crew in Japan and during shelling of the Korean coast, she gave birth to six puppies. They were distributed among the fleet and adopted as mascots. The Mayor and Aldermen Sampson and Brook lunched on board with Comdr Patrick Morgan to recall the ship's commissioning in December 1945 attended by the two aldermen when Ald. Brook was Mayor.

The first voyage of the Constance was as escort to HMS Gambia in September 1946. One member of the final crew, AB John Jollye, came from Copers Cope Rd and he was invited to have a drink with Mayor Curtis in his parlour.

As this was HMS Constance's last voyage this was the end of Beckenham's adoption of her. She was to remain in Chatham with a skeleton crew.

The actor Maurice Denham, best known for his comedy roles in the 'Much Binding' series, left Beckenham for Bedford Gardens, Kensington on 13 September. Born in Beckenham, he was educated at The Abbey in Southend Rd and lived in Kenwood Drive. He appeared in the first 25 episodes of 'Itma' in which he played the charwoman 'Lola Tickle.' His move corresponded with two straight parts that of an airman in the film 'The Purple Plain' with Gregory Peck and in a play called 'Witchcraft' on Saturday Night Theatre. Bob Monkhouse was also in the news———-for careless driving up Anerley Hill. At the time he was living in Crossways Rd and his brother John was in Upper Elmers End Rd.

The new bus garage at Elmers End was opened in May 1954. Originally operated from 1929 by London General Omnibus Company, it had been totally destroyed on 18 July 1944 by a doodlebug that actually flew in through the main doors killing 16 and injuring 37. A plaque bearing the names of nine busmen who were killed and also the plane spotter, John Cunningham, was unveiled. The inscription was to Herbert Leach, Florence M Rarp, Thomas Sharpe, Walter Singlehurst, Michael Smythe, Chas Stares, Frank Stevens, Fredk Westbroom, Alfred Wilbourne and of course John Cunningham who stayed at his post warning the men until the bomb exploded beneath him. The plaque is now in the archives at Acton because the garage closed down in 1986 followed by the London Transport ground in Hawkesbrook Lane in 1999. The door through which the bomb flew was named Cunningham gate and had a special plaque to John Cunningham. Bombed out of his garage, John Smith, the chief depot inspector set up his office in a single decker bus in the forecourt of Elmers End station. Altogether 50 buses had been destroyed together with 14 Greenline coaches that had been converted into ambulances. Staff worked all night to pick out the least damaged buses from the tangled mass and by nine the following morning there were enough buses to provide a service. For three months until the part of the garage still standing was made safe, the streets became the bus garage and the mechanics did the repairs in the open.

Speech Day in November 1954 at the Girls Grammar school gave the Headmistress Miss Henshaw the chance to remind the girls of the efforts of women of the first half of the century to establish the rights of women to a full education. She urged them to use those hard won privileges and be willing to take on positions of responsibility. Indeed she would have had all her girls become headmistresses in their turn! The PTA was pleased to invite the French agent, Odette Churchill GC, to address the parents, staff, Mayor and Mrs Curtis and other Council members about her experiences in France as an agent in WWII. She let the Italians presume that her husband Peter Churchill was a close relative of Prime Minister Winston Churchill, which probably saved her. She had nothing to do in captivity and used to design imaginary dresses for her two children and furnished friends' houses.

We were reminded of a former mayor 1950/51, Alderman E C Dixon, who was one of the trustees of the Azelia Hall and founder of the local branch of the Infantile Paralysis Fellowship. He died at his home in Wickham Way on 24.11.1954 and is remembered by the road called Dixon Place off The Alders.

Twenty
Mayor Cllr William Duncan from a Beckenham family, 1955/56

William Syme and John Duncan formed the building partnership of Syme and Duncan in 1870 when the Copers Cope farmland was being developed for high-class housing. The founder's grandson, William Duncan, became a director of the firm in 1925 and built his own house, Hollybank, in Blakeney Rd, next to the firm's offices and buildings. He was keen on local affairs and became a loyal member of the council for which he stood as an Independent and became an Alderman on the death of Alderman William Sampson in April 1959.

William Duncan presents the darts shield to Mr Semark of the West Beckenham Darby & Joan Club

William Duncan's family possesses many photographs of notable local events, also his jabot, a bronze ash tray and his Alderman's chair, passed on when Beckenham was absorbed by London Borough of Bromley.

Alderman Christie was chosen as Deputy Mayor and the Rev. Donald Knight was called to be Mayor's chaplain for the second time as the Mayor was sidesman at St Paul's church. At the time, the vicar was involved in arguments with the council because he believed that more council housing should be made available on sites in the parish in Brackley Rd and Southend Rd.

There was pressure on the use of land for housing all over the borough. St David's School was threatened with compulsory purchase of land and Mr William Humphreys pig farm was due to go. The 11 acre estate of Eden Lodge, described as a 'green wedge' between the houses of Stone Park Ave and Harvington, has been preserved to this day against the requests from house builders.

The South Norwood sewage farm was soon to close and once the land had dried out there would be 150 acres available for housing, two thirds for Beckenham and one third for Croydon. In the event, the land never became available as it was judged too polluted with heavy metals for housing and now it is a country park. Beckenham still had a desperate need for over 800 dwellings. An application to demolish the ancient Kent House Farm Hotel was likely to be accepted since it was in such a bad state of repair. Built in the seventeenth century, it was the first house in Kent when approached from Surrey, hence its name 'Kent House.'

MAYOR CLLR WILLIAM DUNCAN FROM A BECKENHAM FAMILY, 1955/56

At last the Glebe Way extension was about to begin to join up with the High St West Wickham.

The BBC TV mast at Crystal Palace had reached a height of 430 ft with 210ft to go and television was beginning to make its mark on our lives, although only B & W. A pioneer programme by KCC to use TV in schools was well under way with trials in six schools. The three Ls, Look, Listen and Leave were replacing the three Rs!

The symbols of the 7 squadrons who served at Biggin Hill during the Battle of Britain in 1940 were used for stained windows in the St George's Chapel of Remembrance at Biggin Hill. The designs were by Hugh Easton who was responsible for the Battle of Britain Memorial window at Westminster Abbey. Squadron 32 was a hunting horn, 72 a swift, 74 tiger's head, 79 salamander, 92 cobra, 141 leopard's head and a wheatsheaf for 610.

Driving a grey Maserati borrowed from Stirling Moss, Mike Hawthorn romped home an easy winner in the International Trophy Race at the Crystal Palace on Bank Holiday, 31 July 1955. Stirling had flown home especially from Germany to start the race.

It seemed as though Beckenham's own electricity generating system in Churchfields Rd which, at 55 years old, was one of the oldest in the country, was about to close down. It still supplied nearly half of Beckenham's electricity in the winter.

At Layham's Rd, Keston, you could find the safest area in Kent because the Met trained its police dogs there. Out of 158 dogs, there were two Doberman, two Pointers, 8 Labradors and the rest were Alsatians, all male. They were all gifts from the public but ferocious dogs were not required. Alsatians were the easiest to train of dogs that had a considerable psychological effect on the criminal, not possessed say by a poodle! The dogs were accepted between six and twelve months but only a third passed the course. Then they lived with their handlers eating about 1.5 lbs of meat a day.

The twenty fifth anniversary of the Regal's opening in 1930 was coming up on 20 September which corresponded with its 12 millionth patron, seventeen year old Christine Wright. She was given a pair of tickets to see a performance with her boyfriend. Of the original staff, only Mrs Purvis was still there.

The Mayor was delighted to be asked to present a cheque to Mr Hessey at the Beckenham & Penge Grammar School on his retirement. Not only was the Mayor an old boy himself but his four sons had been Mr Hessey's pupils. He and his five children, John, Robert, Peter and Alan and one girl, Pamela, all attended the Beckenham Grammar schools. Starting in 1916 when the school was at the Technical Institute by the baths, Mr Hessey was affectionately known as 'Nunc.' He was Head of Cator House, taught Geography and took an interest in both hockey and drama.

William Duncan seated on the memorial seat to his wife on his ninetieth birthday in Church Ave. The Town Hall is still there further down the road.

MAYOR CLLR WILLIAM DUNCAN FROM A BECKENHAM FAMILY, 1955/56

The Mayoress, Mrs Duncan, inspects the embroidery with the ladies of the TG at the Azelia Hall

The West Wickhan Operatic Society was preparing to celebrate the twentyfirst anniversary of its opening on Valentine's Day in 1935 with a dinner dance at the Eden Park Hotel. Dr Bennett, first Mayor of Beckenham, saw the first performance of Iolanthe at the Grand Hall, Beckenham and sent a congratulatory telegram to mark the anniversary. The Society mainly produced Gilbert & Sullivan but also Maid of the Mountains, Geisha, Merrie England and Waltz Time.

Poliomyelitis was a current scourge of the young adult population. Dr Alan Goffe was working on a vaccine at the Wellcome laboratories that would soon be available for children and their parents although very little was yet ready for the 70,000 children in Kent who had signed for it. Soon the parents would be offered the polio vaccination with their children. Mayor Duncan was the President of the National Fund for Polio Research and had set out to raise £1,000 in 1956.

By the spring of 1956, new blocks of flats were completed at the bottom of Churchfields Rd, each named after one of the deceased AFS, Aitchison, Maynard and Hudders, and it had been decided to build houses on the Abbey School grounds.

As William Duncan's Mayoralty came to an end, he was commended for his quiet, efficient, sincere manner that had endeared him to all who met him. Cllr Waller in his vote of thanks said there was one thing that would be hard to beat by a future Mayor. During his time of office as Mayor, Cllr Duncan had become a grandfather three times!

Twenty One
Mayor Cllr David Robert Knox-Johnston 1956/57 celebrates the borough of Beckenham's coming of age

25,000 plants were used in Kelsey Park to produce the coat of arms in recognition of the borough's twenty first birthday. Twelve men took a week to plant out the bed with mostly semi-tropical species including Mesembryanthemum cordifolium and Alternanthera paronychaoides raised in the council's nurseries.

Here we see the retiring, Mayor Cllr Duncan, with the new Mayor Cllr Knox-Johnson and the mace bearer arranging the chain.

Mayor Knox-Johnston was born in Ulster. He worked for Ellerman Lines prewar and liked to tell of his job in Greece when he was the 'Deputy Assistant Director of Transportation.'

He was a good mixer, a lively talker, interested listener, enjoying company and social occasions. Cricket, gardening and driving were his hobbies. Alderman Sampson was again chosen as Deputy Mayor and the Rev. Hammond was chaplain.

Civic honours were awarded by the retiring Mayor Duncan to four boys; Chris Walkden for his outstanding achievements in swimming, John Michael Palmer, the Baths Superintendent's son, for rescuing a non-swimmer in deep water at the baths, Albert Maynard, national small bore champion for the Sea Cadets and Anthony Hyett for outstanding courage in overcoming physical disabilities, now walking on artificial feet.

Although Mrs Knox-Johnston's family had lived in Beckenham for at least 80 years, when it came to 'Namesake Day' the Mayor did not know of another Beckenham anywhere else. Readers of the Beckenham Journal soon came to his assistance with the Beckenham Bowling Club in Christchurch, New Zealand and Beckenham by Horse Lake in Saskatoon, Canada. For good measure they added New Zealand's Sydenham and Mitcham, Penge in the Transvaal, South Africa and Langley Park in Washington DC. Langley Park's Charles Emmanuel Goodhart's son Frederick left for the USA in 1920 and married Henrietta McCormick. Changing his name to McCormick-Goodhart, he developed a 550 acre estate in Washington that he called Langley Park.

MAYOR CLLR DAVID ROBERT KNOX-JOHNSTON 1956/57 CELEBRATES THE BOROUGH OF BECKENHAM'S COMING OF AGE

At the end of July, Colonel Cator of Woodbastwick, Norfolk, came to present the prizes at St Christopher's The Hall,. This was the house of Peter Cator his great, great grandfather Joseph's youngest son. His direct ancestor, the eldest son, John Barwell Cator, bought the Woodbastwick property as a shooting lodge in 1807 and a great celebration is planned for this line of the family in 2007, the two hundredth anniversary.

England and Kent cricketer, Colin Cowdrey married Penelope Chiesman, daughter of the Lewisham super store on 15 September at St Nicholas church in Chislehurst.

Former Mayor Cllr Curtis hit the headlines when he sprinted to the Rigden signal box to stop the Harrogate to Leeds train because a Land Rover had spun off the road on to the railway line fifty feet below. Rescuers managed to drag the jeep off the lines sufficiently for another train to miss it by inches. The man trapped in the wreckage survived, although with two broken arms but the soldier who was flung clear died.

On Saturday the 13 October 1956, the Mayor was delighted to officially open the new Cyphers Bowling rink. Still wearing the rose that had been given to him the same afternoon at the Public Hall by Lady Catherine Boyle of TV fame, he put up the first jack of the evening on the new rink. It had been opened twenty years before in October 1936 but after being used as a police food store during the war, it was badly damaged by a rocket in January 1945. The Club tried for a building licence for five years and was lucky last year. The following Monday, the Mayor opened the indoor practice nets at the Beckenham baths taking a mighty swipe at a ball bowled to him by Cllr Adcock. It was noticed that Mayor Knox-Johnston played bowls left handed and cricket right handed!

Do you know what a phillumenist is?

Porter John Ford from Hayes station was the Secretary of the British Matchbox Society. He won the international trophy as the leading collector of matchbox labels of the year and so was presented with the Phillumenist Cup at the Bonnington Hotel, Bloomsbury where he showed 500 Cuban and South American matchbox labels.

As the year came towards its end, the Mayor was one of ten civic heads representing Kent boroughs when the Queen's Own Royal West Kent regiment was presented with eight silver fanfare trumpets, fourteen silver flutes, belts and banners to honour the regiment in its two hundredth year.

Always a sociable man, it was no surprise when the Mayor, his wife and former Mayoresses, Mrs Duncan, Mrs Sampson and Mrs White organised a party for the children of the Council staff. Fancy dress to the theme of 'Cowboys' was judged by Mayor Knox-Johnston and the current song 'Davy Crockett' led the singing. Punch & Judy, clown, conjuror and tea with a magnificent cake made by the Mayoress herself, finished with the release of hundreds of balloons. The Mayor's four sons enjoyed the party, Robin, Richard, Michael and Christopher, all like their father, pupils of Berkhamsted, Herts.

The eldest, William Robert Patrick Knox-Johnston (Robin) was the first person to sail non-stop round the world in Suhaili, in 312 days from 14 June until 22 April 1969. His naval career started as a Royal Naval Volunteer and he worked his way up to his Master's ticket in 1965 when he married. They had one daughter Sara and he now has 5 grandchildren. Among his many Honours are the CBE in 1969, UK Yachtsman of the Year 1970 and 1994, Freeman of Bromley and then he was knighted in 1995.

The spread of TV affected our cinema-going habits and the New Year 1957 began with three local J Arthur Rank cinemas up for sale. Elmers End Odeon with 15,000 seats was £40,000, the smaller Hayes Odeon was £38,000 and West Wickham Gaumont, opened 23 years ago in 1934, was £20,000.

MAYOR CLLR DAVID ROBERT KNOX-JOHNSTON 1956/57 CELEBRATES THE BOROUGH OF BECKENHAM'S COMING OF AGE

Also in January, the £15,000 new library for West Wickham was opened by the Mayor with Dr Bennett in attendance. This was the fourth site for the library. The one opened by Dr Bennett in Jamuary 1938 was at 93 Station Rd. A move to 105 Station Rd, followed by a building opposite the fire station in Glebe Way in 1946 preceded the one we recognise today.

The Rev Donald Knight, much respected vicar of St Paul's church in Brackley Rd, decided to accept the challenge of the new church at Harlow New Town. He was a natural choice for a developing town as he was keenly interested in housing and the associated sociological problems. He had opposed the Council's plans for the Cator Estate since he did not believe that they met the local needs.

The Council was intending to acquire the London Rifle Brigade ground at Eden Park, which was leased to the Eden Beck sports club, to build over 70 1-4 bedroomed houses. Access was to be from Merlin Grove but Mr Larrington would not give permission to use his land. Today it remains an open space used by the Beckenham Football Club, complete with floodlighting!

Beckenham's adopted warship, HMS Constance, was finally to be broken up. The plaque presented by the borough was returned and placed in the vestibule of the Town Hall. Now it is kept in the archive store of the Bromley Museum at Orpington,

Yvonne Antrobus appeared in the local news because of her performance as Lady Macbeth in the Beckenham & Penge Grammar School for Boys production. She showed the boys how to tackle Shakespeare with a spirited performance and subsequently for many years she could be seen appearing on the TV. If you listen today to the plays on radio 4, you may hear that she was responsible for their dramatisation, such as 'Valley of the Dolls' on Woman's Hour.

The ladies from Eden Park TG presented The Five Miss Claymores at the Drama Festival at the Azelia Hall from 3-6 April 1957. The adjudicator judged the production full of atmosphere with excellent costumes and very good acting.

As the Mayoralty was coming to an end, there was a display at Biggin Hill by seven French Mystere II jet fighters. The more familiar Hunter Vs, long and sleek compared with the stockier French fighters, went to Creil airport near Paris. The leader of the Hunters, Squadron Leader Castagnola, had been a member of the Dam Buster Squadron 617 during the war.

Philip Goodhart was elected MP for Beckenham in the by-election caused by the elevation to the Peerage of Mr Buchan-Hepburn and Beckenham's new mayor was to be Cllr H Brook Brown.

The Five Miss Claymores

Twenty Two
Cllr Henry Herbert Brook Brown is Mayor for 1957/58

One of the crowd, this quiet, unassuming man approached his year as Mayor with some trepidation. Musical, occasionally playing the church organ and conducting the choir, a gardener but not by choice, a keen reader when he could find the time, he became a likeable and approachable Mayor.

Cllr Brown was elected to be Mayor of Beckenham well known for his hard work on the council, being especially concerned with the welfare of the elderly although he was not a Beckenham man. Born in Bristol, he did not come to London from the south-west until the early 1930s. Although unwell even during his time as Mayor, he was much appreciated for his sense of duty and ready wit. He had represented Shortlands from 1952 and was a churchwarden at St Mary's church where the civic service was held by the vicar and Chaplain, the Rev. Sugden on 16 June. The Mayor's Deputy was Ald. Boyd Boyd.

Mrs Clark of Gates Green Rd spotted 112 of the 117 'deliberate mistakes' in the local shops and won a prize of £50 from which she donated £5 to the Red Cross. Alderman White, President of the Beckenham & Penge Red Cross Society, presented Mrs Clark with the cheque. The Mayor and Mayoress attended the 'Court of Married Happiness' at the Fair & Flitch on Whit Monday to see that the winners of the side of bacon were Mr and Mrs George Benton.

With temperatures soaring into the eighties, Beckenham's tennis week was a complete sell out for the finals and every standing place was occupied as well. After a damp start on Whit Monday, there was not a cloud to be seen for the rest of the week. The Australian, Mal Anderson beat Herb Flam (USA) in one of the best Men's Finals ever and the favourite, Althea Gibson, just managed to defeat her fellow American, Darlene Hard in three sets.

The unveiling of the Dunkirk memorial to the 4,700 men of the BEF who died took place the following Saturday, 29 June. Relatives were taken to Dunkirk on the SS Invicta and the SS Canterbury, both of which had been involved in the evacuation. Mrs Esther Aylett from Mackenzie Rd had lost her first husband, Frank Jesshope, posted missing on 27 May 1940. She half expected him to appear at the Dunkirk ceremony looking for his lost relatives and Mrs Aylott said she never really believed him dead until then.

The possible relationship between smoking and lung cancer was first announced by the Medical research Council in July but many received the news with sceptism and sales were only down about 10%.

The stage and screen star, Richard Attenborough, was the judge of the ankle competition at the Beckenham Theatre Centre Fete at the Croydon Rd Recreation ground.

CLLR HENRY HERBERT BROOK BROWN IS MAYOR FOR 1957/58

It was won by Patricia Brown whom he rewarded with a kiss. He not only opened the fete but showed great enthusiasm for all the sideshows. He was soaked at the space gun range, tested his nerve on the bell circuit and tried his luck at the horse racing. It was all in aid of the need for a new home for the theatre since it was going to lose its premises at the Harvey Memorial Hall in Fairfield Rd. As a result, the John Lewis Partnership, notable patron of Glyndebourne, contributed a cheque for 100 guineas.

Children completely absorbed at the Croydon Rd Recreation ground

The BBC aerial was completed on Monday 19 August, towering 700 ft as the highest transmitter in the country. During August, the parks were full of entertainments for the children like Punch and Judy and Conjuring and the Games Wardens celebrated their tenth year in the Parks.

Ray Milland opened the Biggin Hill Air Show on 4 September when there was a crowd of a quarter of a million. All three V bombers were flying, there were aerobatics by the Vampires and Meteors and of course the famous lone Spitfire was flown by test pilot Geoffrey Quill.

The autumn issues of the Beckenham Journal featured the past history of Beckenham, highly recommended for those interested in the development of its railways and how things had changed over the years. A meeting of the Beckenham Planning Group a little later had little good to say about Beckenham of the late 1950s. They described the town as dull, drab, dreary, ugly, lacking character and with no sense of civic responsibility! The bombed sites were still not developed, the pavements were uneven, the disused cinemas left empty and the High St was too narrow. Where were a theatre, concert hall, good restaurant, departmental store, museum and what about a Ladies Cricket Team? The Boys Technical School was being moved to Oakley Rd at Keston in January so that another famous name was being lost from Beckenham and the opening of a new Primary School at Shortlands to be called 'Highfield' did not make up for it.

The bus strike started and support was total at the Elmers End garage. Since 1939, the cost of living had increased 170% and the pay of bus drivers had fallen way behind. The wage increases proposed did not apply to all the men but to just one section and so the long strike began.

The worst affected public were the residents of New Addington whose nearest station was four miles away at East Croydon. Manufacturing firms arranged coaches for their workforces, many turned to bicycles and car drivers became very popular. Taking a driving test from Bromley South at this time became a joke.

Buses at Elmers End garage on the first day of the strike

CLLR HENRY HERBERT BROOK BROWN IS MAYOR FOR 1957/58

The High St was so crowded with the extra cars on the road that you just had time to make a short circuit with emergency stops all the time as pedestrians crossed anywhere in front of you and the test was over.

The Beckenham & Penge Sea Cadets were in the news in April. Six boys from T S Sikh, rowed their Admiral, the Duke of Edinburgh, Prince Philip, to shore after his two hour visit to the training ship Ravens Eyot at Surbiton. They were Cadet PO Thomas Hall 19, Leading Seaman Peter Tomkins 16, ABs Robert Meeks, Laurie Drinkwater and Victor Woolgar, all 15 and Ordinary Seaman Gerald Bromley 14. The following Tuesday, the Mayor handed over the Efficiency Pendant awarded to them in 1957.

Francis Cammaerts was the subject on 'This is Your Life' on Monday 28 April 1958. He became a resistance hero after leaving the English staff at the Beckenham & Penge Grammar School for Boys in 1940. His resistance activities, sandwiched between teaching, earned him the DSO, MC and several French decorations. He was captured by the Gestapo when his car was stopped at a road block but he escaped immediately. He became a peace time Head of a school in Stevenage. Harry Reid, another teacher at the Boys School, was also an agent and appeared on the programme.

Twenty Three
Cllr Kathleen Moore is a double first in 1958/59

'The women of Beckenham were most proud of her. At all times she said the right word in the right place and, what was most important, at the right length.'

Cllr West about the retiring Mayor May 1959

Miss Kathleen Moore was both the first lady Mayor and the first mayor to come from West Wickham. The Mayoress was Kathleen's sister, Mrs May Rugg, and the Chaplain was the Rev. Shortt, Rector of St Francis, West Wickham. Cllr William Duncan was the Deputy Mayor.

One of the first social events held by the two ladies was a reception for the Beckenham Branch of World Friends with Swiss and Dutch visitors looking forward to trips to Windsor, Canterbury and the Tower of London.

Then the Mayor, herself a mathematics teacher, paid a visit to the Beckenham Grammar School where the girls had their last garden party at Lennard Rd because the school was moving to Park Langley. Yvonne Antrobus, Heather Thornton, B Horton, V Whitby, Barbara Austin and Anne Carreck were among the girls enjoying themselves dressed up as St Trinians.

August was a busy time for 'The Palace Sack & Bag Co Ltd that in 1955 moved from the Crystal Palace to Thayers Farm Rd. This small firm supplied sacks to farmers over the whole of Kent and was the subject of 'Focus on Industry' in the Kent Advertiser. In these days, our local industries were keen to put out teams and Twinlocks won the knock out cricket contest for the sixth time.

Following a day of sticky heat in August Beckenham was hit by a violent storm which resulted in widespread damage from overflowing streams and sewers that was said to rival the great flood of 1878. Customers at the Bricklayers Arms opposite the Regal cinema were denied their draught beer for the following week as it was all ruined in the flooded cellars. Lakes appeared all over the town in dips in the roads and Corkscrew Hill became a river. In Croydon Rd by the Beckenham Cottage hospital, water was higher than the wheel hubs and at Elmers End the whole of the Green was under water. Passengers alighting at New Beckenham found the station surrounded by water and had to catch a train going to Beckenham Junction since Clockhouse was out of action. The water tore through Kelsey Park like a bore and when the storm was at its height, deep water stretched across the junction at the foot of Church Hill while shopkeepers desperately fought to save their stock. Even after the water subsided in two or three hours, the alarm went out that it was returning and the Beck delivered the build up of water along its length from Springpark.

Towards the end of September, huge crowds were thrilled at Biggin Hill Open Day where Anna Neagle and her husband Herbert Wilcox were the guests of honour. Although missiles and supersonic aircraft were on view, it was still the Spitfires and Hurricanes that reigned supreme. The 250,000 crowd cheered when Alan Brothers, the commentator, read out a telegram, 'Thank you all so much for your kind message. Please accept our very good wishes, Winston and Clementine Churchill.'

The three V bombers, Valiant, Victor and Vulcan, towered above the spectators and there was a model of the Black Knight rocket that was recently launched from Britain's Woomera range.

CLLR KATHLEEN MOORE IS A DOUBLE FIRST IN 1958/59

The nine RAF Hunter and the four USAAF Skyblazers performed their aerobatics rivalled by the three Westland helicopters Wessex, Widgeon and Whirlwind. The perfect formation of the planes while a tanker refuelled three aircraft in mid-air impressed the crowd and the Fairey Rotodyne vertical take-off airliner was for most of the crowd seen for the first time. Perhaps the most striking display came from the FD 2 Snorkel Delta that brought gasps from the crowd as it shot past at supersonic speed followed by the sound of its engines.

The Mayor organised a visit to Bertram Mills Circus at Olympia for children of those who were killed in the Lewisham train disaster of 1957. John and Jean Charlesworth of Keswick Rd and Susan Tidman of Copers Cope Rd joined the children from Lewisham to have a good time.

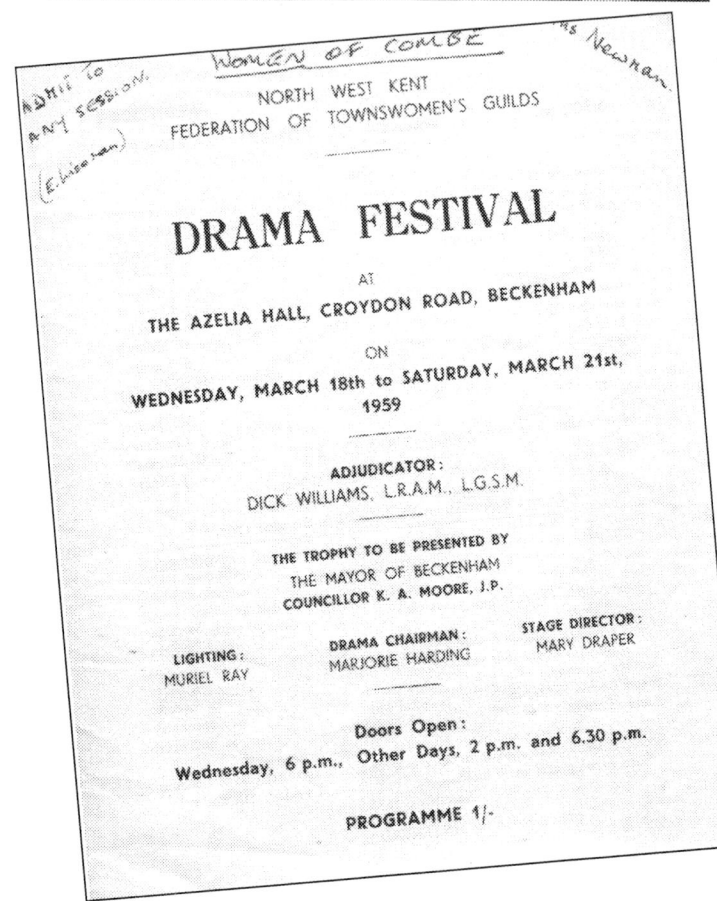

Another new school opened in January 1959. Highfield took its first intake of pupils on 7 January under the Headship of Mr Hevey from Worsley Bridge School and although the new Grammar school at Park Langley had also opened it was too small. Its enlargement started as soon as it opened because of the increased numbers staying on in the sixth form.

The Mayor's Parlour presentation to Marian Vian Secondary School girls, Susan Quickenden, Barbara Everard and Jennifer Branham was for the 100% marks they achieved in the Cycling Proficiency tests.

There were entries from 22 branches of the North West Kent Federation of the TG for the Drama Festival at the Azelia Hall in March and the Mayor presented the trophy. The Eden Park branch did well with the 'Women of Combe' 'except for the brooms and petticoats that looked too new and modern for a play staged at a quayside in North Devon in 1797!'

Glebe Way was in its last stages of linking with the High St. Mayor Kathleen Moore used the same scissors as were used by Cllr Healey on 1 April 1934 to cut the green and white tape by Rose Walk on 21 February 1959. She is remembered for all time by the retirement flats named after her in West Wickham.

It was cup final day when the Mayor forsook her seat by the TV to perform her Mayoral duties. With a small crowd of perhaps 100 non football fans she officially opened the gates to the fifteenth park in the borough.

Since 1945, the council had been looking for land for a park in Shortlands.

CLLR KATHLEEN MOORE IS A DOUBLE FIRST IN 1958/59

The Mayor Kathleen Moore opens the gates of South Hill Park with the Deputy Mayor Duncan

Lord Stamp's garden in Park Hill Rd had been considered but it was too steep for tennis courts and a bowling green. Then lengthy negotiations started for South Hill Wood where the house had been occupied by the Charter Mayor of Bromley, Sir Thomas Dewey, followed by Mr Chilton King, biscuit manufacturer. Only the music room of the old house was kept for a pavilion and new gates were erected using the balance of money put aside six years earlier for the Queen's Coronation. The new Bowling Club with Mr Newcombe, its captain, was looking forward to the match on 4 July with the Mayor's team.

The Deputy Mayor became Alderman William Duncan due to the passing of the Mayor and Mayoress's beloved friend, Alderman Sampson, in April 1959.

Cllr Kathleen Moore's final duty was to award Civic certificates to Queen's Guide, Judith Anne Barton and potential Olympic swimmer Margaret Eileen Toms on 19 May as she retired from office.

Twenty Four
Lancastrian Cllr William Sidney Robbins becomes Mayor 1959/60

'Able to disagree without rancour, win without gloating, lose without spite and a keen sportsman who many a time umpired cricket matches and saved the Mayor's team from defeat'.
From Cllr Hammond's seconding of the nomination for Cllr Robbins as Mayor, 19 May 1959

Cllr Robbins of Shortlands became Mayor at a very important time for the borough because Beckenham was presenting its case for County Borough status to the Royal Commission in Knightsbridge. The delegation comprised Alderman Parkin, who stated the case, supported by Boyd Boyd, Atkins, Moore, the Mayor, and other council officials. Their case was, that after the war, Beckenham stood shorn of many of its former major functions and now experienced a two tier system whereby everything had to go through the cumbersome machinery of Kent County. They considered that the minimum population figure of 100,000 was arbitrary and that Beckenham with its 75,000 had the ability and financial stability to be its own master whether in partnership with Penge or Bromley, both or neither.

The Deputy Mayor was Cllr George White and the Mayor's chaplain was the Rev. Sugden. The Mayoress was only able to attend the civic service and one other function before she had to go to a hospital where sadly she died in August. Also in August we heard of the death of the former Mayor, Henry Brook Brown, who had been a sick man even during his time as Mayor. Shortly afterwards in September, Alderman Charles Percy Christie died unexpectedly, being the third council member to die in 1959, all associated with Shortlands. Cllr Lord replaced him as Alderman.

One of the Mayor's first engagements was to open the fete of the Beckenham Guild of Old Scouts at 54 Beckenham Rd. He met Mr & Mrs West, the Pearly King and Queen, who stayed all day to raise money for Thornton House in near perfect weather.

Shortly afterwards, Terry Hall, the voice of Lenny the Lion, was a great success at the Barnardos Helpers Fete held in the grounds of the Abbey School. Traditionally this was always Beckenham's biggest fete, visited by thousands and Lenny was engulfed by the children.

The Abbey Lane stables were run by a sixteen year old, Jill Platts. She had five ponies that she used to give children rides to help with their upkeep. She hoped to become an efficient, competitive show jumper.

LANCASTRIAN CLLR WILLIAM SIDNEY ROBBINS BECOMES MAYOR 1959/60

Two of her charges were rescues. The 9 year old mare, Kate, was rescued by Ivy Bolsh from Sydenham who noticed that the pony had disappeared from her regular rounds with a Peckham rag and bone man. She traced Kate to a tiny stable with no lighting or bedding and the RSPCA rehomed her with Jill. The other pony, Kerry, was saved from a slaughter house, so weak and thin that Jill did not think he could survive

With Jill's assistance and the support of the Convent school in Foxgrove Rd, the 'Penrick Gymkhana' was organised by the 14 year olds, Anthea Penny and Eileen Rickaby. Kate, the rag and bone man's horse, had just gone to Cheyne Hospital to pull a trap for the handicapped children.

John Simpson of Linden Leas provided the trap and the children were delighted with the chestnut mare with white face and back legs. The BBC made a film of Kate's presentation which was shown that Wednesday on childrens' TV.

The National Swimming Championships were held in Blackpool and the Beckenham Ladies 110 yds freestyle relay team won easily with a 5 second lead over their nearest rivals. A Civic Reception was arranged for the four Ladies for 14 September. They swam in order as follows; Annette Fairbrother, Irene Smith, Maureen Rennie, Margaret Toms.

The Spitfire that led the Battle of Britain Fly-past over London made a forced landing ten minutes later on the Oxo cricket ground at Ravensbourne. Piloted by Air Vice Marshall Maguire of 11 Group Fighter Command, the plane was near Crystal Palace when its engine cut out. The pancake landing on the recently vacated cricket ground cut the stumps in half as the undercarriage was smashed and the propeller ripped off.

LANCASTRIAN CLLR WILLIAM SIDNEY ROBBINS BECOMES MAYOR 1959/60

When the groundsmen, Roy Fay and Raymond Beavis, helped the pilot out of the cockpit and to the pavilion, the pilot was heard to say 'You've got an extra man for tea.'

Two new Secondary Schools opened this term. The first was the only mixed Secondary in the district, at Hayes, where the 400 boys and girls took care mostly to sit apart from each other. The other, a few weeks late, was the new Girls Grammar School at Langley Park. It was opened at the end of October by Mary Trevelyan, adviser to Overseas Students at London University who kept the audience laughing almost continuously. This meant that Balgowan School for Girls could move in to the Lennard Rd school, eventually to become Cator Park.

In November it was the turn of the Mayor to keep the audience in fits of laughter. At the Darby and Joan Club's twelfth anniversary, he obliged with a turn in the entertainment. Broadening his native Lancashire accent, he delivered the classic monologue, 'Albert and the Lion.' Mrs Joyce Fisher, WVS centre organiser, said they'd had all sorts of Mayors but never a theatrical one!

A letter to the KT in December remarked on the missed opportunity in the choice of names for the nine blocks of Council flats in Bromley Rd, Shortlands. Instead of using names of Shortlands people like Grote, Woolley, Craik, Scott and Wilkinson, tree names were used! It was also announced that there were nearly 2,000 houses in Beckenham with no bathrooms and 1,000 with only an outside lavatory.

The Tip Top factory at St Mary Cray experienced an extensive fire on the Thursday before Christmas when they lost 17 tons of bread. The heat from a convector fire had set light to some cellophane wrappings. Together with an unfounded rumour that Ackermans was going out on strike, the bakers were plagued by long queues on Christmas Eve of people trying to buy eight to ten loaves to see them over the holiday. When small bakeries tried to meet the demand by asking their bakers to work overtime, they were let down when people did not honour their orders. It cost them 1s 6d per loaf instead of the usual 1s 1d but they were left with whole batches of unsold loaves.

Nonagenarian John Duncan died at home in Mackenzie Rd on 21 January. Father of Alderman William Duncan, he had come to Beckenham when only one year old from Haywards Heath and at 91 was one of Beckenham's oldest inhabitants. He had been a keen cricketer, member of the Cyphers Bowling Club and Freemason of the Clissold Lodge and Cator Chapter.

Chairman of the West Wickham Community Council, Geoffrey Sargeant, announced that rising costs and lack of support had forced the Flitch to be held on Easter Monday in the hall instead of being part of the Whitsun Fair & Flitch that had started in 1933. He hoped that it was not the end of the occasion as they had raised many thousands of pounds for charity and their dog show had always been a very popular event.

The Mayor recited his own poem 'Mother' at Coney Hall's Over 60s party when the West Wickham Operatic Society entertained them with songs from the shows. The Society celebrated its twenty fifth anniversary with a buffet dance at the Eden Park Hotel on 26 February when Mrs Ida Pool and Mrs Hutt were made Life Members in view of their long and valued service.

Ida Pool is far left with Janet Wynne and Audrey Handy in this production of The Mikado.

LANCASTRIAN CLLR WILLIAM SIDNEY ROBBINS BECOMES MAYOR 1959/60

The Council decided that it was not worth spending money on bringing the mansions Harvington and Homewood in South Eden Park Rd into lettable condition. These historic houses dating from the 1870s were to be demolished although a third, Chalfont, was to be kept for dressing rooms for the footballers and cricketers using the ground. Their lodges are still there. Originally five houses, the first, Elderslie, was pulled down in 1939 to make way for Elderslie Close. The second, Oakfield, seen above, survives to this day together with its renovated stables and lodge.

Another silver jubilee was Mr Palmer's twenty five years as Baths Superintendent organising not only swimming lessons, school attendances and swimming galas but also wrestling, boxing, dog shows and drama competitions to mention a few. He had seen Ronnie Stedman, Margaret Wellington and Chris Walkden chosen for the Olympics. Chris Walkden and Wendy Scripps from West Wickham married at St Paul's, Brackley Rd on 5 March. Henry Cooper was invited by the Mayor to attend boxing matches on 1 April in support of the Mayor's Fund where the best fight was the heavyweight bout between PC Ron Radley of the Met and Sam Sutherland from Downham.

Throughout March 1960, the fate of the closed cinemas at Elmers End and West Wickham was debated. The Elmers End Odeon was to become a 5 or 7 storey office block for Muirheads, hopefully not affecting the houses in Priory Close. The old Penge Empire was also closing. Built during WWI, among its performers were Marie Lloyd, Tommy Trinder, Max Miller, Elsie and Doris Waters, Larry Adler, Hughie Green and Winifred Atwell. Rental of a black and white 17 inch television set cost 9/- per week.

A surprise for the spectators at Muirhead's ground on Bank Holiday Monday was when Petula Clark kicked off the league match between Beckenham and Midhurst.

One of the Mayor's last duties was to present the Cadets of HMS Sikh in Croydon Rd, Penge with their fourth pennant. At the handing over ceremony to the next Mayor, he was commended on his courageous decision to carry on after the loss of his wife, the Mayoress. He had continued with an exacting job in the face of great personal sadness, especially enjoying occasions involving the young and the old. Cllr Robbins accepted the Mayoress's brooch as a memento that he would treasure for the rest of his life.

Twenty Five
Alderman Henry Thomas Parkin is first to wear the double chain 1960/61

This Mayoralty marked Beckenham's twenty fifth anniversary of becoming a borough. Beckenham was fighting for restoration of the powers it had before the war and to be free from the swaddling clothes of Kent County.

The twenty fifth year was the opportunity for a new chain to be added to the first, making a striking double chain for the Beckenham Mayor.

Alderman Parkin should have held office years ago but was prevented by his numerous business commitments that he has had relinquished. He appointed Cllr Waller as his Deputy Mayor and the Rev, Hammond, Rector of Beckenham was his Chaplain.

The Mayor and Mayoress were presented early on in their Mayoralty with bouquet and buttonhole by delighted 'tinies' at the Sports Day on the 1 June of St David's College. The Mayor praised the excellent work of the school. The three year olds were Hilary Schove, Paul Whiting, Penny Waite and David Cumberland. Also on the 1 June, SE England's first motorway opened in time for the Whitsun Bank holiday. It was the 5 miles of the Maidstone By-Pass, the A20 (M).

The fiftieth anniversary of the publication of Robert Borrowman's 'Beckenham Past and Present' fell in June. This lawyer from an old Beckenham family wrote the first history of Beckenham when the population was 33.000, before its amalgamation with West Wickham. Robert died shortly after publication when on holiday in August 1910. He was only 47.

A team comprising representatives of all 24 clubs of the Beckenham & Bromley District Bowling Association was beaten by the last shot of the match at Beckenham Bowling Club's celebration of their Jubilee held at Croydon Rd Recreation ground.

Chris Walkden was making a comeback after giving up training 15 months ago. He came a fingertip second to Rowlinson of Bolton in the 220yds breaststroke as a member of the GB team against Sweden at the Empire Pool, Cardiff, his passport to this year's Olympic Games in Rome in September. He was in brilliant form but the 15 month absence from top class swimming probably cost him his place in the final. However he swam in a final as one of the 4x100m Medley Relay Team.

A review of Beckenham's fifteen parks revealed that they cost Beckenham £65,000 to maintain. The oldest was Croydon Rd Recreation ground opened on 23 September 1891 followed closely by Alexandra Recreation ground. Churchfields' nine and a half acres opened in 1907. Saved from housing development by the efforts of T W Thornton, Kelsey Park was the second largest park, opened in May 1913.

ALDERMAN HENRY THOMAS PARKIN IS FIRST TO WEAR THE DOUBLE CHAIN 1960/61

The pavilion in South Hill Wood Park was the music room of the old house

The largest park was Well Wood in West Wickham with its 43 acres and the smallest, with only two and a half acres, was the McAndrew playing fields. The newest was South Hill Wood, Shortlands opened in 1959 by Mayor Kathleen Moore.

The other parks were Sparrows Den, Harvington, Blake Field, Coney Hall, Cator Park, Crease Park and Elmers End Recreation ground.

Fifty years ago this year, the first Paris to London flight was made by the American John Moisant in a Bleriot monoplane. The landing field at the Crystal Palace was so obscured by spectators that the pilot missed it and made a heavy landing by the tennis courts at the National Provincial Bank Sports ground off Copers Cope Rd. Remember this was 6 September 1910 and people came from all around to see the plane that made the flight.

The Beckenham Theatre had at last found a permanent home at the junction of Manor Rd and Bromley Rd. It was opened by Dick Emery on 30 September. After Diana Knox-Johnston and Catherine Wort presented Dick Emery with a buttonhole, Victor Thornton said that the theatre which began as the Beckenham Children's Theatre in 1948, was an experiment in the fusion of youth and experience. It was started by people who believed in the living theatre where children could employ their imagination and vigour in the make-believe of the play. They had produced 60 one act plays and 7 Christmas entertainments.

The National Schools Life Saving title and Arthur Mothersdale Cup went to Marian Vian School coached by Mrs Brine, Police sergeant Norman Beadle and the Superintendent, Mr Palmer of the Beckenham Baths. The swimmers were Elizabeth Holder, Jennifer Banks, Mavis Bowyer, Doris Withers and Ann Marsh.

The entry to Clockhouse Rd from Beckenham Rd started as an experiment with no right turn into it from Beckenham Rd. In spite of mass condemnation, the rule stayed in place and still exists today, the object being to safeguard pedestrians.

The New Year 1961 started with worries about our lack of knowledge about a nuclear attack. A meeting at the Old Council Offices covered seven questions; how much of the country would be affected, would there be any warning, what were the dangers, what preparation was possible, what should we do at the time, what about fall-out and what would our public services do?

ALDERMAN HENRY THOMAS PARKIN IS FIRST TO WEAR THE DOUBLE CHAIN 1960/61

The Nancy Wiseman concert in recognition of her 21 years devoted to music at the Beckenham Grammar School was arranged by the past pupils of the school, the Adremians. They were especially proud to honour her in this way because Nancy was a past pupil herself. The occasion was marked by the presentation of a conductor's baton inscribed 'With appreciation from the Adremians 1939 -1960' but the sincerity of the concert was apparent in the many past pupils who came to show their expertise to the lady they respected above all other and the jam-packed hall of nostalgic listeners.

Front row:? Daphne Humberstone, Audrey Sarjeant, Monica Duncan, Miss Nancy Wiseman, Anne Emington, Jane Caleym, Brenda and Shirley Porrer. Back Row; Elise Handy, ? Sybil Bell, Mary McIntosh, Elizabeth Mynett, Kathleen Harding, Betty Remound, Patricia Carroll, Valerie Kelsh. (Other performers that I do not recognise in the photograph included Diana Clarke, Ruth Holden, Anne Bellringer and Dorothy Oxley.)

In April 1961 the Mayor and Mayoress visited the Beckenham Telephone Exchange in National Telephone Week. There were 9,250 subscribers for BEC and LODge Hill and new coloured telephones were sold at £3 each. There were five colours, red, topaz, yellow, concord blue and two- tone green.

How two year old Paul Butterworth managed to jam his head in a metal dish holder is not recorded but the fire engine went to Eden Way in May to cut the dish off, leaving Paul unhurt but with a tale to tell. Another young man in the news was Richard Williams from Merlin Grove. He appeared in the film 'The Greengage Summer,' as a nine year old child. Starting as a babe of six months, Richard had already taken part in 12 films with prominent parts in four of them, notably the lead in 'The Heart of a Child.'

ALDERMAN HENRY THOMAS PARKIN IS FIRST TO WEAR THE DOUBLE CHAIN 1960/61

Mayoral Avenue, Harvington

The Beckenham Drama Festival was no longer so popular and audience had fallen from 1,205 in 1957 to 860 in 1951. It was insolvent and was unlikely to continue. However at the TG Drama Festival, Beckenham took the first three places with plays all produced by Greta Raiks. Central Beckenham scored 90% closely followed by Eden Park and Hawes Down each with 87%.

The planting of an oak tree in Harvington by the retiring Mayor had lapsed since 1955 but the Mayor planted three on behalf of himself, the late Brook Brown and Knox-Johnston and others by previous Mayors Duncan and Robbins. Mrs Rugg deputised for Kathleen Moore. The intention was to make a country walk from north to south through an oak avenue.

By the end of his term, the Royal Commission recommended that as Beckenham and Bromley had so much in common that they should merge. At Bromley's annual civic dinner, the guest, Mr Harold Macmillan recalled the time when he had been MP for the constituency of Beckenham, Penge and Bromley. The 1961 census numbered Beckenham's population at 77,265 against Bromley's 68,169 and at a poll of Beckenham's rate-payers, it was agreed that they would rather be a 'big noise' as part of Kent than a very small authority in SE London

Twenty Six
Cllr Alfred Waller's daughter becomes the youngest Mayoress 1961/62

One of the first official functions was at the dedication of the Sampson memorial at St George's church placed on the South wall of the nave. It was made of Welsh slate surrounded by a moulding of nabrasinia and read 'William Joseph Sampson born 1894 died 1959, Freeman of Beckenham.'

With Cllr Smithers as his Deputy and the Rev. Webber as his Chaplain, Cllr Waller became Mayor on 22 May 1961. Educated at Christ's Hospital, he served in both wars. The Mayor had lived in Beckenham for thirty years and was a churchwarden at St John's church, Eden Park. Being a widower, he enlisted his twenty two year old daughter, Rosalind Waller, as his Mayoress. She was a Croydon teacher and keen member of the Beckenham Ladies lacrosse club. He became one of the ten Aldermen in the new Bromley Council in 1964.

The Mayor opened a new kind of shop for the time at 7 High St. This was the charity shop for Save the Children Fund that raised £68 on its first day. Sadly it was found that valuable silver items like a silver cigarette case had been stolen from a showcase. He also opened the new gas showrooms at the corner of Burrell Row in the High St, commenting that the only oasis of light during the recent electricity blackout was Eden Park station, lit by gas!

Another official visit was to the Beckenham Grammar School for Girls concert presented by Nancy Wiseman's Second in Command, Miss Hawkins although Nancy appeared in the madrigals sung by a staff group. The varied programme included Katherine Edmonds' horn solo, Lloyd Webber's Pavane by Hannah Forbes, flautists Gillian Whitworth and Pauline Burden and the popular Ann Whiley on the piano. Helen Mynett sang 'Songs of the Smuggler's Lass,' Pearl Johnson accompanied the clarinets and the strings were Elizabeth Beldry with Elaine Fox and Margaret Try.

Some well known English tennis players were at the Beckenham tennis where Christine Truman lost the singles final but won the Ladies Doubles with Ann Haydon beating the Australians, Margaret Smith and Lesley Turner. The picture shows Christine in action. It was a two hour thriller won in the third set 9-7 when Margaret Smith missed a smash!

CLLR ALFRED WALLER'S DAUGHTER BECOMES THE YOUNGEST MAYORESS 1961/62

The Chitty report in August, concerned with the development of the Cator Estate, emphasised the great importance of a generous long term policy of planting to link Beckenham's open spaces along the rivers. A former Director of Kew Gardens observes that he knows of no other piece of suburban landscape planting of riverside greenways to compare with Beckenham's Cator Estate.

Does today's Green Chain Walk fulfil this hope of nearly 50 years ago?

Snow fell continuously from 7.00 am on the last day of the year putting a damper on New Year celebrations and few people ventured out. It was followed by a night of such low temperatures that the snow froze solid and caused traffic chaos on road and rail. The snow weighed down the branches of the trees, weakening them so that when gale force winds followed many branches were whipped off causing widespread damage. Well Wood in West Wickham was one of the hardest hit with more than fifty trees blown down including a very large sweet chestnut.

'Petticoat Pirates' starring Charlie Drake was showing at the Regal and we had our local 'filmstar' taking part. She was Gret Stott from Elmers End who had appeared in several films using her judo skills. Her film career started after she won the British Women's Open Judo championship for three years in a row. She put on a display in the foyer of the Regal where she threw Mr Sullivan the Assistant Manager.

Judo class 1967, Insert - Gret Stott

There were nearly 1,000 entries in the Beckenham Canine Association dog show at the Grand Hall, reckoned one of the best shows in the South of England. Mr J Walkden's toy poodle won 'Best of Show.' The Superintendent of the Baths, Mr Palmer, who made sure that all the events held there ran smoothly, was to retire in the summer, to be replaced by Mr Lusher on 1 July.

The Mayor started his Mayoral year as Councillor but was elected Alderman to replace Alderman Jackson who retired in March. It was as Mayor Alderman Waller that he presented the much-coveted burgee to the Beckenham & Penge Sea Cadets on 1 May. For six consecutive years the cadets had received an efficiency pennant and had thus earned the burgee.

The Mayors of both Beckenham and Bromley attended the tenth annual dinner of the Beckenham & District Soroptimists Club where Nancy Wiseman was President. The Mayors spoke of the coming amalgamation of their boroughs and were very polite to each other. Mayor Cllr Latter of Bromley said that Beckenham had the advantage because it was the home of the Soroptimists to which Mayor Alderman Waller replied that Bromley had the advantages of trains that actually stopped there, a theatre and a straight High St!

CLLR ALFRED WALLER'S DAUGHTER BECOMES THE YOUNGEST MAYORESS 1961/62

The Misses Wiseman, Tompson and Halpin, Soroptimists

The Mayoress, Rosalind Waller, turned waitress serving refreshments at the fete at her old school, St Christopher's where she had been Head Girl in 1955. She was commended by the Chairman of the Governors, Dr Gordon Lyle, for the charm and enthusiasm she had shown as Mayoress during her father's term of office.

One of the last official duties of the Mayor and Mayoress was to cut the tape at the opening of the garden for the blind at the Croydon Rd Recreation ground. Over fifty varieties of scented plants had been planted in a garden between the café and where at one time there was a putting green. They had been given by the Beckenham Ladies Circle.

Twenty Seven
Former Deputy Mayor, Cllr Edward R Smithers succeeds as Mayor 1962/63

To be Mayor at this time in Beckenham's history is not a task to be taken lightly. Far reaching changes will call for wisdom, tact and understanding.

Remarks by Cllr Mrs West as Cllr Smithers became Mayor

Edward Smithers of Hayes Chase had lived in West Wickham since 1935 and was first elected to the council in 1954. He chose Cllr Johnson as his Deputy and the Rev. F C Waghorn of St Mary's, West Wickham was his Chaplain. He was known for the energy that he put into all his activities including cricket, bowls and even dancing the 'Twist.' The newly elected Mayor's first task was to congratulate Sheila Parsons from The Grove, West Wickham, for achieving Civic Recognition. Pupil at the Beckenham Grammar School for Girls and paralysed from the waist down because of polio as a young child, she has done well scholastically and is a valued violinist in the school orchestra.

As the time for the union of the districts for the London Boroughs approached, a federal system was suggested where councillors would be able to exercise the widest possible powers in relation to their own areas. What a good idea that seems today where each of the original five districts feels that its views are minimalised!

Plans were afoot for the building of a new grammar school for the boys and it may come as a surprise today to know that the council were considering land that would be severed from the Bethlem Royal Hospital by the projected new ring road, Parkway E. The existing playing field land at Park Langley next to the girls' school would need additional land to be purchased from Wellcome's or Dunstan's.

The private school, Woodbrook, with its Head, Miss Dredge, was in the news as it had won the shield for best entry in the Fellowship of Independent Schools in the annual literary competition. Carolyn Thoday and Monica Brooke had each won first prizes.

The Mayor and Mayoress attended a Royal Garden Party at Buckingham Palace on Friday 13 July, which was lucky for some. Soon afterwards they were cheering on the tug-of-war teams in the children's sports at the Beckenham Flower Show.

St Pauls's church Autumn Show was very popular with Christine and Lesley Kobrak and Penny Withers when their decorated cakes did well by the judges.

FORMER DEPUTY MAYOR, CLLR EDWARD R SMITHERS SUCCEEDS AS MAYOR 1962/63

For nearly thirty years, West Wickham had been asking for its swimming pool and now it looked as though the council was thinking that Bromley or Orpington would be a more suitable site for the borough of the future. Councillors Olga Roberts and Frank Cooke were furious. They pointed out that this was a meeting of the Beckenham Council not the proposed new London Borough! Alderman Duncan, Chairman of the Baths Committee, said that even if Bromley and Orpington were considered, the logical geographical location was still West Wickham and that its planning was already far advanced. It was announced that the new borough would have a population of nearly 300.000, making it the eighth largest of the 32 suggested boroughs. The Mayor helped to cut the cake at Alice Linsell's one hundredth birthday held at Thornton House in Bromley Rd.

Dredging of the two hundred year old lake of Kelsey Park brought many spectators to watch two old traction engines, Iris and Mavis, dredge 2,300 cu yds of silt from its bed. Refilling in December from the River Beck would use at least 5 million gallons of water.

We watched the Beckenham Cottage Hospital 'decant' into temporary buildings in Croydon Rd Recreation ground from 2005 onwards to be rebuilt as 'The Beacon' medical centre not a hospital at all because it will have no overnight beds.

Suggestions made over fifty years ago that the Beckenham Hospital might close in the future were dismissed as 'ridiculous' by Mr MacCallum of the Hospital's Welfare Committee. He was attending the bed presentation ceremony to the memory of the late Aneurin Bevan by the Penge Local Labour Party. Another local hospital that is no more was the Beckenham and Penge Maternity Hospital in Stone Park Ave where the chapel was dedicated on 1 December 1962.

There was to be a new Headmaster at the Beckenham & Penge Grammar school to succeed Mr White from January 1963. He was David Anthony Raeburn, senior classics master at Alleyn's School, a master dedicated to productions of Shakespeare.

The snow blizzard started on Saturday night 29 December and we woke to see the deepest snow for many a year. The Evan-Jones family, David, John and Peter, in Whitmore Rd built an igloo to see in the New Year and the Signals unit of the TA took Meals on Wheels for the WVS to 35 stranded pensioners in West Wickham. It cost the council £500 per day to keep the 24 miles of main roads clear but it was impossible to clear the 86 miles of side roads which became deeply frozen ruts. Even if you could manage to put your car on the road, the car parks had not been cleared. Sport became snowbound and the icy weather went on and on until by the beginning of February, the snow clearance bill was £15,000 with salt and grit running short. Skating was not permitted in Kelsey Park because the successive layers of snow had resulted in ice of irregular thickness although the keepers kept the ice broken at the sides for the water birds. Householders had to wait for coal as they watched their supply dwindle away and residents in Kent House Rd were without water for days as the water main had frozen. The first Mayor and Freeman of Beckenham, Dr James Bennett, died aged 96 on 21 January after living for 50 years in the borough.

Snow was still falling as Mr Stow, managing director of Whitbread's, pulled aside the Union flag over the inn sign of the Greyhound in Beckenham High St at its official opening in January 1963. The fibreglass mural incorporated features of brewing; ears of barley, the sun, the copper mash tun and the final cask.

> In memory of
> Miss Wiseman
> House Mistress
> of
> Goodhart House
> 1948-1963

The new inn stood on the site of Beckenham's nineteenth century village Greyhound. Today a block of offices shares the site with the brewery.

This was a sad time for the girls of the Grammar School as their much respected music teacher, Miss Nancy Wiseman, died from ovarian cancer. Herself a former pupil of the school she had not only been Head of Goodhart House for some years but had become the Deputy Head to Miss Henshaw. She has never been forgotten by her pupils however successful they became. See chapter 32 for the remarks of Patricia Carroll.

A fifty foot water spout appeared at Clockhouse on Sunday 8 March from a burst water main but it soon froze bringing grief to pedestrians, cyclists and motorcyclists alike. Colin Derrick of Ravenscroft Rd was taking some friends to a dance in his new car bought only the day before when he skidded onto the pavement bringing their evening out to a premature end.

Do you remember the Belgian Georges Cuisenaire system of rods to teach primary mathematics to the borough's children? Supported enthusiastically by Mr Hevey of Highfield School, the boxes containing large numbers of ten different sized coloured rods became standard teaching of the rules of mathematics in all the borough's schools for some years. What caused their demise?

The Mayor supported the 'Freedom from Hunger' campaign by planting symbolic wheat at the War Memorial on Saturday 16 March. Token ears of wheat were being sold all along the High St in an effort to raise £10,000 during the year. Organisations were asked to hold their own wheat planting sessions, bingo and whist drives.

Miss Nancy Wiseman sits on the left of Miss Henshaw surrounded by the Prefects in 1961/1962

FORMER DEPUTY MAYOR, CLLR EDWARD R SMITHERS SUCCEEDS AS MAYOR 1962/63

The Handy string quartet with Peter Handy and his sister Shirley on violin and cello and Elise Handy (née Beeton), Peter's wife, on the viola. Rosemary Johnson is the second violinist.

Also in March, the boys had a day's holiday from school at Hawes Down. Neil Blick from South Eden Park Rd and John Anderson from Cherry Tree Walk nearly drowned at Keston Ponds when trying to cross the ice. Their friend, Richard Varney, scrambled to safety but the other two were left clinging to the broken ice where the water was 8ft deep. They were saved when Richard raised the alarm and an off duty policeman, Keith Jones, rescued them.

A charity effort that went wrong was held by the Beckenham FC as a repeat of the successful 'All Stars' football of 1961. Although Pete Murray was mobbed there were only about 800 spectators instead of the expected 1,250. There was an unfortunate clash of date with Harry Secombe's cricket XI playing Colin Cowdrey's XI at Bickley and even though the All Stars won 7-5, the Beckenham FC lost financially.

In April, Henry Cotton returned for a visit to the Park Langley Golf Club where he had started his professional career. He was asked to advise on future course improvements with the club's current professional, Wally Hitchcock.

Twelve year old Richard Varney

Twenty Eight
Mayor Cllr Mrs Daisy West of West Wickham 1963/64

Headmistresses the Misses Henshaw and Dixon both retired in 1963. It was said that they excited the admiration of all who came in contact with them and their successors would have great difficulty in keeping up with their standards.

As the new Mayor took over, one of Beckenham's most well known and respected citizens, Victor Thornton died aged 61 at his home in Kelsey Way on 24 May 1963. His Deputy Editor and drama writer, David Shellan wrote warmly of his former friend and employer.

> 'Editor of the Beckenham Journal and member of the Light Rescue Service of the ARP, his health had declined after the war. He had been a keen sportsman, playing hockey and cricket, and member of the Beckenham Swimming Club. He had won prizes as a baritone at the Beckenham Festival and he was famed for his work in the world of drama. A favourite topic was cats and his two pet black cats provided almost daily bulletins.'

Among the many comments upon hearing the sad news were the following. Philip Goodhart MP said

> 'An editor of a local newspaper can do much to enrich the life of the community and Victor Thornton was that kind of editor.' A lifelong friend from Falmouth, R L Eagle said 'I first met him in 1925 when I joined the Beckenham Shakespeare Society. He was outstanding in any kind of part and I have never known an amateur actor to equal him. I particularly remember his Quince in A Midsummer Night's Dream in 1928 and his Caliban at Sandhills.'

Always ready to step in to entertain, his 1953 production of the Merry Wives of Windsor in Kelsey Park to celebrate the Queen's coronation was exceptional as were the concert parties 'ARP Follies' and 'The Four of us' where he joined forces with Violet Graham-Williams, Ida Pool and Vernon Jones. A reading of 'Under Milk Wood' at the Beckenham Theatre Centre was given by his fellow actors in his memory later in the year. An exhibition in the foyer celebrated his legendary production of 'Peer Gynt' in 1928.

Historian Miss J Chreseson came from Carlisle Grammar School to replace Miss Henshaw at Beckenham Grammar School for Girls and Mr J S Denham, previously Head at a Shirley School, took over from Miss Dixon at Worsley Bridge, both appointed from the beginning of September 1963.

The stage of 'The Merry Wives of Windsor 1953

MAYOR CLLR MRS DAISY WEST OF WEST WICKHAM 1963/64

A pleasant duty for the Mayor was to distribute certificates to six Beckenham Ladies and one Beckenham Swimming Club member who had 'covered themselves with glory and brought distinction to the borough.' These were the well known Judy Gegan, Margaret Toms, Diana Harris, Judith Kelly, Mary Williams, Mary Piper and Christopher Tomkins.

Dr Kildare, Richard Chamberlain of TV fame, spent Christmas with the Harvey family in Wickham Way. Eric Harvey met Richard in LA where he was a friend of his American brother-in-law and invited Richard here for Christmas. Arriving on Christmas Eve, the actor was amazed to find that he was a 'star' in a foreign country and he became the Hon President of the Trubeats Jazz Fan Club. He went to lots of parties, was encouraged to try Morris dancing and found out about the Beatles. BBC 2 opened on 20 April 1964.

After Christmas, the family of the former Mayor, Knox-Johnston, moved from The Avenue, Beckenham to a 23 roomed haunted house in Rookery Rd, Downe. It was reputed to be haunted by the ghosts of a Cavalier and two boys who were killed in the house while trying to escape from the Roundheads.

Left: Colin Watts and Cliff Watkins in the garden

Above: the bridge over the River Beck

Lantern slides made by the late County Alderman John Bennett who died aged 90 in 1953, were catalogued by Rob Copeland and handed over to the Beckenham libraries. The Kentish Times of 20 March 1964 has a double page spread on pages 4 and 5 showing many of these historic old slides including the old Tilling horse bus going from Catford to Beckenham via Forest Hill and Sydenham.

Mr Davies from 60, The Drive had been a founder member of the Church Drive Garden Association that in 1927 had purchased three quarters of an acre of land at the rear of houses in Church Ave and The Drive. He had been Chairman for more than 26 years and said the River Beck had been a constant source of enjoyment flowing as it did through the garden. Only six of the original inhabitants were still in residence in 1964 but over forty years later the garden is still there.

The first black and white hunting dog of the breed Basenji to be born in Europe was a bitch puppy, Soubrette-Noire of Tenki. She was bred by Miss Juniper of Belvedere Rd, Anerley. The Africans of the Belgian Congo regarded them as very lucky, even more precious than their wives!

MAYOR CLLR MRS DAISY WEST OF WEST WICKHAM 1963/64

Although Beckenham's days as a borough were numbered, the Town Hall curtains were falling down and the Mayor insisted on replacing them herself in February 1964 because it would still be an important public building. She also continued the tradition of planting a tree in Harvington's Mayoral Avenue. At the annual civic dinner at the Public Hall she said, 'During the past year, I have been privileged to witness the enthusiasm of all I have visited. I have become so proud that within the borough are firms bringing fame to Beckenham in the many products they are making.

One of her last official duties was to award the certificate of Civic Recognition to 15 year old Diana Harris for her breaststroke performance in the National Swimming Championships.

As this Mayoralty gave way to Beckenham's last, the first meeting of the council of the London Borough of Bromley was already being held, presided over by Sir Cuthbert Ackroyd, the Charter Mayor. Alderman Parkin, a man well known throughout the country in local government, was elected Chairman. He said,
'We must all have the basic aim to serve the interests of 300,000 people. Our prime responsibility must be to the new borough.'

Twenty Nine
Cllr Alfred Johnson JP becomes Beckenham's last Mayor 1964/65

'There is still a year's work to be done for Beckenham. It is my intention to endeavour to lead the borough in the furtherance of the efforts made in the past. Although the borough may become extinct, it will have done a service for its fellow citizens of which we should all be proud.'
Cllr Johnson as he took over his office on 29 May 1964

Cllr Maxwell Williams was the Deputy Mayor and the Rev. Sugden of St Mary's, Shortlands, was the chaplain.

The best entry ever for the Beckenham Tennis Tournament included many world class players. Among the women were the previous year's Wimbledon singles champion, Australian Margaret Smith and the Brazilian, Maria Bueno, who had won Wimbledon in 1959 and 1960.

Although Christine Truman could not play as she had injured her arm, she attended with the other Wightman Cup British players, Deirdre Catt, Ann Haydon-Jones, Elizabeth Starkie and Angela Mortimer. Among the men were Manuel Santana, Ken Fletcher, John Newcome and Fred Stolle. After five days of brilliant sunshine, the weather broke on Saturday and rain washed out the finals. There was only one outright champion, John Newcome, who beat Fred Stolle. Margaret Smith and Maria Bueno had to be satisfied with sharing the championship. The Kent girl, Virginia Wade, also came and played well.

The National Recreation Centre at Crystal Palace was opened by Prince Philip on 13 July 1964 and followed by a walk around Penge with the Rt Hon Quinton Hogg MP.

The Mayor and Mayoress presented the trophies when thirteen schools competed for the Borrowman Swimming Cup in the Primary Schools swimming Gala which was won by Worsley Bridge School. The trio of the Beckenham Ladies swimmers, Judy Gegan, Diana Harris and 16 year old Linda Ludgrove was waiting anxiously to see if they would be selected for the Olympic Games in Tokyo.

It was the centenary of St Paul's church in Brackley Rd in July. It was the oldest church building in Beckenham. Remember that St George's church was rebuilt at the turn of the nineteenth into the twentieth century. When St Paul's was opened in 1864, under the jurisdiction of the Parish church, it only consisted of the nave and north porch. The baptism register runs from 1870 and the other registers run from 1872 when St Paul's became independent

Back row: Janet Needham, Helen Jarman, Ian Spiers, Jane Taylor, Roger Boxall, Paul Jessup, Jack Edmonds.
Front Row: Martin Jones, Philip Manning, David Manning, Judith Johnson, Ruth Baker, Jennifer Ward.

The quiet study extension at Beckenham reference library came into use on Saturday, 25 July 1964 and is still used as much as ever today

In August 1964, Norman Reid from Brabourne Rise was appointed Director of the Tate Gallery in Millbank, London, a post to begin on 1 October 1964. The famous ballerina, Antoinette Sibley, with parents in Cromwell Rd, Beckenham, married another prominent member of the Royal Ballet, Michael Somes. Antoinette became famous overnight when the leading ballerina, Nadia Nerina was taken ill before a performance of Swan Lake five years before.

The Mayor cut the first turf for the Hayne Rd Day Centre with the words, 'The first thought of the Council must always be for the people.' He hoped that it would be ready in time to hand over to the new authority in April 1965. By December, the Old Peoples' Welfare Committee was already feeling threatened by the 'dictatorial' attitude of the co-ordinating committee feeling that local matters should not come within the province of such a committee. The centre was eventually opened by Mayor Alderman Parkin on 7 May 1965 and was called the Rachel Notley Centre.

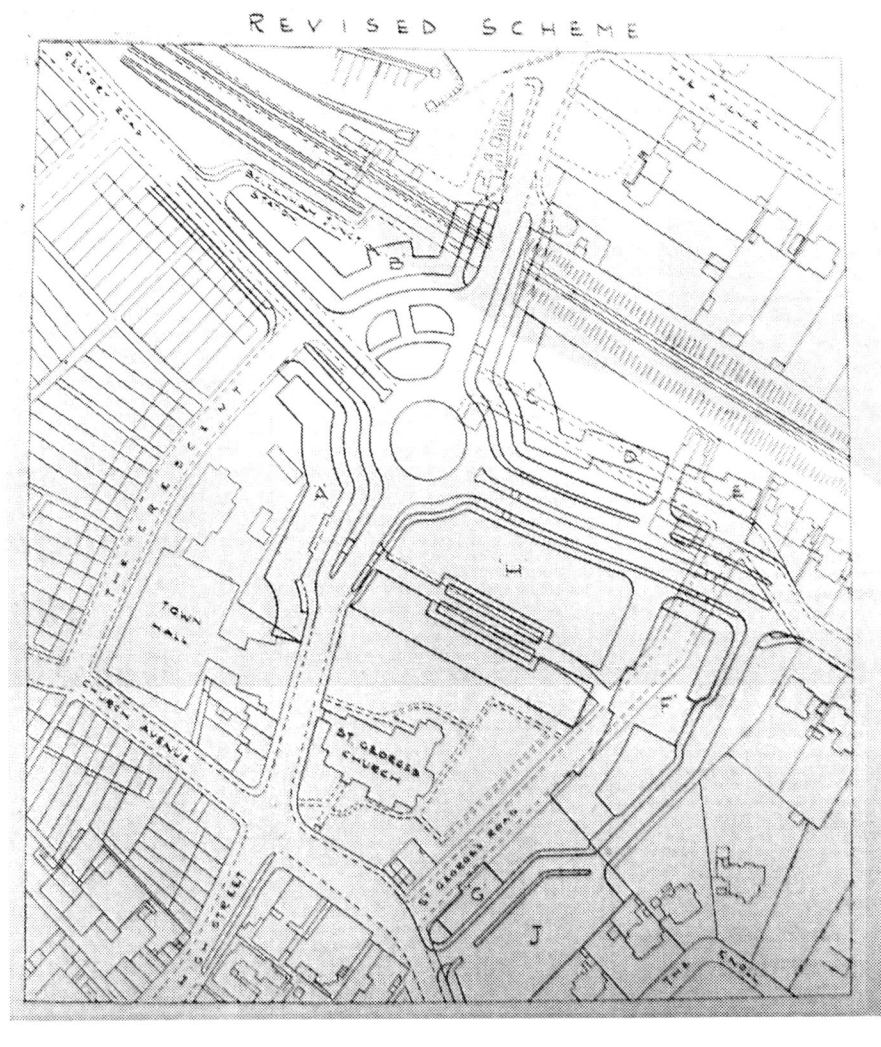

Unfortunately borough engineer Dove's plan of a roundabout and town centre was long forgotten

CLLR ALFRED JOHNSON JP BECOMES BECKENHAM'S LAST MAYOR 1964/65

Development was underway all over Beckenham. The large private houses at nos 60, 62 and 64 Wickham Rd were being demolished by Wren Properties to make way for 21 houses and 18 flats in three blocks. The cottages built about 1870 in Burrell Row had gone to be replaced by office accommodation. After twenty years of negotiations with Charringtons and the Midland Bank, the council had at last finalised the purchase of the necessary land in North Central Beckenham to rebuild on the doodlebug destroyed property by St George's church and Albemarle Rd. The old post office and other buildings would have to go to allow the straightening of Albemarle Rd and the construction of Beckenham Green etc.

News of our Olympic team was released. Linda Ludgrove and Judy Gegan were among the swimmers, West Wickham teacher, John Cooper, was expecting to run both the 400m hurdles and the 4x 400m relay, cyclist Terry West and Beckenham hockey club players Alan Page and Roger Sutton completed out local members. John Cooper won two silver medals and was not only greatly appreciated at his reception at Hawes Down School but also appeared on the Billy Cotton Band Show as one of 15 successful Olympic medal winners

Two gold medals were won by Carol Bryant at the Tokyo Paralympics. Paralysed from the waist down by polio, Carol was a telephonist at Syme & Duncan's in Blakeney Rd. She won both the wheelchair slalom and the 60m wheelchair race. She had started taking an interest in sport seriously at Stoke Mandeville Hospital in 1961. Her colleagues at work had sent her off with a giant iced cake bearing the Olympic symbols.

The versatile Beckenham composer, Carey Blyton, presented an evening of his work in October at the Music Group of Arts & Music. His 'Music for Children' was a mixed bag of action songs with words by his aunt Enid Blyton. This was followed by 'Fun with Figures' and 'Dining Room Ballads' ending with a selection of piano pieces for Grades IV and V examinations.

News came in December 1964 of the production of a measles vaccine by the Wellcome laboratories in Beckenham that was going for trials at the Medical Research Council. Already the foundation had contributed to vaccines for whooping cough, diphtheria, polio, cholera and typhoid.

The death of Sir Winston Churchill and his funeral in St Paul's cathedral on Saturday 30 January emptied the High Sts as so many watched the funeral on TV. Head teacher of Alexandra Primary School, Miss Harding, attended the service as a Friend of St Paul's cathedral. She said it was a happy service and not sad at all. The wooden holders for the six orange candles at the catafalque had been used for the funeral of the Duke of Wellington a century before. Mayor Johnson represented Beckenham at the funeral at St Pauls' and also at the memorial service on Sunday afternoon at the parish church of St George's. The prayers were led by the Rev. Yarker of St Francis, West Wickham. On Sunday evening at St Mary's, Shortlands, the Mayor's chaplain, the Rev Sugden, paraphrased Churchill's own words with,

'Never in the field of human history did so many owe so much to one man. Let there be no doubt that Winston Churchill was used by God to save this country when all hope seemed lost and all other potential leaders seemed to have failed.'

A muffled peal of bells at the parish church, rung by 10 bellringers, lasted nearly three and a half hours.

Sweeny Todd was the Eden Park TG's production for February 1965 which was described as original and inventive. Vera Newman as Sweeny Todd gave a marvellous performance and Dr Lupin was gorgeously funny.

Dr Lupin, clergyman and Mrs Lovatt piemaker

The Mayor and Mayoress were there to hand over the trophies.

There was a great argument about the provision of robes for all the new councillors at a cost of £3,600 and votes were 31 to 27 for the robes but there was public uproar especially when the new borough's first budget was for £16 million. This meant an average rate increase of 5d in the £ with Beckenham paying 6d and Orpington 8d.

Frederick Gazeley, Beckenham's mace bearer for the last six years was to continue for the new borough with Mr Scaplehorn of Bromley as Deputy. He was to take charge of all the regalia and robes and of course would still be responsible for Beckenham's mace even if it did have a new badge. The cinquefoil design of the College of Arms was approved by the Council on 9 February although Alderman Bray from Orpington would have liked the motto 'Servive Populo' to be in English.

Mayoress and Mayor Johnson

And so we came to the final civic dinner for Beckenham borough in the Public Hall on 12 March 1965.

Philip Goodhart MP proposed the toast to the Beckenham Corporation saying that to a large extent the hopes held out some thirty years ago had been fulfilled. So many leaders in the community had given their whole lives to the service of the borough. Cllr Mayor Johnson replying commented that it was to their credit that West Wickham had managed to remain a separate entity especially culturally.

There was little celebration at the end of March 1965 when Beckenham became part of the new London Borough of Bromley on 1 April 1965 although there was a farewell dinner at the Public Hall on Wednesday 31 March.

The Mayor, Councillor Alfred Johnson, presided and answered to the toast proposed by Dr Edden to the 'Borough of Beckenham.'

There were to be some 70 members in the new council to cope with the new role of local authorities.

While losing the 'cosy feeling of the parish puddle' they should all gain in opportunity, wisdom and strength.

The Mayor, Councillor Alfred Johnson, the last Mayor of the 'Borough of Beckenham.'

Thirty
The Borough 19 Story

'We are entering a critical period, not a going concern but a new type of authority without organisation, premises or officers.'

Alderman Parkin at the first full meeting of the council May 1964

By 1963 it was clear that four and a half councils would be united into Borough 19. The residents of Beckenham, West Wickham, Penge, Bickley, Chislehurst, Orpington and Petts Wood were anxious to retain their names and identities for postal and other purposes. Little Penge especially had resisted all attempts at take-over bids and won all its battles except this one. West Wickham already knew what it was like to be amalgamated when it became part of the Beckenham Borough. The CS entwined on the Chislehurst and Sidcup badge below would no longer apply since Sidcup was set to join Bexley, although the MPs Dame Patricia Hornsby Smith and John Lubbock tried hard to split B19 into two and keep Sidcup.

The Mayors of Bromley and Beckenham tried hard to clear the air because the joint advisory committee had recommended the name 'Bromley' for the new Borough. This was firmly rejected by 17 votes to 10 when the Beckenham Council debated the subject. Councillor Read declared it had been chosen for Bromley's self-glorification. Councillor Gordon-Smith had three suggestions, Kentgate, Ravensbourne and Churchill. Alderman Duncan favoured Ravensbourne saying that the people of Beckenham would never support the name Bromley but others said that the river was little more than a ditch these days so hardly suitable for the new borough's name. It was suggested that Bromley was only waiting for the opportunity to spend Beckenham's money.

For all her struggles to remain independent, Penge had to go the way of the rest.

However Alderman Parkin thought that Bromley was a good choice because Bromley was the oldest and best-known town in the area with a centuries-old market and was situated in the centre of the new borough. He also suggested that if we did not decide for ourselves, Whitehall would decide for us.

Bromley's Arms were granted in 1904. The three ravens flying across the middle of the shield represented the river Ravensbourne while the broom in the first quarter and on the crest came from the name Bromley. The second quarter's sun was from the Manor of Sundridge and the gold scallop shell in the third quarter and the crest was from the Arms of the See of Rochester. The silver horse was of course the horse of Kent.

Beckenham's Arms were granted in 1932 with the rivers Beck and Chaffinch as wavy lines across the centre, two white flowered horse chestnut trees above and the Kent horse below. The crest bore the Cator lion. In 1935, the West Wickham Tudor supporters were added with the coming of the Charter. (frontispiece)

Orpington became an UDC in 1934 and was granted arms with the River Cray in the centre of the shield that was edged with a green band to represent the green belt. Two red mural crowns represented the urban development and the Kent horse formed the crest. Although given five years to become used to the idea, it was a bitter pill for the areas of Beckenham and West Wickham, Penge, Orpington and Petts Wood, Chislehurst and Bromley when they were forced to relinquish their individuality and combine into a single London Borough in 1965.

Of course, ultimately Borough 19 became Bromley and new Arms and motto were devised.

A cinquefoil in the centre of the shield was used to represent the unification of the five councils. The scallop shell was for the Diocese of Rochester, the numerous acorns were for the Kentish oaks and the silver horse was the horse of Kent. The remaining symbols of dragon and crossed swords were symbolic of London. In this way, the new borough was set in a background of old and new without causing offence to any of the preceding councils. All the old mottos were replaced with the new 'Servire Populo' It is interesting that the old Beckenham Mace was retained with the new Bromley arms and that the Beckenham Mayor's chain of office is still occasionally worn.

One man who lasted throughout Beckenham's life as a Borough, Alderman Henry Parkin, continued to serve the new Bromley Borough for a further twenty years. One of the ten new Aldermen elected at the first full meeting of the council, he was also the Chairman in charge until he was elected the first Mayor of the London Borough of Bromley eleven months later. Since no civic building existed capable of housing all the departments, the best use had to be made of the offices of the former authorities. The Beckenham Town Hall became the home of the Borough Engineer, Surveyor and Planning and Penge Town Hall accommodated the Borough Architect. Thomas Webster Fagg from the Chislehurst and Sidcup UDC became the Town Clerk with his offices at the Bromley Town Hall, the Medical Officer went to the Walnuts at Orpington and education, formerly managed by Kent was housed at Sunnymead, Chislehurst.

We were fortunate that a gifted accountant, Thomas William (Tom) Sowerby, had come to be Beckenham's treasurer in 1961 in readiness for the change. An ex Squadron Leader, with over twenty five years experience in local government, most recently for Worcestershire County Council, he was used to dealing with thousands rather than the hundreds of pounds in Beckenham's accounts. He valued the sterling qualities of Beckenham's Councillors and stayed in the new Borough until 1977. He had spent 43 years in local government and had come to suspect that Whitehall was seeking to infiltrate it. He warned that the Government would soon be telling the local authorities exactly how to spend the budgets allowed. Tom left his job as Bromley's Borough Treasurer to join the money brokers Butler Till. In his day he was a keen cricketer and as a member of Beckenham Cricket Club he would open the bowling with Derek Underwood at the other end. He retired to Beckenham to enjoy the parks and tree lined roads and where he could watch Kent play at their new ground in Copers Cope Rd.

On 15 April 1964 at the inaugural lunch at the Town Hall Bromley, the Charter Mayor, Sir Cuthbert Ackroyd, presiding, included in his speech, 'We stand today in the presence of history and I emphasise that the five authorities concerned in the coming amalgamation will still remain local communities with their own local loyalties.' Looking back over more than forty years we can see that this has not always been possible but it is still worth fighting for.

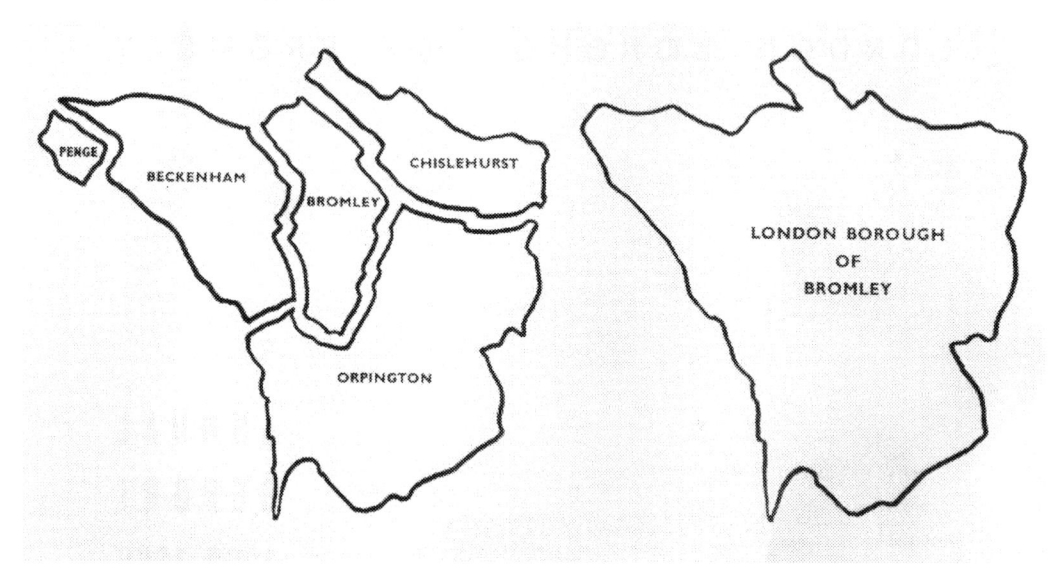

The Arms of the London Borough of Bromley

Thiry One
Rob Bonnet tells of his childhood in Beckenham

Beyond the asparagus bed - and through a hole in the wire fence - was the National Provincial Bank Sports Ground and while in the early years, I was happy to swing a bat or kick a football on the garden lawn, it was really that hole in the fence that defined my childhood. It opened onto tennis courts once described as the best in Southern England outside London SW19, so much so that Wimbledon champions and challengers would come and practice there in June.

I was born in Woolwich and spent three years as a baby and toddler in Eltham but my parents - Harold and Mary Bonnet- moved to the bottom end of Copers Cope Road in 1955. Just beforehand, my father had been made secretary of the National Provincial Bank Sports Club which had its grounds behind the house and whilst he had an office in the City, it naturally also suited him to live close to the club.

Post-war rationing was over but some signs of conflict remained...pre-fabricated single story dwellings further up the road towards Beckenham...a bomb-site down at Lower Sydenham where I'd soon be riding my bike with friends....the circular mark on the grass at Cyphers Cricket Ground in Kings Hall Road where a German V2 had fallen short of its central London target.

Here we see in 1948 a cricket match in progress where the V2 fell. Cyphers are playing a match versus Davidson's. We are looking through a hole in the wall of the damaged indoor bowling green.

ROB BONNET TELLS OF HIS CHILDHOOD IN BECKENHAM

Some of the more elderly neighbours still described the centre of Beckenham as "the village" - a romantic notion for what was a developing and relatively prosperous London suburb. Still, the curiously-named Copers Cope Road retained a country feel. Large horse-chestnuts lined the road's grass verge, which in turn featured two gravel paths (one for pedestrians and the other - more narrow - worn away by cyclists for whom the road surface was too treacherous.) The road itself was also unmade - bare and pitted in the middle but awash with pebbles to the side; along with others in the area (Park Road, Brackley Road, Lawn Road, and Worsley Bridge Road) it helped form a pocket of pseudo-rural tranquillity to the south of the terraced streets of Sydenham and Penge.

The road would flood in the winter and create large pot-holes; and it would be dry and dusty in the summer, when the local council would send round the "water-cart", a large lorry with a tank and sprinkler to damp down the dust. Naturally, the local children - me included - would run alongside as it trundled past, daring each other to get a soaking. The driver - meanwhile - would shake his fist at us for coming so close, but he was barely travelling at 5 miles an hour...and we were nimble. The large Victorian houses at the upper end of the road gave way further down to the more modest but still substantial dwellings where we lived. My house - number 141 - was one of maybe about thirty of its kind and was built at the turn of the twentieth century. How do I know? Because my father showed me a picture taken early in its first decade in which the half-built houses bristled with scaffolding. The first owners will have had social aspirations no doubt; the houses had two storeys plus a cellar and an attic and when we moved into 141 it still featured a network of bells for the maid and tradesmen. But my parents installed tenants in our attic, not servants!

At first, we lacked the household amenities that the British now take for granted. A pantry but no fridge...a rudimentary coke-fuelled AGA that caused panic at meal-times and grumbling when it was time to empty the ash. Heating came only from original fire-places that my father then destroyed according to wanton mid-sixties vogue...and there was a primitive washing machine filled via a hose directly attached to the kitchen taps, plus a mangle that looked - and sometimes behaved - like an instrument of torture.

And there was no car. My father must have reckoned that he didn't need one when the boundaries of his life were defined by the daily train from New Beckenham up to Cannon Street station and weekends spent 200 yards down the road at the sports ground. Besides which, the car would have taken a dreadful hammering amongst the pot-holes...and the rest of us had bikes. Eventually my father bought a green MG 1100, but not before modest modernisation to the house. The pantry disappeared, the kitchen was extended and a fridge installed, a gas cooker replaced the AGA, a fitted washing machine was plumbed in...and central heating followed, but only on the ground floor. And fitted carpets - the ultimate luxury - spread though the hall and sitting room and eventually into the bedrooms.

And yet amidst this spending, financed by my father's promotion at the National Provincial Bank, the bathroom and lavatory were strangely neglected. Elsewhere in the road, householders were pushing forward into the brave new dream world of en-suite or second bathrooms. But at 141, the bathroom stayed the same for thirty years...cold linoleum floor, limited hot water and no real privacy in one of the rooms where you might think adults would crave it most. My parents shared it with the lodgers throughout....and also, if she could make it up the stairs, with my Granny.

ROB BONNET TELLS OF HIS CHILDHOOD IN BECKENHAM

My mother's mother lived in the back room on the ground floor and - if nature demanded and her arthritis allowed - she'd haul herself painfully up to the first floor. I lived in fear of discovering her in a crumpled heap at the bottom step but her apparent fragility disguised a fierce determination - and a good sense of balance - and she never put a foot wrong.

Instead it was me who finished in the heap...inspired perhaps by watching the winter Olympics on TV, I once launched myself from the top of the stairs in a bath tub. I must have imagined I was going for bobsleigh Gold. It ended in tears...I smashed my face on the hall stand at the bottom and broke some of the best family glassware inside. My mother was a constant source of love and care. Not only did she put me back together again after the bobsleighing but also soothed my nightmares when I thought the walls were closing in and once carried me - bloodied and bruised - all the way home from a friend's house after I'd fallen off his swing and onto the concrete below. Meanwhile she was dedicating 20 years of her life to her mother in that back-room...and also to Suzanne Bonnet, the daughter of my father's first marriage, who still calls her "mum" as naturally as if she really were her own.

Suzanne left in the early sixties to pursue a career in nursing but Granny stayed. Her room had double doors through to the conservatory - her "summer sitting room" - and beyond of course was the garden, long and narrow, lawn and flower beds at the top end, orderly rows of vegetables towards the bottom. My war-generation parents must have thought they were still digging for victory. And when, during the sixties, they really splashed out and bought a freezer, the kitchen was converted into a mini factory, with my father dumping arm-loads of carrots, beans and peas onto the draining board while mum frantically tried to keep up with the processing, packing and freezing.

The pride and joy, however, was the asparagus bed at the very bottom of the garden - supplying produce of an altogether more exotic nature. Dad read the books, dug in the manure, bought the special serrated knife and then watched with pride every successive spring as this fertile corner of his garden helped re-define him in the eyes of lunch guests as more than just a "meat and two veg" kind of a fellow. Asparagus was served - after all - as an "hors d'oeuvre".

Our neighbours seemed mysterious. The Harrises at 139 appeared a little bohemian...after all, the father had a dark beard and the mother - if I remember rightly - wore flowery dresses. A hippy, maybe, before her time? They had a son, Christopher, with whom I played occasionally but this was never going to be a strong friendship because he wasn't interested in cricket or football and instead kept frogs and newts in an artificial pond beneath their kitchen window. Somehow, my parents conveyed to me that they were not our sort of family.

And at 143, the Hogbens. An elderly couple...she from Texas with greying hair that fell down behind her knees, but which was usually kept in a bun. And he, a heavily set man, a little frightening maybe with a deeply intellectual air. He was a professor of music at Coloma College in West Wickham but was also a keen amateur astronomer who - on a clear summer's night - once invited me to look through his telescope at the moon and the stars beyond. This was a magical, unforgettable moment, probably at about the time of Yuri Gagarin and John Glenn, but I usually feared contact with Mr Hogben because he would be the one eyeing me darkly from their back-room when I clambered across the fence to collect a carelessly struck tennis ball. They would play music together, he the cello and she the violin. It seemed very high-brow and had long since marked them down as unusual, given my parents' determinedly middle-of-the-road tastes, which went no further - once they finally bought a record player - than Bert Kampfert, the leader of band music which was chronically bland. Mrs Hogben, meanwhile, was a successful gardener, who tended her lawn and roses with enormous care (hence their disapproval of flying tennis balls!).

But the most eye-catching aspect of the Hogbens' garden were the red-painted bottles, inverted on long sticks and placed at strategic intervals along the fences and amongst the flower beds. These, they said, scared off seed-hungry pigeons. My father always raised a sceptical, amused eyebrow at this eccentric theory...though if he'd had half a chance to remove the bottles and fling them at the cats desecrating his asparagus bed, he'd have taken it.

ROB BONNET TELLS OF HIS CHILDHOOD IN BECKENHAM

I played there first with my mother - and then with friends - but it was on the football pitches and in the cricket nets where I truly developed my love of ball sports. My favourite football team was Manchester United - a name associated both with glamour and post-Munich sympathy at the time - but my first football shirt was in the gold of Wolverhampton Wanderers and I wore it at a number of sports-ground-based birthday parties that amounted to little more than football kick-abouts with baked beans on toast to follow. No girls. There was real privilege on those pitches...27 acres of extended back garden where I was free to come and go with friends, provided we kept off the cricket squares and the pavilion roof. Occasionally we'd be chased off by the head-groundsman, especially if he caught us making dams in the river beyond the pitches, but we were mostly tolerated, even if our games owed more to a child's imagination than to any coaching manual.

When accompanied by my father, of course, there was no danger of expulsion...but his Sunday morning cricket net sessions were serious affairs. My father was an able cricketer, an all-rounder who'd once played to minor counties standard and was still performing for the Bank's 1st XI. He wanted much of the same for his only son and so coached me in the virtues of a straight bat and upright action from an early age.

He'd pace out his run - short at first, but longer as I grew older - and bowl over after over at me, pausing only to correct my backlift or shot selection. Sometimes these words of advice developed into lengthy lectures and I'd grow impatient for the next opportunity to try to hit the ball back over his head, the only airborne shot he'd allow. Otherwise, the ball had to be played along the ground; my father, after all, had matured as an instinctively cautious bank manager.

And when I was bowling, there was the banker's financial incentive. He'd place a handkerchief on a good length in front of him; I got a sixpence every time I hit it. And behind him on his middle stump, he'd place a half crown - a small fortune to a boy whose weekly pocket money was only a shilling. I won enough sixpences to open a junior bank account...but his half crown only once. He was never one to give away his wicket, but I remember the smile on his face nevertheless.

The New Beckenham/Lower Sydenham area contained a whole range of business-house sports grounds...occasional venues for me and my friends for other, more surreptitious games of "three and in" - accompanied by breathless commentaries in the style of Kenneth Wolstenhome (or so we thought!). However the summer highlights were always the so-called Saturday Sports Days when cricket matches were replaced by athletics and bank staff from across the country would come to compete. Today, it would be called corporate bonding. Whether at the NP, Lloyds Bank across the road or the Midland Bank beyond New Beckenham station, these were occasions for excitement and glamour.

It was as if the circus had come to town. Lorries delivered acres of white canvas and within a day the cricket pitches were lost beneath cavernous marquees where, after the erecting gangs and ground-staff had gone home, we'd invent any number of games.

Hide-and-seek, toboggan-down-the-canvas roof, throw-the-cricket-ball-over-the-roof, indoor-tennis...and occasionally loosen-the-guy-rope-and-see-what-happens.

And even more exciting were the slides and swings that came too; ready by Friday evening, but not dismantled sometimes till Monday morning, we treated them as our very own and they exhausted us until well after dark throughout the weekend. Still, the shouts of our play high on the slide were drowned out by the sounds of the Saturday evening's concert from deep within the main marquee. My father was responsible for booking the stars and enjoyed this brief annual contact with the world of showbiz. One year he booked the singer Marion Ryan and - after dragging me inside from the slide - made his introduction. I wasn't especially cute - in fact I was dirty and smelly from the slide - but La Ryan covered my face both with bright red lipstick and confusion. It was my first kiss from anyone beyond the family.

One of these corporate Saturday sports days was different from the rest...the club across the river next to Lower Sydenham station featured egg and spoon races rather than serious sprinting and middle-distance running, with the whole afternoon accompanied by music on the PA. My father was a sports purist who had no time for trivial games or the pop charts and he complained to the organisers. They simply turned up the volume. I was in the NP cricket nets with a friend as usual but stopped to listen to this fresh, raw sound floating across the field. It was introduced by harmonica and then followed by a simple lyric. "Love, Love me Do...You know I love you...I'll always be true...so Plee-ee-ee-ease. Love Me Do!" I didn't know it then but this had been my first experience of The Beatles.

These were the days of the Home Service and the Light Programme, received at home on an old bakelite radio which matched the telephone. We had no record player and so first awakenings to pop music - even before the Beatles - came over games of Monopoly at my friend David Manning's house along the road. Tommy Steele and his "Little White Bull" left me cold...but Buddy Holly's Greatest Hits were bright and full of energy. "Peggy Sue", "It Doesn't Matter Any More", "It's Raining in my Heart". They also came from the distant yet fascinating USA.

Later came a new portable radio with the 208 wavelength clearly marked. I'd take it to the NP Bank's tennis wall where I would be Neil Fraser and Rod Laver for alternate shots in the Wimbledon final but I'd come away knowing the composition of the entire Radio Luxembourg top twenty. And later, I'd hide the radio under my bedclothes and only allow myself to sleep after I'd heard the rich melodies of the Beach Boys' "I Get Around" for a second time.

Early school days were at Woodbrook in Hayne Road, then at Bromley Road Infants in Beckenham opposite the fire station. I was pathetically terrified on my first day but quickly settled and took comfortably enough to the three "R's" but - significantly perhaps - my most vivid memory is of cricket matches in the playground involving the elderly janitor. It seemed as if the whole school was lining the pitch as he bowled and we - in turn - defended the three stumps chalked on the school kitchen wall. The smell of boiled cabbage drifted through the open window but it was my taste for school sport that was developing.

ROB BONNET TELLS OF HIS CHILDHOOD IN BECKENHAM

Next came Worsley Bridge Road Junior School, though only after a first year spent in the Bromley Road annexe. This felt like proper school. It had modern bright classrooms, a big playground and playing fields with two football pitches and an artificial cricket strip. It also had teachers who were more than mother substitutes.

My second year teacher Mrs Jewry was strict, both in the classroom and in swimming lessons, where - as a Beckenham Ladies coach - she had special expertise. We splashed lengths behind polystyrene floats, but I wasn't a natural swimmer and longed for the five minute play time at the end when we could either duck-dive or show off to the girls.

Ah...the girls. The playground was segregated, not so much to prevent forbidden games of kiss-chase as to protect the girls from the rough and tumble of the boys. And yet - as ten and eleven year olds - something was stirring. Others were more courageous than me and boasted of stolen kisses, especially in the summer when we played at the top end of the field where the teachers rarely patrolled. But I was hopelessly timid. Fearful on the one hand of rejection and on the other of teacher or parental disapproval, I merely flirted with flirting. Pathetic. Still, I did eventually summon up the courage to ask one class-mate if I could walk part of the way home with her and this eventually became a regular after-school 'date.' And once I even held her hand. Briefly.

In my last two years at Worsley Bridge I was in the class of Mr Griffiths, my first male teacher. He was an altogether different proposition from even Mrs Jewry. He seemed severe and demanding and would occasionally administer a clip round the ear. I didn't like that much and resolved to get in his good books.

Worsley Bridge Football team 1963/64. L to R back row; Mr Griffiths, Jack Edmonds, Roger Boxall, Kenwood (goalie), Robert Bonnet, Barry King, Mr Thomas. Front row; Tony Else, Tony Martin, Peter King, Graham Sheppard, Paul Jessup, Richard Brough, David Manning.

He could see through mere obsequiousness, so it had to be hard work in the classroom and on the playing field, where he coached both the football and cricket teams. He'd tuck his dark suit trousers into his football socks and drill us in the basics - "the side of your foot boy, not your toes!" - and then faithfully supervise the Saturday games against other local junior schools.

We were good and beat most of them except Hawes Down from West Wickham. Graham Sheppard, David Manning, Roger Boxall, Tony Else, Barry King...all had skill and stamina. And so - to much the same extent - did I. And although I was timid in front of the girls, I was an out-and-out glory seeker on the pitch. I had to play centre-forward and I had to score the goals. Once I got six against Alexandra and was chaired off the pitch. Paradise.

Mr Griffiths would have approved even more when I offered to write match reports in my final year for the school magazine...the first awakenings, maybe, of a career in sports journalism? However, the perspective was laughably personal and self-serving..."a superb shot from Bonnet", "Bonnet heroically cleared off the line", "Bonnet played on regardless of injury". Team-mates occasionally received a grudging mention. These testaments to a child's vanity, hammered out two-fingered on my mother's typewriter, still exist somewhere deep in family storage. Rob is front row, second from left.

Worsely Bridge Cricket Team 1963/64

Elsewhere there was Sunday School and cubs at St Paul's Church in Brackley Road...I was asked to join the choir but had been traumatised at Junior School when the music teacher asked us to stand one by one and recite scales. Mortified, my attempt fell somewhere between refusal and catastrophic failure and I still won't sing up on Christmas morning in church. Cubs was better than Sunday school because it involved a moderately violent version of ball-he and a football team...and also because they gave me lots of badges to wear on my uniform.

So this pre-teenage childhood was safe, healthy, happy (apart from the bobsleighing and singing) and full of certainties, if maybe a little limited. Saturday nights were invariably spent in the NP bar, where I eventually drank my first shandy but preferred to get my dad to play me in marathon games of table-tennis. My parents rarely entertained or went to the West End....if ever we did it was to the Lyons Cornner House, a Brian Rix farce or the Royal Tournament.

Nevertheless, present recollection casts sunlight over all these memories, maybe because they're also suffused with the warmth of a child's freedom. My parents, of course, had warned me about talking to strangers, but the reality is that the quiet leafy roads, the well-tended gardens and grassy acres of the sports ground held no danger other than the occasional sprained ankle and so I was lucky enough to live a childhood in which I was entirely free to express myself in work, play and sport. Once Graham Sheppard and I went on a Sunday morning bicycle adventure all the way up to Trafalgar Square and back again, a round trip via Catford, Lewisham, New Cross and Elephant and Castle of about twenty miles. I suppose we were about ten or eleven.

ROB BONNET TELLS OF HIS CHILDHOOD IN BECKENHAM

True, we felt rather brave and adventurous at the time, but the traffic was a thousand times less intense than now and our parents' scolding was tinged - I suspect - with admiration. They - too - were free to let us spread our wings, which we both did later at Dulwich College. Today that same trip would be a polluted, dangerous slog, even on a Sunday. And Copers Cope Road - of course - has changed almost beyond recognition. It was metalled in the mid-sixties and became a Beckenham/Catford rat-run. The large Victorian houses at the top of the road have given way to modern blocks or cul-de-sacs; those few that remain have mostly lost their previous identities as family homes....each front porch has a collection of door bells, one for each flat. Planning constraints still mean that the sports grounds resist housing development, but they no longer form the weekend's social focus. The corporate loyalty that once filled the pitches during the afternoons and the bars in the evenings of the fifties and sixties has largely evaporated - despite the heavy subsidies that meant cheap sport and beer. A few old-timers still visit - and maybe play the odd game of bowls - but if twenty or thirty somethings want sport, they'll play for their local club. Or watch it on Sky.

Kent County Cricket Club now occupies the old Lloyds Bank Ground...they've built a smart new pavilion as a magnet for a more metropolitan fan base than they can achieve in Canterbury. The hard tennis courts across the road from 141 have given way to modern housing. The National Westminster Bank - as it became - already had the old Westminster ground at nearby Norbury and eventually abandoned Lower Sydenham to a management company. The Bank still plays at the re-branded "Fitness Exchange" but the days of running five cricket teams on a Saturday are over. And so is the tennis...the grass courts have been converted to football pitches.

My parents had moved out of 141 in 1985 and taken a ground floor flat in central Beckenham.

Five years later my father died and after his cremation my mother and I had to decide where to scatter his ashes. We chose the old NP Bank's 1st XI cricket square where he'd nurtured my hero worship by hitting sixes onto the pavilion balcony. So on a bleak February afternoon we were joined by my sister for a quiet ceremony that was certainly informal but lacked nothing in irony. We were returning him to the scene of his cricketing triumphs but trespassing on it at the same time. How often, after all, had I heard him bellow "Get off the Square" at unknowing children, mischievous teenagers or even ignorant adults who'd failed to appreciate the unspoken sanctity of the cricket pitch. These incidents always produced the Captain Mainwearing in him.

Still, he became mellower in his retirement, and might even have smiled at the way his dust gathered under my finger nails as I tried to scoop it from the plastic bag. And then again, as it occasionally blew back into my face in the wind. Embarrassed at my clumsiness and lack of foresight, I dropped twenty yards behind and - unseen by my mother and sister - eventually emptied the remaining contents of the bag by holding it between thumb and forefinger like a young boy might scatter crumbs for hungry birds. I haven't visited the sports ground since then.

I last drove down Copers Cope Road about two and a half years ago, shortly before my mother moved out of the area. Naturally everything seemed smaller - and maybe neater - and those images of the late fifties and early sixties refused to superimpose themselves on the view through the windscreen. I stopped outside 141, half afraid that the occupiers would ask what the hell I was doing, but half wanting them to ask all the same, so that I could explain and they would invite me in to satisfy my curiosity. But the curtains were closed and the front door remained shut. Surely it has at least two state-of-the-art bathrooms now? And central heating throughout?

Rob with his daughters, Clare (left) and Eleanor at the Great North Run in 2004

Thirty Two
Some Personalities of the time

Carey Blyton (1932-2002)

Carey was born in The Drive and was 6 months old when Prince George passed his home on the way to open Beckenham's new Town Hall in 1932. The Prince departed but Carey lived in Beckenham for the next 30 years. He was educated at Bromley Road, The Grange in Wickham Road and at the Beckenham County Grammar School for Boys (BCGS).

He came close to death in 1944 when a V1 landed diagonally opposite his house in The Drive and again three years later when he was struck down by polio. Hitler's flying bomb forced an evacuation for Carey and his Mother to the West Country where he confronted the English class system, deepened his affinity with the natural world, and learned the elements of capitalism bartering cheap jewellery with American GI's for their cigarettes.

In 1947, his GCE O level results were delivered by BCGS head 'Jumbo' White to Farnborough Hospital where he told Carey that they were 'the best in school' that year. After months in hospital, the tedium of his long convalescence at home was changed by a neighbour who suggested Carey learn to play the piano. This "therapy" became converted into a passion for music and when Carey returned to BCGS in 1948 he joined the Music Society, a joint venture with the Girls County School.

Writing in the Beccehamian, the BCGS magazine, Carey - for whom music was close to an all consuming interest - complained about the passive interest of the girls. He was not doing them justice as some six were on the Music Society Committee and some of these, with others, also took part in the highly successful annual BCGS drama productions.

In 1949, the Girls County School sixth formers invited the boys to a dance in the hall in the school in Lennard Road. The boys were told to "come as you are". With his legs in irons, Carey could not dance so he suggested the boys provide some entertainment, an idea endorsed with enthusiasm by his colleagues and several, like Brian Sanders, Mike Hopkins, Francis Weiss, John Miles and Peter Mitchell, vividly remember how Carey, dressed in a black cloak as the anarchist, Count Bombski, led the BCGS sixth form on a "band storming" march to Lennard Road via Penge High Street and the astonished constabulary of the police station.

In the Girls School hall, Carey provided decorations in the provocative form of sets of three balloons and later he startled everybody by throwing his "bomb" - a black painted ball cock - onto the dance floor. This behaviour horrified Miss Henshaw and it was not surprising that girls were absent from the next Music Society meeting.

With this exuberance behind them, Carey and a small group of friends took part in concerts, one being at Elm Road Baptist Church Hall and another in the Arts & Music series held in the BCGS hall.

Carey and Benita Powell

SOME PERSONALITIES OF THE TIME

They were organised by Tom Williams who had been a senior English master at the school and who also found time to set the questions for the BBC radio programme, 'Top of the Form.' In 1952, Carey and a local actress, Benita Powell, appeared in the film 'The Blue Beads' shot in Kelsey Park and Beckenham High Street.

From these beginnings emerged the Beckenham Salon 1952 to 54, described by Carey as 'a collection of arts-interested young people in "downtown Beckenham" who wrote music, poetry, plays, took "artistic" photographs, etc.' Their members included Carey, David Munro, Mike Hopkins, David Roberts, Arthur Dodd. Jack Frost, Hugh Bean, Benita Powell, John Vosser, and Mollie and Geoffry Russell-Smith. They performed five public concerts and other in the drawing rooms of the fine houses in Beckenham. The Salon's President, Sir Arthur Bliss attended several events.

Standing: David & Phyllis Munro, Jean Tresize (all worked at Beckenham Library) Seated Carey Blyton, Marcia Parkin, John Vosser, Mike Hopkins, Jean MacGregor, Benita Powell, It was Phyllis's 21st birthday. NB Marcia was the daughter of Alderman Parkin who lived in Wickham Way.

Writing to a fellow composer, Mike Cornick, in 1997, Carey said 'As I think more and more of my beginnings as a composer, and thus of "early days" the more I realize how very crucial were the years 1949 to 1953 - the Beckenham salon was clearly seminal.'

Most of the 100 solo and choral songs were written early in his career, several being premiered in the Salon Concerts. In 1953, he started his four year music degree at TCM (London) where obtained all three college diplomas and was awarded a 10 month scholarship to the Danish Conservatoire in Copenhagen. He returned in 1958 to be music editor for Mills Music and became Professor of Harmony, Counterpoint and Orchestration at Trinity until 1973. For the next 10 years he was Visiting Professor at the Guildhall School of Music and Drama where he pioneered tuition in composition for Films, TV and Radio.

Carey wrote music for films, TV (including Dr Who series) and radio and advertising commercials. He worked with and wrote music for schools and gave private tuition as well as later freelancing as a music editor. He wrote a number of short stories. Friends and colleagues recall his charisma which reflected his love of the natural world and a whacky but infectious humour - involving puns, pseudonyms, limericks, and nonsense verse.

One piece of nonsense versus was concocted on a long car journey as a soporific for his first son, Matthew. This was Bananas in Pyjamas (BIP) which his wife, Mary, urged him to write down the words and music. A collection of his nonsense songs and poems was published in 1972 by Faber. Ten years later, BIP videos were produced by the Australian Broadcasting Corporation (ABC). Since then, ABC has issued licences world-wide for over 1000 items of BIP merchandise: books, toys, toothpaste, toothbrushes, clothing etc

In 2002, Carey was delighted to learn that the infant pupils of his first school - Bromley Road - had created a mural depicting their favourite song, Bananas in Pyjamas, a copy of which was presented to his youngest son Daniel.

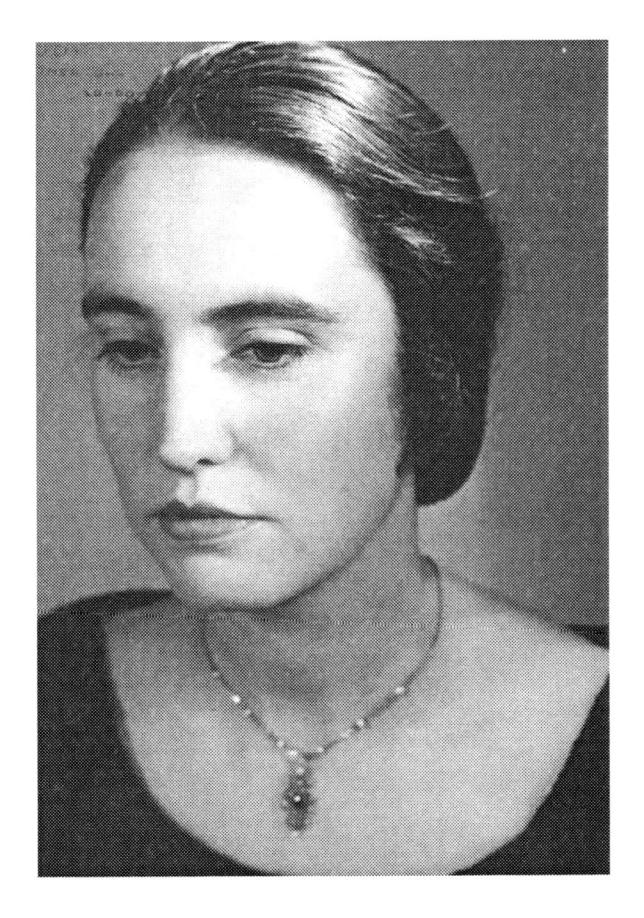

Patricia Carroll, concert pianist

Born in Beckenham, Patricia's musical talent soon impressed her fellow pupils at the Beckenham County School for Girls. Her impetuous personality, beautiful individual interpretation of the work and technical skill merged to produce unforgettable vital performances with such meticulous attention to detail. If only Patricia's outstanding performances of those school days of ours could have been recorded! If you ask Patricia about those school days she says she remembers them with enormous pleasure, particularly Nancy Wiseman and Sylvia Cutler on the staff who were so enthusiastic and encouraging. Patricia also played piano and violin sonatas and the violin in a string quartet.

She began playing at the age of five and at 10 years old she had already entertained British and American troops at many war time concerts. She won a scholarship to the Royal College of Music where in 1951 she won the Chappell medal for piano playing and was forecast as one of the leading young pianists in the world. The Directors of the London Symphony Orchestra heard her play Rachmaninov's Third Concerto in D minor at a college concert and asked her to play at the Royal Festival Hall in 1952 under George Stratton. Her interpretation was true to the music, rising to moments of greatness in the cadenza of the first movement and the finale. In 1962 she played the Grieg concerto at the first night of the Proms, conducted by Sir Malcolm Sargent and in 1965 Patricia was one of four solo pianists in a performance of 'Les Noces' by Strawinsky. She studied at Paris under an exchange scholarship and returned to perform frequently for the BBC. Another scholarship to Vienna heralded recitals travelling all over the country. She won an international competiton in Germany and studied with Arturo Michelangeli in Italy.

In 1978 she was one of two pianists in the film 'Lillie' with Francesca Annis playing Lillie Langtry 'Piano Parlour' was a programme of Victorian piano music for radio 4, where she introduced and played pieces such as those familiar to home pianists as well as brilliant show pieces for travelling concert artists. Patricia was Professor of Piano at the Royal College of Music for many years and says that perhaps her most extraordinary experience as adjudicator was in Hong Kong in 2002 when she heard 1600 pianists in three weeks!

After a lifetime of music, Patricia retired to study and recently graduated with a BA Hons. in Humanities with History of Art. She married in 1959 and became Patricia Newman. Her three children, son and two daughters, have been successful in their various ways.

Patricia in period costume for Piano Parlour

Alison Prince, author and illustrator

Alison hated school.

> 'It was so boring. I spent most of the time dreaming up adventures, which never happened of course. That's how I came to write the stories about the school Mill Green where they really do happen.'

Having attended the same school, I can read between the lines and see the origin of many of her ideas. I can see her sitting uncomfortably on a stool while our chemistry teacher demonstrated the component parts of crude oil thinking that if she really wanted to know she could look it up in a book. We all appreciated Alison's distinctive style of drawing and she was certainly a great success in the part of the Grocer in the 1944 production of 'The Knight of the Burning Pestle.' It was said that 'the invasion of the platform by the sturdy Grocer and his wife was carried out with exhilarating vigour sustained by a prodigious supply of apples.'

As well as illustrating and writing, Alison has worked in television (remember Trumpton?) and at the zoo (serving teas at the Penguin Bar), sold newspapers, gilded picture frames, run a smallholding (getting up at dawn to milk the cows), driven a cattle truck, painted scenery and hitch-hiked across Europe. She is responsible for the drawings in 'Hello to Ponies' and Hello to Riding' and she wrote and illustrated 'The Good Pets Guide.' 'The Sherwood Hero' won the Guardian Children's Fiction Award and 'The Summerhouse' has been a recent success.

At present Alison lives on the Isle of Arran where she is a member of the local council. Her children are all over the world. Samantha, a writer, lives in the Cevennes in S W France. Ben and his Chinese Malaysian wife are currently in China. Andy, with Ruth and their two children, is a farrier and restorer of houses in Australia. Eldest son John manages a bus network in Edinburgh.

The one and only Nancy Tonkin (née Banks)

There was nothing that Nancy Banks could not accomplish if she set her mind to it. After her brother, Kenneth Banks, died in May 1945 when his Spitfire crashed in a field near York, it was left to Nancy to give her shattered parents a reason for living. Her mother never recovered from the shock of losing her son so cruelly three weeks after the end of the war and died from cancer nineteen months later leaving Nancy with the task of being both son and daughter to her bereft father. She became the first woman to become the club champion of her father's fishing club. Later on she was selected for the male preserve of the National Championships. As this was on her wedding day, she postponed her wedding to go fishing instead!

Bill and Nancy Tonkin had the perfect family of two boys, Kenneth and Michael followed by two girls, Susan and Alison. They were always busy. They did not just collect stamps but made specialist collections and entered (and won) competitions. With Nancy in charge, the family always made the most of everything. They were all good swimmers, especially the girls who were members of Beckenham Ladies. And what do they do today? Kenneth is a wealthy business man with a talent for choosing the saleable product. Michael owns the family business in Croydon. Susan is one of only eight woman Wing Commanders in the RAF and Alison runs the Coney Hall preschool nursery.

Nancy was the Secretary of the Adremians from 1975. She organised the committee to perfection and was the leading light in celebrating the school's diamond jubilee by producing the school plate and two patterns of mugs, with a magazine depicting the events of the past fifty years.

She discovered a talent for writing that she put to good use as co-author with Eric Inman of the book 'Beckenham' that has run to two editions. Her passion for collecting led to the assembly of postcards and other memorabilia shown to perfection in the 'Beckenham' book. Since her death at the age of 69 in 1995, her husband, Bill Tonkin, has catalogued her postcard collection to make it more easily accessible to posterity.

Nancy with her year's trophies at the S Norwood Angling Club dinner

SOME PERSONALITIES OF THE TIME

Boxer and footballer, Frank (Dot) Morris

Frank showed his skills as both footballer and boxer while a schoolboy when he earned his nickname 'Dot' as he played in the seniors at Oakfield School in Penge when still in the Juniors.

He was schoolboy boxing champion of Great Britain.

As a young man in the army, it was boxing that took up his time.

In April 1951, after a well matched fight in the REME Boxing Championships at Shepherds Bush, Frank was awarded the verdict in the Featherweight Contest for his better technique and strong left hand. After much success as a Lightweight, Frank turned to his other love, football.

He played on the left wing as a part time professional for Crystal Palace until no more part timers were allowed and went to Tunbridge Wells United for a time before moving to nearby Beckenham Town. As skipper, he inspired the team which cruised to many a victory. For a year he elected to become player manager for Beckenham Social in 1962, near to where he lived in Churchfields Rd but soon returned to Beckenham Town.

He encouraged his family to follow him into the world of sport and Susan born in 1955 responded by becoming a Kent backstroker for Beckenham Ladies. Patricia born 1958 became a singer. Richard born nine years later was an all round sportsman but favoured the business world of computing. Granddaughter Alex kept up the tradition as a Southern Counties swimmer.

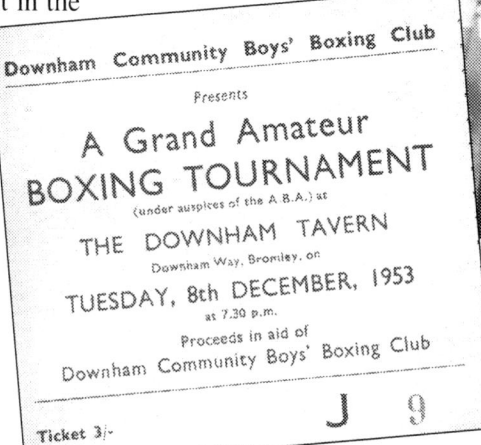

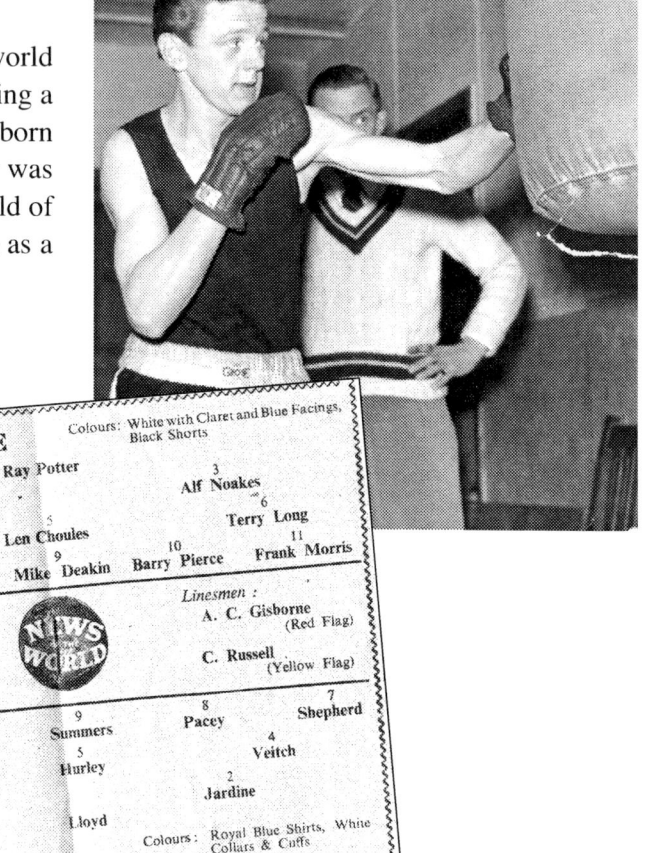

SOME PERSONALITIES OF THE TIME

Mollie Lunggren formerly Frost (née Russell Smith)

Mollie was thirteen when her family moved to Cromwell Rd in Beckenham. She went to the Beckenham Grammar School for an interview with the 'fearsome' Miss Fox. Her mother was asked if she was any good at Maths and when the reply was that although very good at English, she was not good at Maths, Miss Fox recommended that she went to Woodbrook. As she had come from Tunbridge Well Grammar School, Woodbrook's small classes were a great contrast. The summer uniform made from a pattern provided by the school was in cream tussore silk. Low waisted 1920s style (this was 1936) with long pointed collars, the dresses sound most impractical but they were actually comfortable, hardwearing and easy to wash and iron.

At that time, Miss Mead and Miss Elvin were great friends with Miss Neville, the Head of the Tavistock Clinic and pioneer in Child Psychology. Visiting the school to give interviews and intelligence tests to the children, she unearthed Geoffry Russell Smith's musical talent and invited Miss Rose of the Royal College of Music to hear the 9 year old play the piano. The result was that he was made a junior exhibitioner at the college. His talent was further encouraged at the Beckenham & Penge Grammar School for Boys by a young Australian music master, Hubert Clifford who was able to persuade the LCC to take other children from outside the London area. Geoffry went on to a musical career in composing, publishing, conducting, adjudicating and writing and has now retired to Australia. Miss Mead and Miss Elvin would be justifiably so proud!

Mollie enjoyed herself at Woodbrook especially when she played the lead in the school plays and realised that Miss Fox had probably been right. Mollie started evening classes at the Beckenham Art School while still at Woodbrook and at 15 became a full time student there. Henry Carr, the principal, painted her portrait and she did well in the drawing exams but when the bombs came too close for comfort during 1940, the family wearied of crouching in the Anderson shelter and retreated to Suffolk to stay with an aunt.

She joined the East Anglian School of Painting and Drawing and started working alongside the portrait painter, Lucien Freud and Kathleen Hale who created Orlando, the Marmalade Cat.

When Mollie reached call up age, she worked at a Ministry of Health Day Nursery opened to cope with evacuees and when the Head collapsed with measles, Mollie found herself running the nursery single-handed. During a stint in the Civil Defence, she managed to have her first painting exhibited in a West end gallery as a CD artist. Returning to Beckenham, she became an inspector of electrical engineering at Creed's of Croydon and even became a member of a small 'hush hush' team inspecting bomb sights for aircraft.

Mollie's brother, Geoffry, became a friend of Bob Monkhouse and Mollie remembers them playing together at the Elm Rd Youth Club the Lonnie Donegan number, 'Does the spearmint lose its flavour on the bedpost overnight?' Geoffry also brought his friend Jack Frost home and as a bass baritone and composer and he became one of the Elm Rd crowd. Mollie and Jack married and Mollie's life in the world of Art took off. She exhibited at the Women's International Art Club meeting contempory women painters as well as older women like Laura Knight. She made her first painting trip to Paris with the painter Delia Massey and locally joined the Beckenham Salon as the only female member. Carey Blyton, David Munro and Mike Hopkins were founder members.

SOME PERSONALITIES OF THE TIME

Prior to 1952, when Mollie's daughter Eleanor was born followed by her son Garnet in 1953 Mollie had taught in the kindergarten at Woodbrook. When the children were three and four years old, Mollie's first marriage had broken down and she moved to Cromwell Rd to live with her mother. After training as a mature student at Stockwell College.

There followed 10 years as a teacher at Balgowan and 12 years as a painter tutor in Adult Education. Hung four times in the Royal Academy Summer Show, member of the Print Makers Council, published four collections of verse set to music by her brother and a book about biblical Harlots and Heroines, founder member of the Piccadilly Poets.

Oddly enough Mollie became most widely known for the children's action song, 'The Dingle Dangle Scarecrow.' This standard children's song by Mollie and Geoffry has become a classic, recorded, broadcast and televised across the world.

In 1963, Mollie married again, this time to Eric Lunggren, her neighbour in Cromwell Rd where Mollie lives to this day. Her artistic talents passed on to both her children and to Mollie's delight to her grandchildren as well. I met Mollie at Woodbrook where our children were in the kindergarten together with Rob Bonnet. A small world indeed!

Epilogue

The London Monument to the Battle of Britain

'I think the design is absolutely first class and will make a world class tribute to 'The Few.'
Winston S Churchill

Founded in 1996, the Battle of Britain Society launched an initiative to erect a monument to all the Allied aircrew that fought in the Battle of Britain. The monument, the design of John Mills, shows not only the pilots but all the ground support that enabled the pilots to fly and fight. It was unveiled on the Victoria Embankment near Westminster Bridge by Prince Charles on Sunday 18 September 2005.

Biggin Hill was of especial importance to Beckenham and indeed the whole of the London Borough of Bromley because it was the favoured airfield chosen to protect London. Squadrons of the RFC had begun to occupy the airfield as early as 1917. In November 1937, squadron 32 of Biggin Hill took part in the first radar controlled experiment when three Gauntlet fighters intercepted a Dutch air liner at 6,000ft en route to Croydon.

Their first kill of WWII was when Hurricanes shot down a Dornier on 21 November 1939 and it was on 15 May 1943 that the Biggin Wing claimed its thousandth enemy aircraft. Hornchurch and Biggin Hill were the two most frequently bombed airfields in Fighter Command and they were in the thick of the Battle of Britain fighting. In fact the code words scramble, pancake, angels and bandits were devised at Biggin Hill.

Planes that flew from Biggin Hill during the Battle of Britain were Spitfires, Hurricanes, Defiants, Gladiators and Beaufighters.

The London Monument to the Firefighters

Long after the end of the war, the Queen Mother insisted that the AFS should have the special memorial which we can see in St Paul's courtyard. It was created by John Mills, the son in law of the West Ham Chief Officer, Cyril T. Demarne. The original maquette had been produced by the Chief Officer in memory of his firemen and is housed in the Hall of Remembrance of the London Fire Brigade at Lambeth. The large memorial was unveiled by the Queen Mother on 4 May 1991 in Old Change Court near St Paul's Cathedral. It has the names of 1027 of the dead firemen and woman on its hexagonal base. The font used for the inscription is that on the ration books, 'Gill Sans.'

The Women's WW2 Memorial

A third WW2 memorial designed by John Mills stands next to the Cenotaph in Whitehall. Made of bronze, it depicts the women's roles in the form of seventeen sets of clothing and uniforms. These symbolise the hundreds of different kinds of work carried out by women in WW2 from digging coal, building ships and growing food to serving in the armed forces. Like the firemen's memorial this also uses the typeface used on the wartime ration books.

Answers to the local crossword from Christmas 1952

Index

1948 Olympics 33
A S F Butcher 55
Abbey Lane stables 92
Abbey School 30, 92
Ackroyd, Sir Cuthbert 109, 116
Action stations 40
Adcock, Cllr 84
Adler, Larry 95
Adremians 60, 98, 129
Adyes, Charles 6
Adyes, Frederick 6
Aerograph 33
Agate, Ernest Stanley 41
Aitchison, P C 24, 82
Akehurst, Marjorie 59
Alan Boyden 12
Alan Brothers 89
Alcock 9
Alexandra Recreation ground 96
Alexandria School 78, 112
Ali Baba and the Naughty Thieves 8
AMGOT (Allied Military Government Occupied Territories) 27
Anderson, John 106
Anderson, Mal 86
Andrews, Evelyn 59
Andrews, Julie 62, 63
Andrews, Mr 48
Annis, Francesca 127
Antrobus, Yvonne 85, 89
Area K 40
Area L 40
Arthur Mothersdale Cup 97
Atkins, Cllr J H 38, 48, 52, 92
Attenborough, Richard 86
Atwell, Winifred 95
Austin, Barbara, 89
Aylett, Esther 86
Azelia Hall 69, 75
Bagg, Company Officer 44
Bagg, Mr 45
Bailey, Henry 41
Bailey,Ron M 52, 45
Baker, Graham 50
Baker, Ruth 110
Baldwin, Mrs 72
Balgowan School for Girls 94, 132
Bananas in Pyjamas 126
Banks, Jennifer 97
Banks, Kenneth 51, 129
Banwell, Freda 63
Barber, A C 24
Barclay & Perkins Co. 40
Barrett, Vera Eileen 54
Barrett, Vivien 77
Barry Curtis 78
Barry, 4th Baronet Sir Rupert Rodney Francis Tress 47
Barry, Francis Tress 40
Barton, Judith Anne 91
Battle of Britain 17, 133
Baxter, David 67
BBC TV mast 81, 87
Beacon, R 23
Beadle, Ernest 23, 75
Beadle, Norman 97
Bean, Hugh 126
Beard, Dorothy 35
Beavis, Raymond 94
Beccehamian 125
Beckenham & District Soroptimists Club 101
Beckenham & Penge Grammar School for Boys 18, 131
Beckenham & Penge Sea Cadets 26, 101
Beckenham Bowling Club 11, 83, 96
Beckenham Cottage Hospital 104
Beckenham Cricket Club 116
Beckenham FC 106
Beckenham Grammar School for Girls 107
Beckenham Green 32, 112
Beckenham Horticultural Society 68

Beckenham Philatelic Society 28
Beckenham Rotary Club 11
Beckenham Swimming Club 78, 108
Beckenham Telephone Exchange 98
Beckenham Tennis Tournament 110
Beckenham Theatre 97
Beckenham Town FC 11
Beckenham's War Weapons 22
Beeton, Elise 34
Belarus 58
Beldry, Elizabeth 100
Bell, Sybil 98
Bellringer, Anne 98
Bencurtis Park 77
Bennett, Ald. Dr James Henry 5, 15, 27, 82, 85, 104,
Bennett, John 108
Bennett, Nell 7
Bennitt,W. 43
Berkhamsted 84
Berry, Rev. 8
Bevan, Aneurin 104
Biddle, Fireman 63
Big Daddy 56
Biggin Hill Open Day 89
Billy Cotton Band Show 112
Billy Mole's Orchestra 36
Bismark 17
Biswell, Auxiliary Fireman 42
Black, Jimmy 74
Blackham, Mr 36
blackout 22
Blake Field 97
Blakemore, Archibald 56
Blick, Neil 106
Blinkhorn-Hay, Gladys Muriel 41
Blyton, Carey 112, 125, 131
Blyton, Enid 112
Blyton, Daniel 126
Blyton, Mary 126
Boadella, Don 76
Bolsh, Ivy 93
Bonell (née Tonkin), Susan 51
Boniface, Ian 52
Bonnet, Harold and Mary 117
Bonnet, Suzanne 119
Bonnet, Rob 62, 122, 132
Bonnett, Clare 124
Bonnett, Eleanor 124
Borough Charter 1
Borrowman Swimming Cup 110
Borrowman, Robert 66, 96
Bowles, Kenneth J 24, 39
Bowles, Mollie 39
Bowyer, Mavis 97
Boxall, Roger 110, 123
Boyd, Canon 23
Boyd, Cllr Boyd 61
Boyd, Cllr Thomas Boyd 53, 92
Boyle, Lady Catherine 84
Boys Technical School 87
Brackley, Mrs 25
Branham, Jennifer 90
Bray, Alderman 113
Bray, David 77
Breck, Alfred 24, 25
Brett, Rev. George 57, 60
Bridges, Christine 59
'Briggy' Brigden 74
Brine, Mrs 97
Bromley,Gerald 88
Brook Brown 99
Brook, Mayor Ald Guy 36, 68
Brook, RP 74
Brook, Wendy 35
Brooke, Monica 103
Brough, Richard 122
Brown, Henry Brook 92
Brown, Jack 56
Brown, Patricia 87
Browne, Harold 41

Bryant, Carol 112
Buchan-Hepburn, Mr 85
Bueno, Maria 110
Bunting, Fred 32, 60
Burden, Pauline 100
Burgoine, Mr 8
Burnham, G P 43
Burns, Edward (Ted) James 19
Burton, Frank 41
Burtonshaw, Thomas Richard 45
Butler-Jones (nameplates) Ltd 38
Butterworth, Paul 98
C A Burt 43
Cadet Flt Sgt Crafter 76
Cadet West 52
Caleym, Jane 98
Cammaerts, Francis 88
Campbell, Edward 6, 9, 14, 23, 33
Campbell, Mrs 9
Carden, H J 24
Carl. Maison 23
Carr, Dorothy 8
Carr, Henry 131
Carreck, Anne 89
Carroll, Patricia 98, 127
Castagnola, Squadron Leader 85
Cator Park 94, 97
Cator, Colonel 84
Catt, Deirdre 110
Chalfont 95
Chalk, Vernon 48
Chalmers, D H 23
Chamberlain, Richard 108
Chambers, Doreen 37, 59
Chancery Lane 77
Chappell. Peter 51
Charlesworth, John and Jean 90
Charringtons 112
Chartwell 34
Chavasse, Dr 60
Cheshire, Mary 64
Cheyne Hospital 93
Chiesman, Penelope 84
Chreseson, Miss J 107
Christie, Don 76
Christie, Charles Percy 92
Christie, Mayor 67
Christie, T H 55
Chulsa Estate 41
Church Drive Garden Association 108
Churchfields Rd 9
Churchfields Recreation Ground 68, 96
Churchill, Odette 79
Churchill, Peter 79
Churchill, Winston 17, 34, 38, 63, 69, 89, 112, 133
Clapp, Auxiliary Fireman 42
Clapson, Station Officer 63
Clark, Michael 19
Clark, Mrs 86
Clark, Petula 55, 95
Clarke, Diana 98
Clarke, Marjorie 63
Clifford, Hubert 131
Clockhouse Rd 97
Cole, F G 43
Coleman, Frederick 69
Colthorpe, Audrey 37
Compton and Edrich 64
Coney Hall 97
Coney Hall Putting Green 60
Conway, Percy John 50
Cooke, Frank 104
Cooper, Fireman 43
Cooper, Henry 95
Cooper, John 112
Copeland, Rob 108
Copers Cope Rd Ratepayers and Residents Association 72
Copers Cope Road 124
Cordy, Leading Fireman 43
Cornick, Mike 126
Coronation of George VI 8
Cotton, Henry 106
Couldrey, Noel Robert 48
Court Downs Rd 23

Court of Married Happiness 9
Cowdrey, Colin 84
Cowper, Sidney 65
Cox, Major Simon John 47
Craik (née Mulock), Dinah 10
Crawford, Jim 74
Crease Park 97
Crease, Cllr James 5, 23
Crease, Gerald 23
Crickenden, Dave 78
Croydon Rd Recreation ground 96, 102
Crush, Derek 76
Crystal Palace 63
Cuisenaire, Georges 105
Cumberland, David 96
Cunningham, John 79
Curtis, Cllr C B 27, 77
Curtis, Phyll 31
Curtis, Valerie 31
Cutler, Sylvia 127
Cyphers 50, 117
Davies, Mr 40
Davies, Mr 108
Day, Fireman 63
Day, Robin 5
Deans, R J 24
Demarne, Cyril T. 134
Denham, Maurice 63, 64, 79
Denham, Mr J S 107
Derrick, Colin 105
Dewey, Sir Thomas 91
Dibley, Joan 36
Dictatorships 8
Dingle Dangle Scarecrow 132
Dixon, Alderman E C 79
Dixon, Miss 107
Dixon, Mr & Mrs 72
Dodd, Arthur 126
doodlebugs 30, 32
Dors, Diana 61
Dove, Mr 14
Dowsett, Alan 18
Dowsings 33
Drake, Charlie 101
Dredge, Miss 103
Drew, Charles 3
Drinkwater, Laurie 88
Drysdale, Janet 25
Duncan, John 80, 94
Duncan, Monica 98
Duncan, Mrs 84
Duncan, Alderman William 81, 82, 89, 91, 99, 104, 114
Dunkirk 17
Dunkirk memorial 86
Duplock, Pat 34
Durbin, Deanna 34
Eagle, R L 107
East Anglian School of Painting and Drawing 131
Easton, Hugh 81
Edden, Dr 113
Edden, Felicity 12, 35
Edden, Michael 12
Edmonds, Jack 110, 122
Edmonds, Katherine 100
Edward Laycock, Rev. 8
Edwards, Ina 57
Elderslie 95
Elgood Playing Fields 9
Elgood, Alderman 33
Elm Road Baptist Church 125
Elmers End garage 87
Elmers End Odeon 84
Elmers End Recreation ground 97
Else, Tony 122, 123
Elvin, Miss 62, 131
Emery, Dick 97
Emington, Anne 98
Empire Day 9
Endean, Daisy 46
Endean, F J 24
Evan-Jones family 104
Evans, Elizabeth 34
Evans, Mr 40
Everard, Barbara 90
Fagg, Thomas Webster 115

Fairbrother, Annette 93
Farley, C 24
Farley, Raymond 46
Farmer, R B 43
Fay, Roy 94
Field, Bill 34
Field, Lil 30
first night of the Proms 127
Fisher, Gay 61
Fisher, Joyce 94
Fitzgerald, Denis 23
Flack, Thelma 37
Flam, Herb 86
Fletcher, Ken 110
Florence Petley 63
Foll, Mr 36
Footner, N 57
Forbes, Hannah 100
Ford, John 84
Forsyth, PO 42
Fox, Elaine 100
Fox, Miss 29, 131
Frake, Capt 38
Franks, Mr 36
Frazer, Arthur 30
Freedom from Hunger 105
Freud, Lucien 131
Frewer, Mr 45
Frinton 58
Frost, Jack 126, 131
Fry, Mr F W 55
Furley and Baker 10
Gale, Mr & Mrs 72
Gammon, David 18
Gammon, Olive 18
Gammon, Sidney 18
Garland, Judy 21
Gazeley,Frederick 113
Gear, Mr 40
Geddes, Aukland Sir 14
Gegan, Judy 108, 110, 112
George Benton, Mr and Mrs 86
George Montagu Rochfort Lord JP 68
George, Leonard 41
Gibson,Althea 86
Glebe Way 81, 90
Godfrey, H M 57
Godwin, Ivy 61
Goffe, Dr Alan 82
Goldthorpe 31
Goodchild, Fred 30
Goode, M 43
Goodhart, Philip 85, 107, 113
Goodison, Mary 37
Goodman, Sheila 63
Gordon-Smith, Councillor 114
Gosling, Victor 48
Grace, W G 6
Graf Spee, Admiral 16
Graham-Williams, Violet 107
Gray,Mr 62
Green, Hughie 95
Greengage Summer 98
Gregory, Mr 75
Greyhound 104
Griffin, Mr 40
Griffiths, Mr 122, 123
Grove Dancing and Dramatic Club 64
Guille, Frank 60
Gussie, Gorgeous 61
Gyi, Thelma 31, 34
Brook Brown, Cllr H 85, 99
H C Wotton 24
Hale, Kathleen 131
Hall, G J J 24
Hall, Terry 92
Hall, Thomas 88
Hamer, Olive 45
Hamer, Stanley 45
Hammond, Cllr 92
Handy string quartet 106
Handy, Audrey 57, 61
Handy, Elise 98
Hard, Darlene 86
Harding, Kathleen 98, 112
Hards, Charles 24
Harris, C F 43
Harris, Diana 108, 109, 110
Harris, Leading Firemen 44
Harvey, Eric 108

Harvington 12, 61, 95, 97, 99
Harvington Estate 77
Hawes Down School 112
Hawkins, Miss 100
Hawthorn, Mike 69, 81
Hawthorndene 44
Haydon-Jones, Ann 110
Hayes School 94
Hayes, Miss 63
Hayne Rd Day Centre 111
Hazelgrove, William 50
Hazelton, Alan (Banger) 46
Hazelton, Bill 46
Hazelton, Doris 46
Healey, Alderman 3, 8
Healey, L T 24
Healey, Mrs 5
Helen Mynett 100
Henshaw, Kathleen 31, 33, 37, 67, 79, 105, 107, 125
Hessey, Mr 81
Highfield School 90
Hillary 75
Hitchcock,Wally . 106
HMS Constance 79, 85
HMS Cossack 16
HMS Sikh 26
Hogg MP, Rt Hon Quinton 110
Holden, Ruth 98
Holder, Elizabeth 97
Holloway, Rupert 74
Homewood 95
Hopkins, Mike 125, 126, 131
Hopkinson, Grace 7
Hornsby Smith, Dame Patricia 114
Horton, B 89
Hourston, Miss 67
Howard, Trevor 75
Howden, Canon 28
Hudders, S R 23, 82
Hughes, Rev. Bernard 77
Humberstone, Daphne 98
Humphrey, William 80
Hunter (nee Radford), Jean 32
Hurst, Leslie Frederick 41
Hutchinson, Miss 58
Hutt, Mrs 94
Hyett, Anthony 83
Inman, Eric 51, 129
Invicta Squadron 131 17
J B Pillin Ltd 33
Jackie Palo 56
Jackson Ritson, Rev. Caleb 26
Jackson, Cllr 27, 32
Jameson, Column Officer 30, 42, 45
Jane, Sylvia 59
Jarman, Helen 110
Jay, Margaret 34
Jeff, Mayor R W 21
Jeffries, Carol 7
Jeffries, Sir Charles 7
Jenner, Tom 74
Jennings, Jennifer 59
Jesshope, Frank 86
Jessup, Paul 110, 122
Jewry, Mrs 122
Joan Burns, 37
Johns, Pamela 30
Johns, Rob 8
Johns, Tony 19, 20, 27
Johnson, Cllr Mayor 113
Johnson, Judith 110
Johnson, Pearl 100
Johnston, Brian 64
Jollye, AB John 79
Jones, Keith 106
Jones, Martin 110
Jones, Percy 70
Jones, Vernon 16, 45, 76, 107
Juniper, Miss 108
'Jumbo' White 125
Jutton, Mr 48
Kedward, P M 43
Keen, Mr 25, 60
Keen, S A 43
Kelly, Judith 108
Kelsey Park 96, 104

136

Kelsh, Frank 74
Kelsh, Valerie 98
Kent County Cricket Club 124
Kent House 80
Kenwood 122
Kildare, Dr 108
Killick, Stephen 1
King, Miss 31
King, Mr Chilton 91
King, Pat 59
King, Peter 122
King, Rev Guy 8
King, Barry 122, 123
Kingfisheries 68
Kitchener, Ken 78
Kite, A V 24
Kite, Albert 46
Knight, Laura 131
Knight, Rev. Donald 68, 80, 85
Knight, T F 43
Knox- Johnston, Diana 83, 97
Knox-Johnston, William Robert Patrick 84, 99, 108
Kobrak, Christine and Lesley 103
Kramer, Josef 34
L T Ralph 43
Lampards 10
Langley Park 90, 94
Lathwood, Ernest Stanley 41
Latter, Mayor Cllr 101
Laycock, Canon 56
Leach, Herbert 79
Lee, June 57
Leeks, Assistant FFC Reginald 45, 68
Leeks, Mavis 35, 37
Leeks, Tony 20
Lenny the Lion 92
Lewis, G F 43
Lightfoot, Pat 28
Lightfoot, Roy 28
Lillie 127
Links Rd 30
Linsell, Alice 104
Little Mo 74
Lloyd, Marie 95
Lomax, Senior Sister 35
Longhurst, Mrs 63
Looe Rocks 25
Lord, Cllr 92
Lovatt, Mrs 112
Lowe 75
Lubbock, John 114
Ludgrove, Linda 110, 112
Lunggren, Eric 132
Lunggren, Mollie 131
Lupin, Dr 112
Lusher, Mr 101
Lyle, Dr Gordon 102
Lynch-Watson, Mayor Alderman 22
Lynn, Jack 51
MacCallum, Mr 104
mace 3
MacGregor, Jean 126
Macmillan, Harold 34, 38, 99
Magrath, Sub Officer 63
Maguire, Air Vice Marshall 93
Maidstone By-Pass, the A20 (M) 96
Mallett, Tom 57
Maltman, Stephanie 23
Mann, John 55
Manning, David 110, 122, 123
Manning, Philip 110
Manser, Geoffrey 69
Marian Vian School 17, 90, 97
Marsh, Ann 97
Martin, Tony 122
Masters, Auxiliary Fireman 42
Maunder, Raymond 50
Maynard, Albert 83
Maynard, Cllr 35
Maynard, Hilda 45
Maynard, J 23, 45, 82
McAndrew 97
McCormick-Goodhart 83
McIntosh, Mary 98
McKibben, Leading Firemen 44
McManus, Mick 56
Mead, Miss 62, 131
measles vaccine 112

Meeks, Robert 88
Michelangeli, Arturo 127
Midland Bank 112
mile of books 26
Miles, John 125
Milland, Ray 87
Miller, Max 95
Mills, John 133, 134
Milne, Margaret 12
Minter, A E 24
Minter, Ann 46
Miss E M Fox Prize for Creative Work 29
Mitchell, Barbara 59
Mitchell, Peter 125
Mitchenson, Joe 50
Moisant, John 97
Monkhouse, Bob 54, 79, 131
Moore, Councillor Kathleen 28, 89, 90, 97, 99
Moore, Frederick 23, 92
Moore, S H 43
Morgan, Comdr Patrick 79
Morgan, Company Officer 44
Morgan, Jack 45
Morgan, Luke 30
Morley, Mr 63
Morley, Mrs 63
Morris, Frank (Dot) 130
Morris, Shirley 45
Morrison, Alita 10
Morrison, Betty 37
Mortimer, Angela 110
Moss, Stirling 81
Mountain, G. 43
Mountford, Beryl 57
Mountjoy, Norman 23, 75
Mountjoy, Olive 23
Mrs Douglas 62
Muirheads 36
Mulloy, Gardnar 74
Munro, David 126, 131
Munro, Phyllis 126
Mynett, Elizabeth 98
Namesake Day 83
National Provincial Bank Sports ground 97, 117
National Recreation Centre at Crystal Palace 110
Neagle, Anna 89
Needham, Janet 110
Netherhurst, Chief Officer, A. N. 40, 42
Neville, Miss 131
New, Reginald 22
Newcome, John 110
Newman, Patricia 127
Newman, Vera 112
Nickols, Charles 7
North West Kent Federation of Townswomens Guild 62
Notley, Rachel 111
nuclear attack 97
Oak Lodge School 58, 78
Oakfield 95
Odeon cinema at Elmers End Green 14
Old Palace School 23
Oldfield, Leading Fireman 42
Oldfield, Olly 78
Olympic Games 96, 112
Osborne, David 48
Oswald, Elsie 50
Oxley, Dorothy 98
Pack, Bob 58, 78
Page, Alan 112
Palmer, John Michael 83
Palmer, Leslie 23
Palmer, Mr 95, 97, 101
Panton, Felicia 37
parakeets 62
Parcell, F G 24
Parfett, M C 24
Parkes, C M 56
Parkin, Alderman 92, 96, 109, 114, 115, 126
Parkin, Marcia 126
Parkway E 103
Parsons, Margaret 53
Parsons, Sheila 103
Peacock, Mrs 69
Pearly King and Queen 92
Penny, Anthea 93
Penrick Gymkhana 93
Percy, Dorothy 37
Perkins, Polly 62
Petchey's Orchestra, Mr 2
Petleys 12
Philip Vian, Captain 16
Piano Parlour 127

Pilbrow, Arthur Gordon 55
Piper, Mary 108
Pite, Hugh 78
Plaistow Rd, West Ham 23
Plant, W C 24
Platts, Jill 92
Player, Beryl 50
Pollock, George 55
Pool, Ida 16, 94, 107
Poplar school 42
Porrer, Brenda and Shirley 98
Powell, Benita 125, 126
Preston, Pamela 59
Price, Cllr 69
Price, Mr and Mrs 60
Prince Charles 133
Prince George 125
Prince Philip 88, 110
Prince, Alison 128
Princess Elizabeth 60
Pringle, Barbara 7
Prosnall, Doreen 57
Proud (nee Burtonshaw), Laura Elizabeth 45
Purnell, Ted 74
Purvis, Captain Charles 40
Purvis, Mrs 81
Putnam, David 22
Queen Mother 134
Queen's Own Royal West Kent 84
Quickenden,Susan 90
Quill, Geoffrey 87
Rabson, Miss 31
Radcliffe, George 50
Radford, J F 32, 60
Radley, PC Ron 95
Raeburn, David Anthony 104
Raiks, Greta 99
Rainger, Mr 25
Rarp, Florence M 79
Rayner, Joan 63
Read, Councillor 114
Ready, Stuart 36
Redman, Mr 56
Reid, Harry 88
Reid, Isabel 37
Reid, Norman 111
Remound, Betty 98
Rennie, Maureen 93
Rev. F C Waghorn 103
Rev. Hammond 83, 96
Rev. Llewellyn- Davies 26
Rev. Shortt 89
Rev. Sugden 92, 110, 112
Rev. Webber 100
Rev. Yarker 100
Rich, Firewoman Trixie 44
Richard, Mrs 30
Rickaby, Eileen 93
Ridler, Pat 31, 37, 59
Ripley, George 30, 41
River Chaffinch 56
Robbins, Cllr 92, 99
Robbins, Pamela 31
Robbins, Beryl 31
Roberts, David 126
Roberts, Olga 104
Rodgers, Charles 51
Roger, Boxall 122
Rooney, Mickey 21
Roots, L 24
Rose, C I 43
Rose, Miss 33, 131
Round, Dorothy 10
Rugg, May 89, 99
Russell Smith, Geoffrey 131
Russell-Smith, Mollie and Geoffry 126, 131
Ruthen & Perkins 10
Sampson Challenge Cup 43
Sampson, Alderman 5, 21, 29, 22, 43, 72, 100
Sampson, Eileen 28
Sampson, Mrs 84
Samuel, Mr 38
Sanders, Brian 125
Sandhurst School 27
Sands, Pamela 37
Santana, Manuel 110
Sargeant, Geoffrey 94, 69
Sargent, Margaret 53
Sargent, Sir Malcolm 127
Sarjeant, Audrey 98
Sarjeant, Geoffrey 69
Sawyer, Auxiliary Fireman 42
Scaplehorn,Mr 113
Scarr, Mr 14
Schove, Hilary 96
Schove, Mr 78
Scripps, Wendy 95
Seath, Florence 30, 41

Seath, Reginald 30, 41
SEM (Small Electric Motors) 33
Semark, Mr 80
Sharpe, Thomas 79
Shellan, David 107
Sheppard, Graham 122, 123
Sherpa Angnima 75
Sherwood Hero 128
Shipsey, Edward 5
Shipsey, Maurice 5
Short, Stanley 23
Sibley, Antoinette 111
Simpson John 93
Sindall, Mr 38
Singlehurst, Walter 79
Smith, Christine 30
Smith, Gordon 45
Smith, Irene 93
Smith, Margaret 100, 110
Smithers, Cllr Edward 100, 103
Smythe, Michael 79
Snazell, Frank 50, 51
Snowy White 60
Somerville, Frank 24
Somerville, William 24
South Hill Wood 91, 97
South Norwood sewage farm 80
Sowerby, Thomas William (Tom) 116
Sparrows Den 97
Spiers, Ian 110
SS Canterbury 86
SS Invicta 86
St Christopher's School 68, 102
St David's College 78, 96
St Michael's church 36
St Paul's church 56, 110
Staddon, C Eric 23, 43
Stamp, Baron Josiah 25
Stamp, Baroness Olive Jessie 25
Stamp, Hon Arthur Maxwell 25
Stamp, Hon Katharine Mary 25
Stamp, Hon Wilfred Carlyle 25
Stamp, Rt Hon Trevor Charles 25
Stamp, Sir Josiah 1, 8, 14, 54
Stanwell, Gerald 64
Stares, Chas 79
Starkie, Elizabeth 110
Stedman, Kathleen 59
Stedman, Ronnie 33, 55, 64, 95
Stembridge, Henry Charles 50
Stevens,Frank 79
Stock, Mr C 14, 55, 68
Stokes, Captain 26
Stolle, Fred 110
Stone, Fireman 63
Stow, Mr 104
Stratton, E. 43
Strong, Fireman 44
Sullivan, Mr 101
Sutherland, Sam 95
Sutton, Kingsley 24
Sutton, Roger 112
Swallow, Alfred 55
swimming scholarships 64
Syme & Duncan 112
Syme, William 80
Talbot Turner, Bradwell 16
Taylor, Carl 23
Taylor, Jane 110
Tensing 75
The Navy's here 17
Thoday, Carolyn 103
Thomas, Alan 76
Thomas, Eric 52
Thomas, Mr 122
Thompson, Sheila 34
Thornton, Heather 89
Thornton, T W 96
Thornton, Valerie 78
Thornton, Victor 8, 14, 16, 25, 27, 64, 68, 76, 97, 107
Three Tuns 63
Thurnscoe 31
Tidman, Susan 90
Till, Butler 116
Tilling's 40
Timms, Cpl 38
Tip Top factory 94
Tom Smith, Mr and Mrs 9
Tomkins, Christopher 108

Tomkins, Peter 88
Toms, Margaret Eileen 93, 91, 108
Tonkin (née Banks), Nancy 51, 129
Tonkin, Bill 129
Tookey, Geoffrey 55, 68
Tookey, Richard 55
Tovey, Barbara 52
Training Ship Sikh 66
Tresize, Jean 126
Trevan, Dr 36
Trevelyan, Mary 94
Trinder, Tommy 95
Triton Diving Goons 78
Trost, Miss 37
Truman, Christine 100, 110
Trumpton 128
Try, Margaret 100
Turner, Lesley 100
Twinlocks 33
Underwood, Derek 116
Unwin, Elsie 25
Varney, Richard 106
vertical take-off 90
Vian, Charlotte 17
Vian, Claire 17
Vian, Marjorie 17
Vian, Miss 48
Vian,Captain Philip 26
Vick, E W 24
violent storm 89
Vosser, John 126
Wade, Virginia 110
Wageningen 49, 60
Waite, Penny 96
Walkden, Chris 78, 83, 95, 96
Walkden, Mr J 101
Walker, Kay 62
Walklin (Jeffries), Carol 5
Walklin, Jane 7
Waller, Cllr 96
Waller, Rosalind 100, 102
Ward, Jennifer 110
Wardle, DJ 74
Wardle, G A 50
Wardle, Willie 74
Warman, Jeanine 34
Warner, Company Officer 44
Warner, Mr 45
Waters, Elsie and Doris 95
Wath-on-Dearne 31
Watkins, Cliff 45
Watson, Alan 78
Watts 25
Wauchope-Watson, Phyllis 77
Waylett, Cllr 56
Wayne Tank Co 36
Weeks, Leading Firemen 44
Weiss,Francis 125
Welch, Mr 15
Well Wood 97
Wellcome laboratories 112
Wellington, Margaret 36, 55, 95
West Wickham Residents Association 78
West Wickham Operatic Society 82, 94
West, Mr & Mrs 92
Westbroom,Fredk 79
Wheatley, Brenda 21
Whiley, Ann 100
Whitby, V 89
White, Alderman 86
White, George 57, 92
White, Mr 104
White, Mrs 25
White,Mrs 84
Whiting, Paul 96
Whitworth, Gillian 100
Wickham Common Infants School 8
Wilbourne, Alfred 79
Wilcox, Herbert 89
Wilkinson, Dr Sam 58
Williams, Cllr Maxwell 110
Williams, Mary 108
Williams, Richard 98
Wilson 9
Wingham, George 41
Wiseman, Nancy 29, 63, 76, 98, 100, 101, 105, 127
'Wis' Wisdon 74
Withers, Doris 97
Withers, Penny 103
Woodbrook School 62, 103, 121, 131, 132
Wooderson, Sydney 49
Woodland, W J 24

Woods, C J R 43
Woolgar, Victor 88
Woolley, Frank 74
Worsley Bridge School 78, 90, 107, 110, 122
Wort, Catherine 97
Worthington, George 74
Wotton, Bryan 46, 47
Wright, Christine 81
Wright, Mr & Mrs 22
Wynne, Janet 57
Yabsley, Mr 5

Jenna Publishing

www.pickpatspage.homestead.com

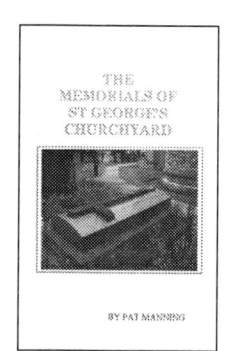

Memorials of St. George's Churchyard

Jenna Publishing
36pp A5   £2.00 (+ £1.50p+p)

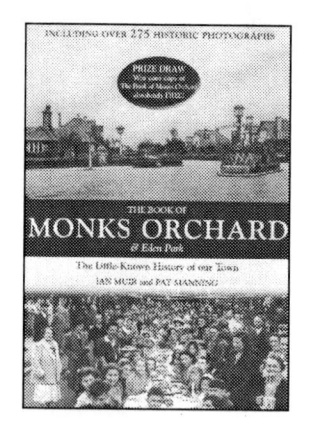

Monks Orchard & Eden Park

Halsgrove
160pp A4   £19.95 (+ £3.00p+p)

Memories of Beckenham's Rivers

Jenna Publishing
52pp A5   £5.00 (+ £1.50p+p)

Beckenham The Home Front 1939-45

Jenna Publishing
104pp A4   £8.00 (+ £2.00p+p)

The Cators of Beckenham & Woodbastwick

Authors on line
76pp A5 £9.95 (+ £1.50p+p)

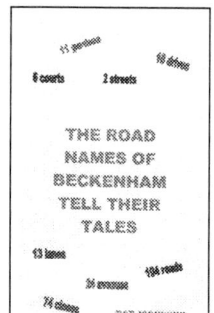

The Road Names of Beckenham Tell Their Tales

Jenna Publishing
84pp A5 £5.00 (+ £1.50p+p)

Beckenham's 30 Glorious Years 1935-65

Jenna Publishing
144pp A4   £11.99   (+ £2.25p+p)

All books are available from The Beckenham bookshop and Bromley Libraries or can be purchased by sending a cheque including postage and packing from
Pat Manning, 29 Birchwood Ave. Beckenham. BR3 3PY